MEASURED DRAWINGS
OF
OLD ENGLISH OAK FURNITURE

MEASURED DRAWINGS OF OLD ENGLISH OAK FURNITURE

JOHN WEYMOUTH HURRELL

DOVER PUBLICATIONS, INC.
NEW YORK

Published in Canada by General Publishing Company, Ltd., 30 Lesmill Road, Don Mills, Toronto, Ontario.

Published in the United Kingdom by Constable and Company, Ltd., 10 Orange Street, London WC2H 7EG.

This Dover edition, first published in 1983, is an unabridged and unaltered republication of the edition published by B. T. Batsford, London, in 1902, with the title *Measured Drawings of Old Oak English Furniture Also of Some Remains of Architectural Woodwork, Plasterwork, Metalwork, Glazing, Etc.*

Manufactured in the United States of America
Dover Publications, Inc., 180 Varick Street, New York, N.Y. 10014

Library of Congress Cataloging in Publication Data

Hurrell, John Weymouth.
Measured drawings of old English oak furniture.

Reprint. Originally published: London : Batsford, 1902.
1. Furniture—England—Drawings. I. Title.
TT196.H86 1983 749.22′022′2 83-5259
ISBN 0-486-24521-7

PREFACE.

FOR ingenuity and quaintness of design, richness of moulding, or profusion of ornament, the old Oak Furniture of England, and the internal woodwork and plasterwork of our old English Mansions of the seventeenth and eighteenth centuries are probably unsurpassed by the contemporaneous work of any other country; while the numerous smaller country houses still left to us are full of most interesting detail of a more simple kind, but possessing the same originality and quaintness of spirit. It is therefore somewhat surprising that whereas so many valuable works have been published, especially of late, dealing in a more or less pictorial manner with the domestic buildings of this period, no carefully detailed work has hitherto been published particularly devoted to their furniture and internal finishings.

It would require many volumes to adequately illustrate the rich abundance of this domestic work throughout the country: I have therefore selected some of the more simple examples of domestic furniture, panelling, ceilings, etc., together with a few examples of church furniture for illustration in this volume. It should be observed that my object has been to represent, by accurate measurement and careful delineation to scale (without the aid of pictorial effect), the true spirit of the work in exhaustive detailed analysis of its construction and design, with the mouldings and ornamentation drawn full size wherever practicable. It is my belief that this will make the book a valuable one for reference to the Architect, Designer, and Craftsman, whose business it is to produce similar work in modern times. It should also be of much interest to the Antiquary, who will trace in it a natural development of design culminating in the revival of classic form at the beginning of the nineteenth century.

Upon the 110 Plates of which the volume consists are represented a great variety of subjects, all of which are so completely detailed that further explanation is unnecessary.

JOHN WEYMOUTH HURRELL.

MANCHESTER,

June 1902.

SUBJECTS OF THE PLATES.

MEASURED DRAWINGS
OF
OLD ENGLISH OAK FURNITURE

OLD OAK CABINET ~ Lancashire
Modern cornice
Centre
for mould ornaments see details
for mould ornaments see details
A
A
B
B
B
118 3/4"
13 1/4"
B
B
B
B
B
B
Centre meeting joint of doors
floor line
12 9 6 3 0 1 2 3 feet.

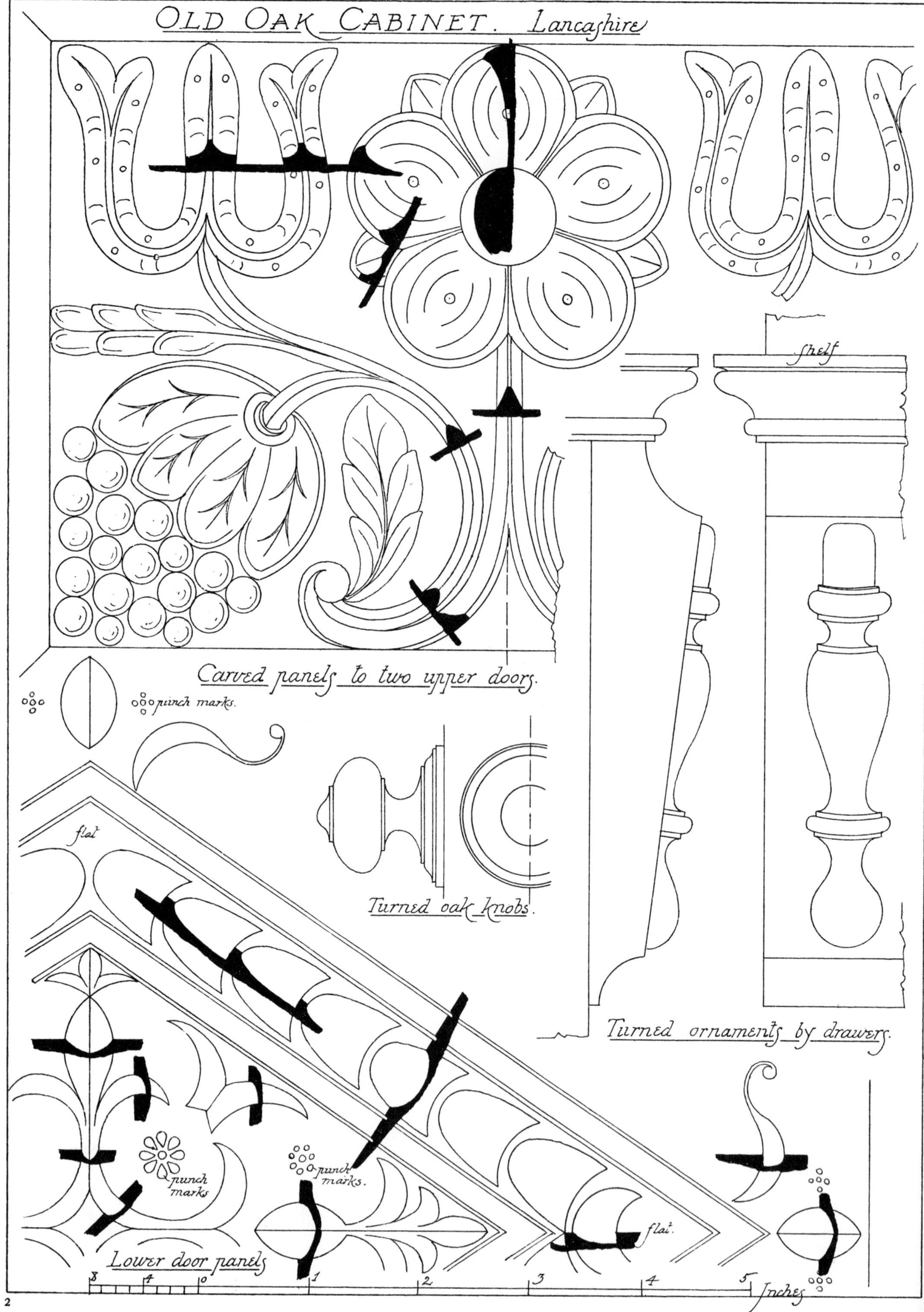
OLD OAK CABINET. Lancashire
shelf
Carved panels to two upper doors.
punch marks.
Turned oak knobs.
Turned ornaments by drawers.
flat
punch marks
punch marks.
flat.
Lower door panels
8
4
0
1
2
3
4
5
Inches

OLD OAK CABINET ✗ Lancashire.
Incised line
finely punched ground.
Incised line
Incised line
Incised line
Sunk
Sunk
Half of fixed centre panel.
Turned pilasters to upper cupboard.
Turning reversed for lower half.
Centre
Plan
0
1
2
3
4
5
6
Inches.

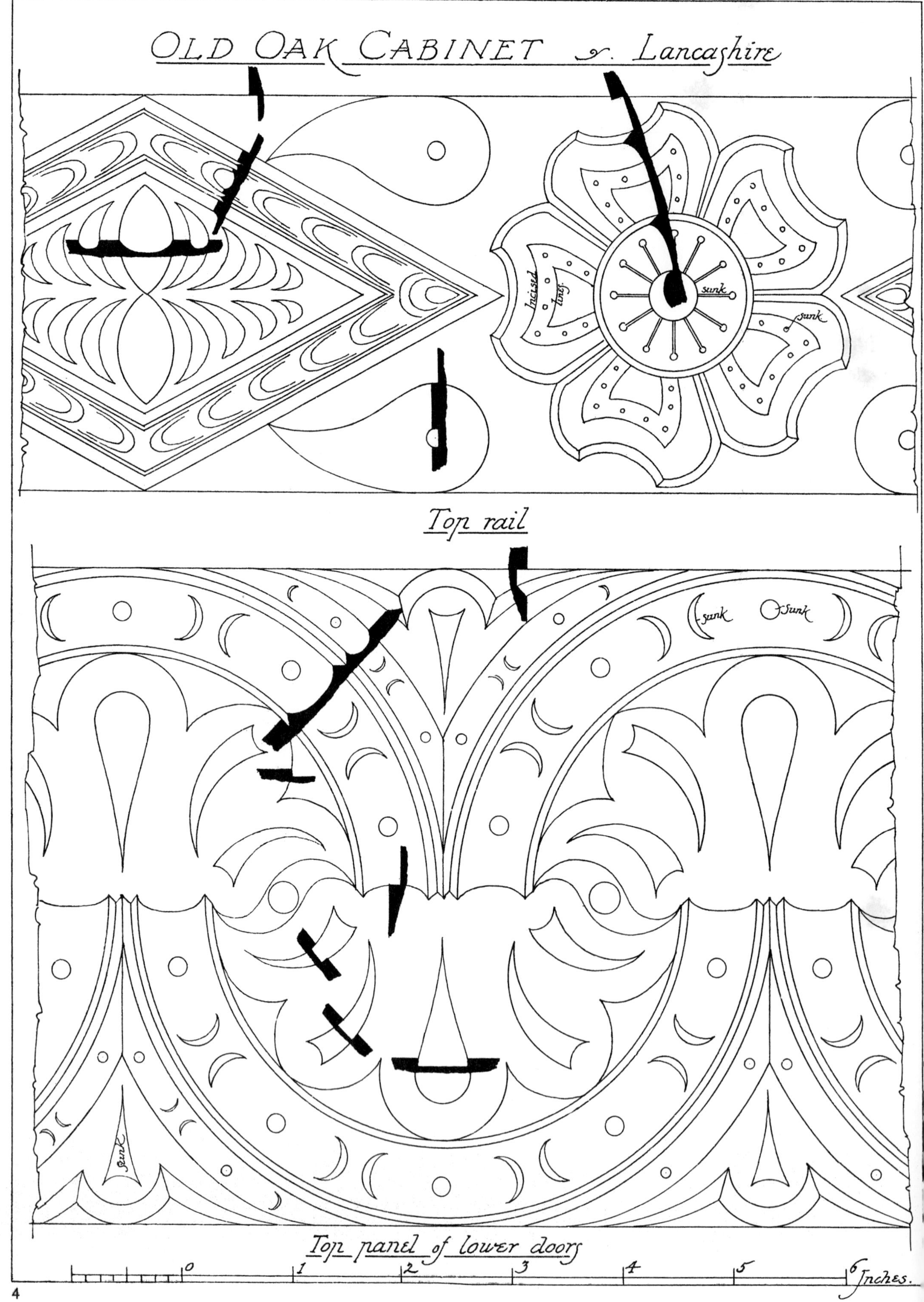
OLD OAK CABINET &. Lancashire
Incised lines.
sunk
sunk
Top rail
sunk
Sunk
sunk
Top panel of lower doors
0
1
2
3
4
5
6 Inches.

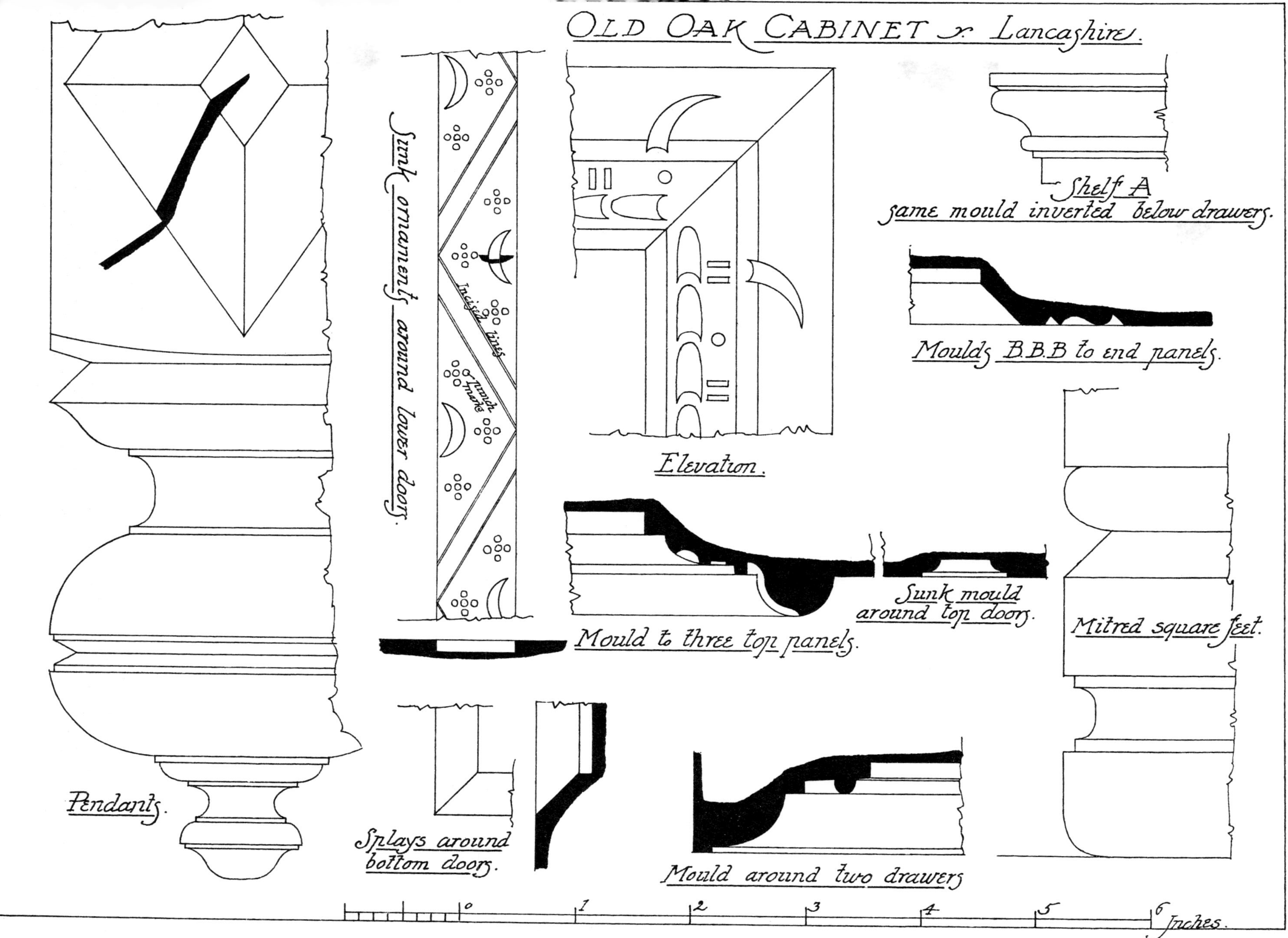
Old Oak Cabinet – Lancashire.
Shelf A
same mould inverted below drawers.
Moulds B.B.B to end panels.
Elevation.
Sunk ornaments around lower doors.
Incised lines
Punch marks
Mould to three top panels.
Sunk mould around top doors.
Mitred square feet.
Pendants.
Splays around bottom doors.
Mould around two drawers
0
1
2
3
4
5
6
Inches.

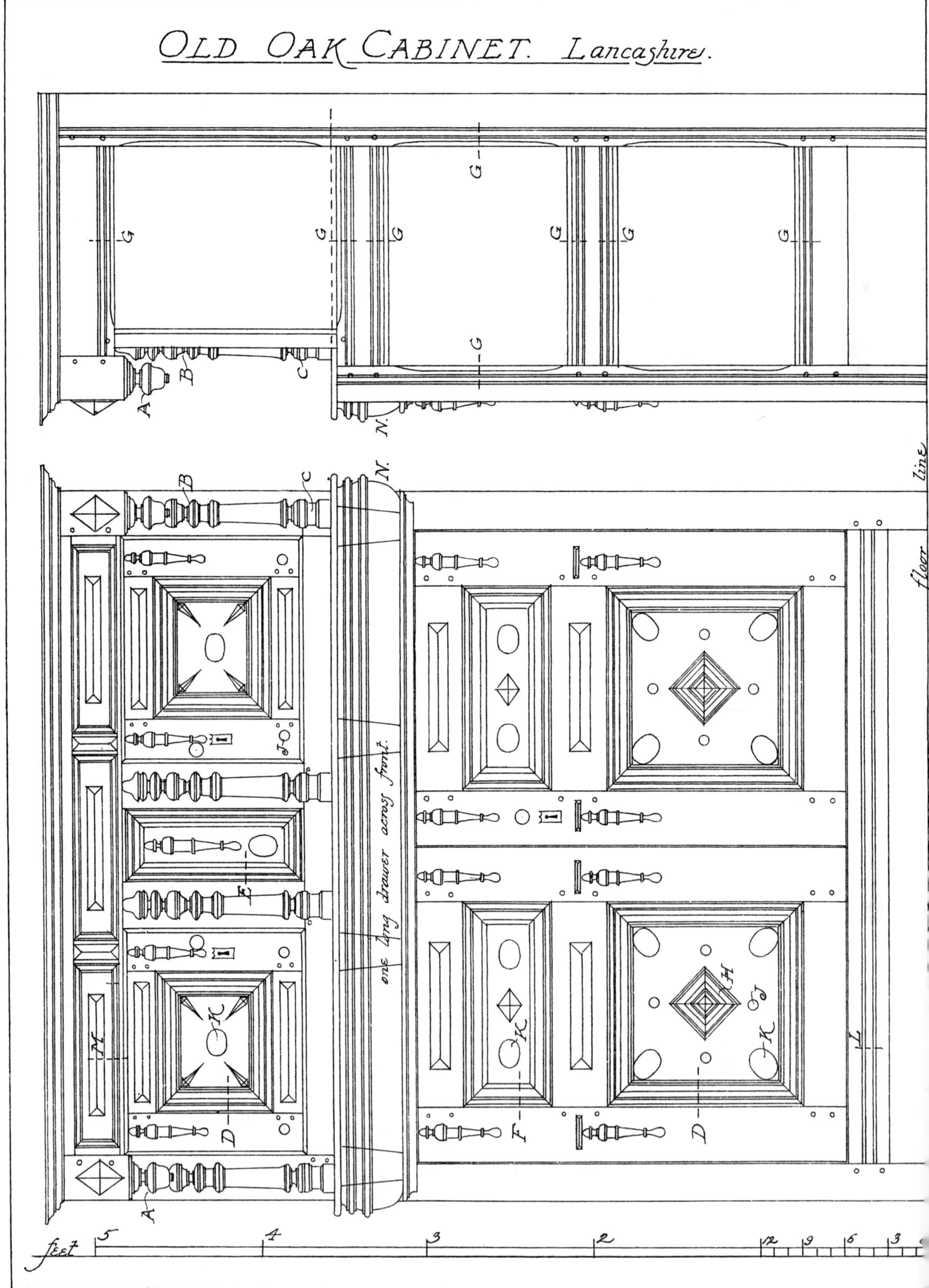
OLD OAK CABINET. Lancashire.
one long drawer across front.
floor line
feet
5
4
3
2
12
9
6
3

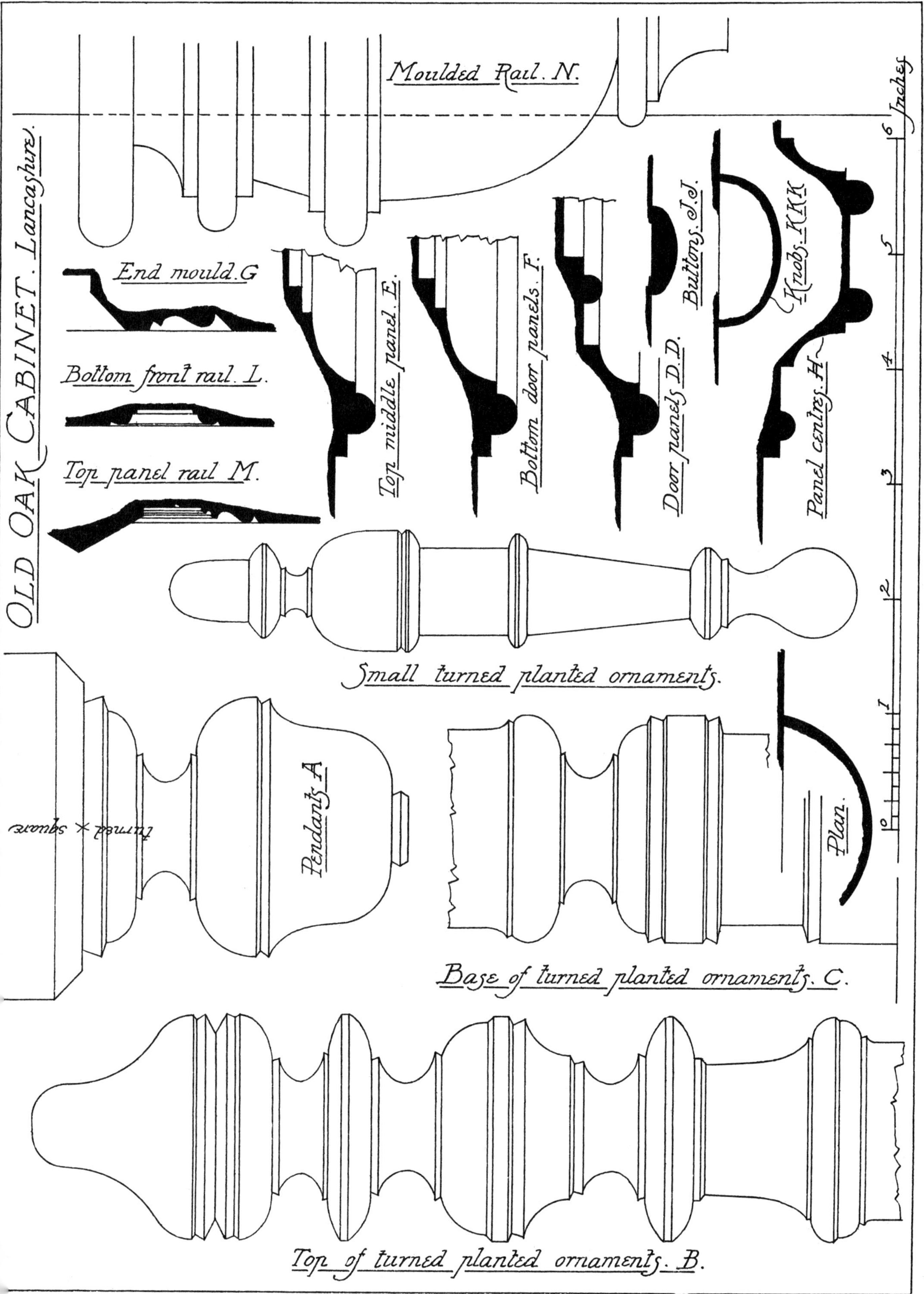
OLD OAK CABINET. Lancashire.
Moulded Rail. N.
Inches
6
5
4
3
2
1
0
End mould. G
Bottom front rail. L.
Top panel rail M.
Top middle panel. E.
Bottom door panels. F.
Door panels D. D.
Buttons. J. J.
Knobs. K.K.K.
Panel centres. H.
Small turned planted ornaments.
turned × square
Pendants A
Plan.
Base of turned planted ornaments. C.
Top of turned planted ornaments. B.

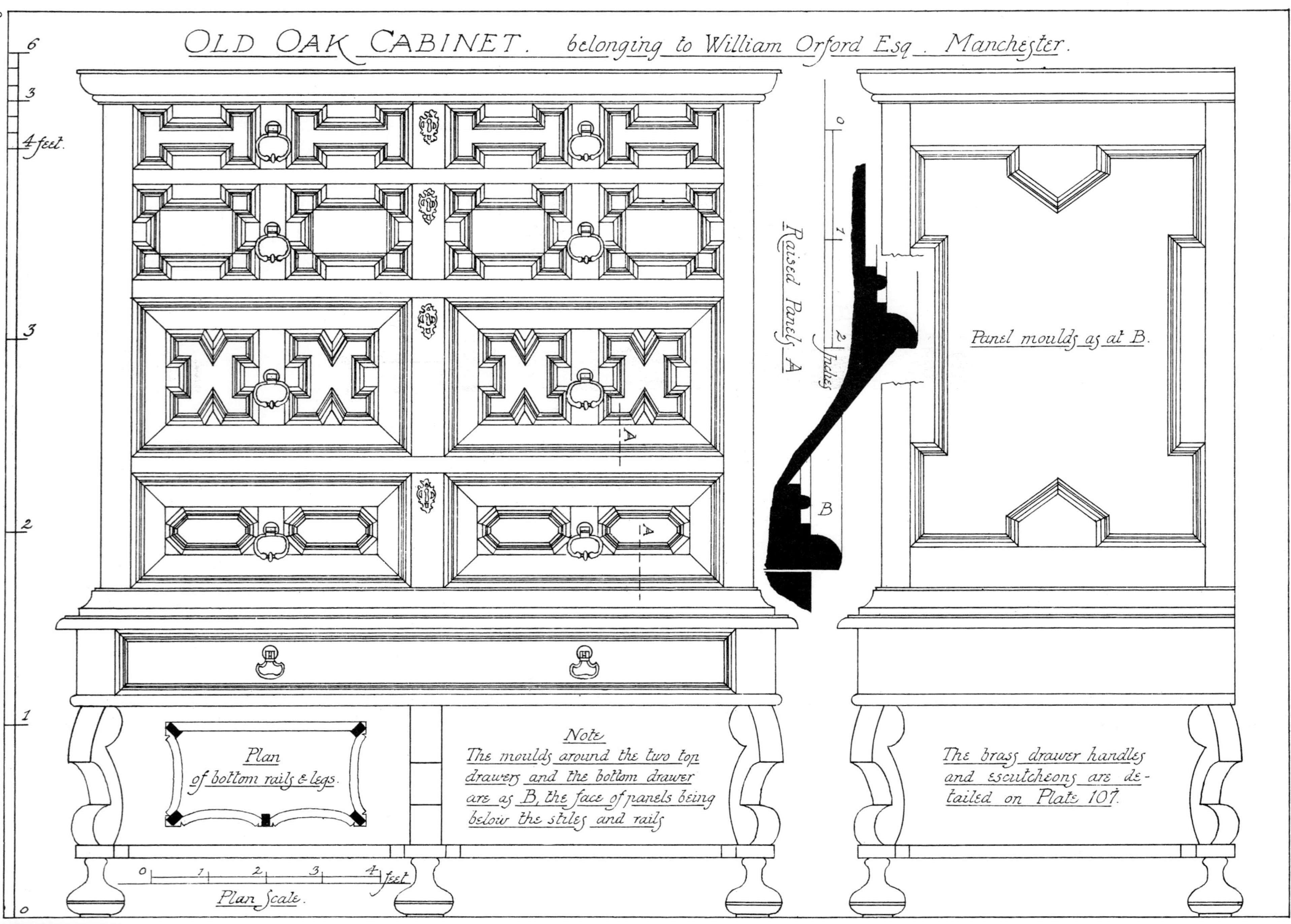
OLD OAK CABINET. belonging to William Orford Esq. Manchester.
4 feet.
Raised Panels A
Inches
B
A
Panel moulds as at B.
Plan of bottom rails & legs.
Note
The moulds around the two top drawers and the bottom drawer are as B, the face of panels being below the stiles and rails
The brass drawer handles and escutcheons are detailed on Plate 107.
Plan Scale.
4 feet

OLD OAK CABINET. belonging to Mr. John Forsyth. Eccles.

Moulds at B.

Moulds at C.

This raised panel with double moulds also at D.

The plain spaces A are slightly splayed upwards towards the centre about 1/16 of an inch keeping below the fillet at E.

The centre upright panels are all slightly convex vertically including the moulds.

half bead

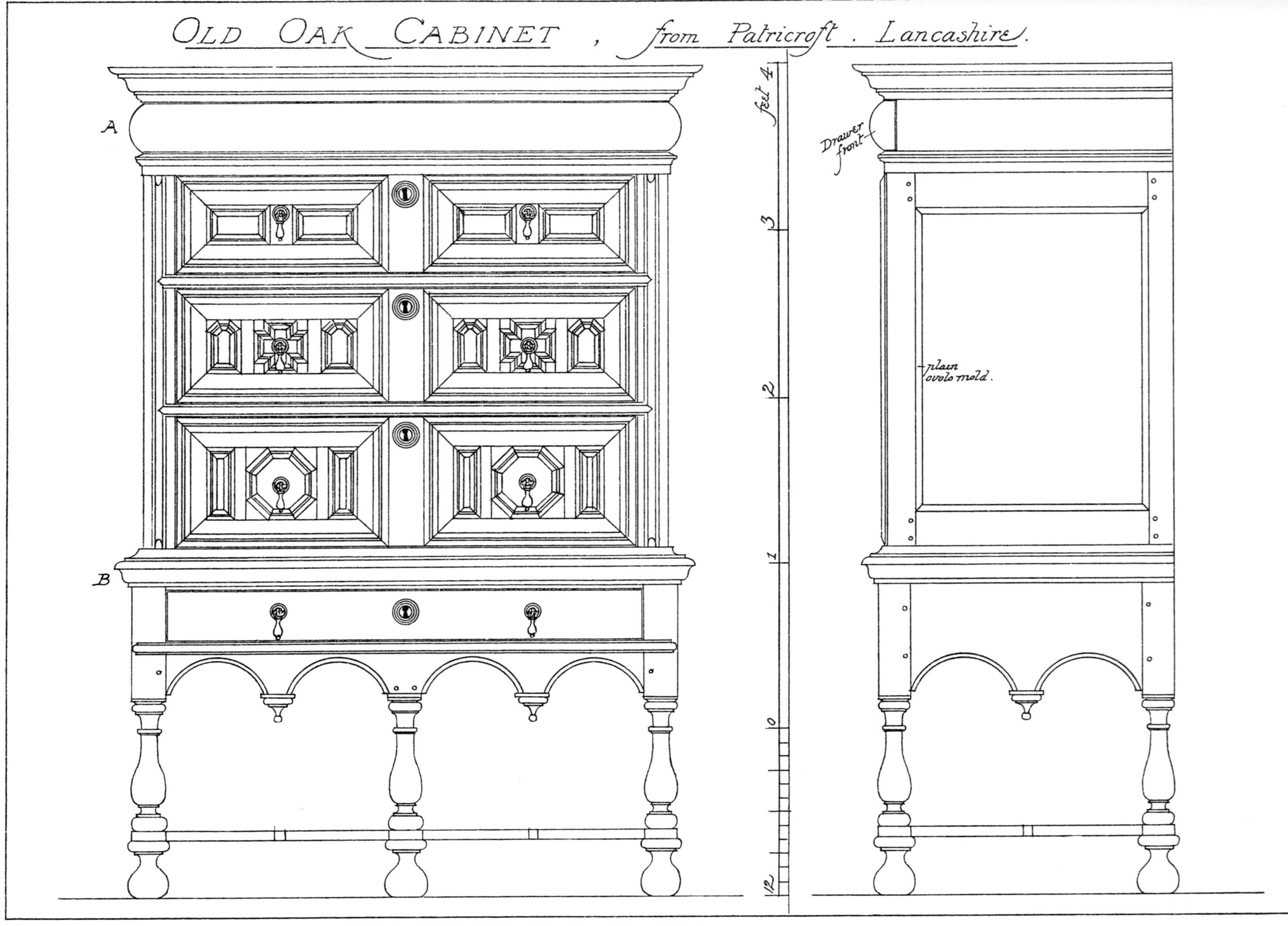
Old Oak Cabinet, from Patricroft. Lancashire.
A
B
feet 4
3
2
1
0
12
Drawer front
plain ovolo mold.

OLD OAK CABINET from Patricroft Lancashire.

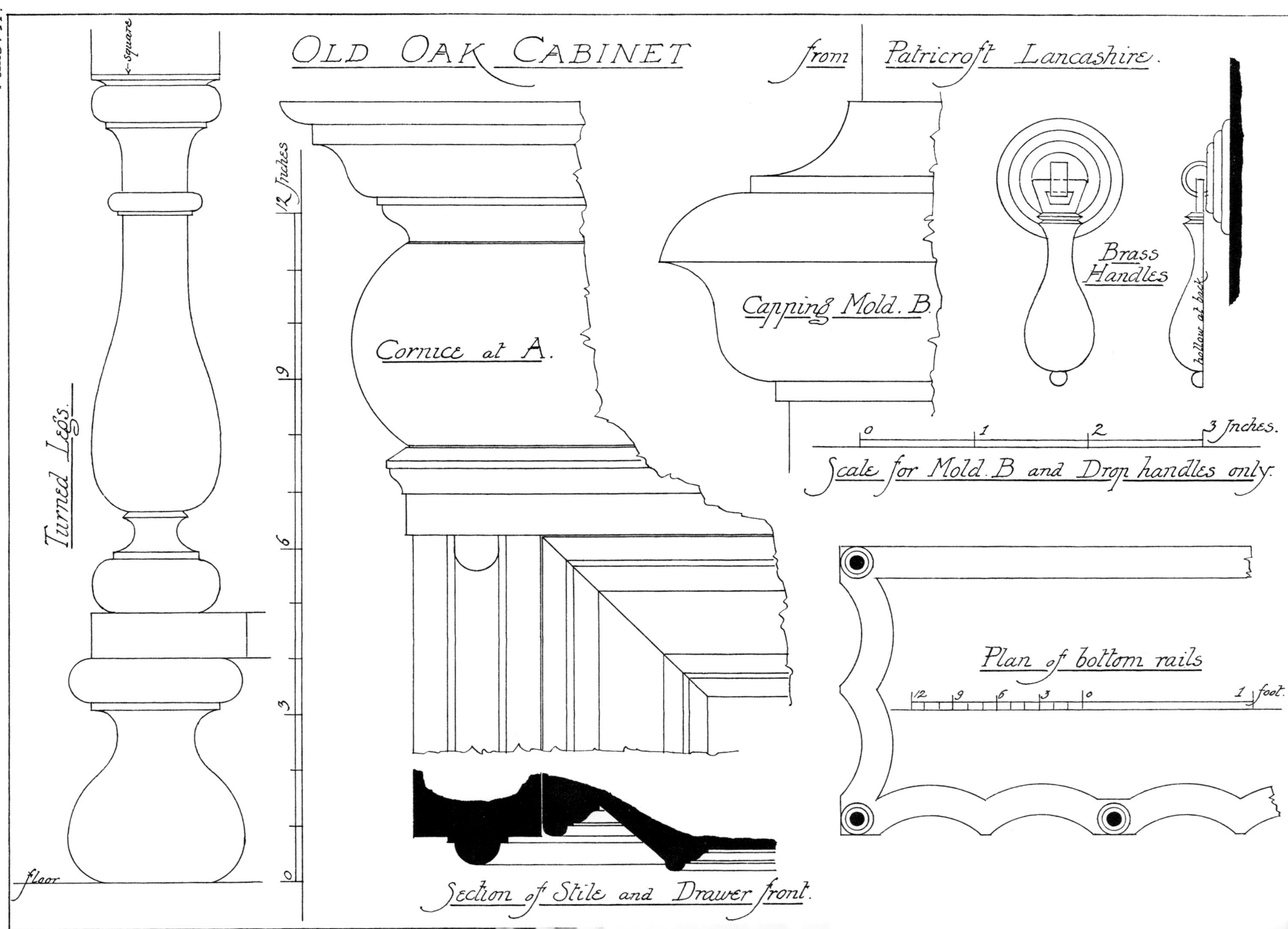

Old Oak Cabinet — Manchester.

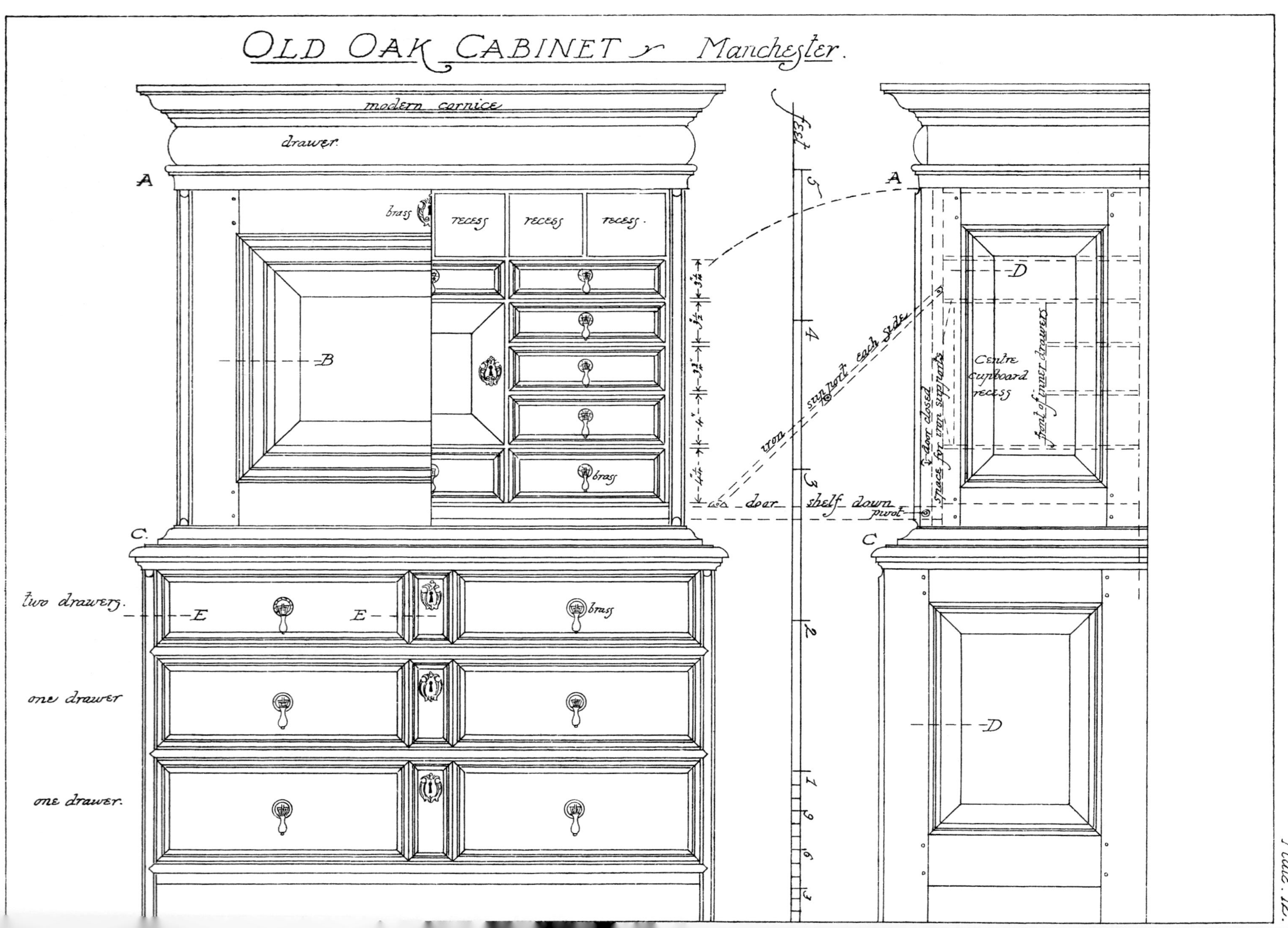

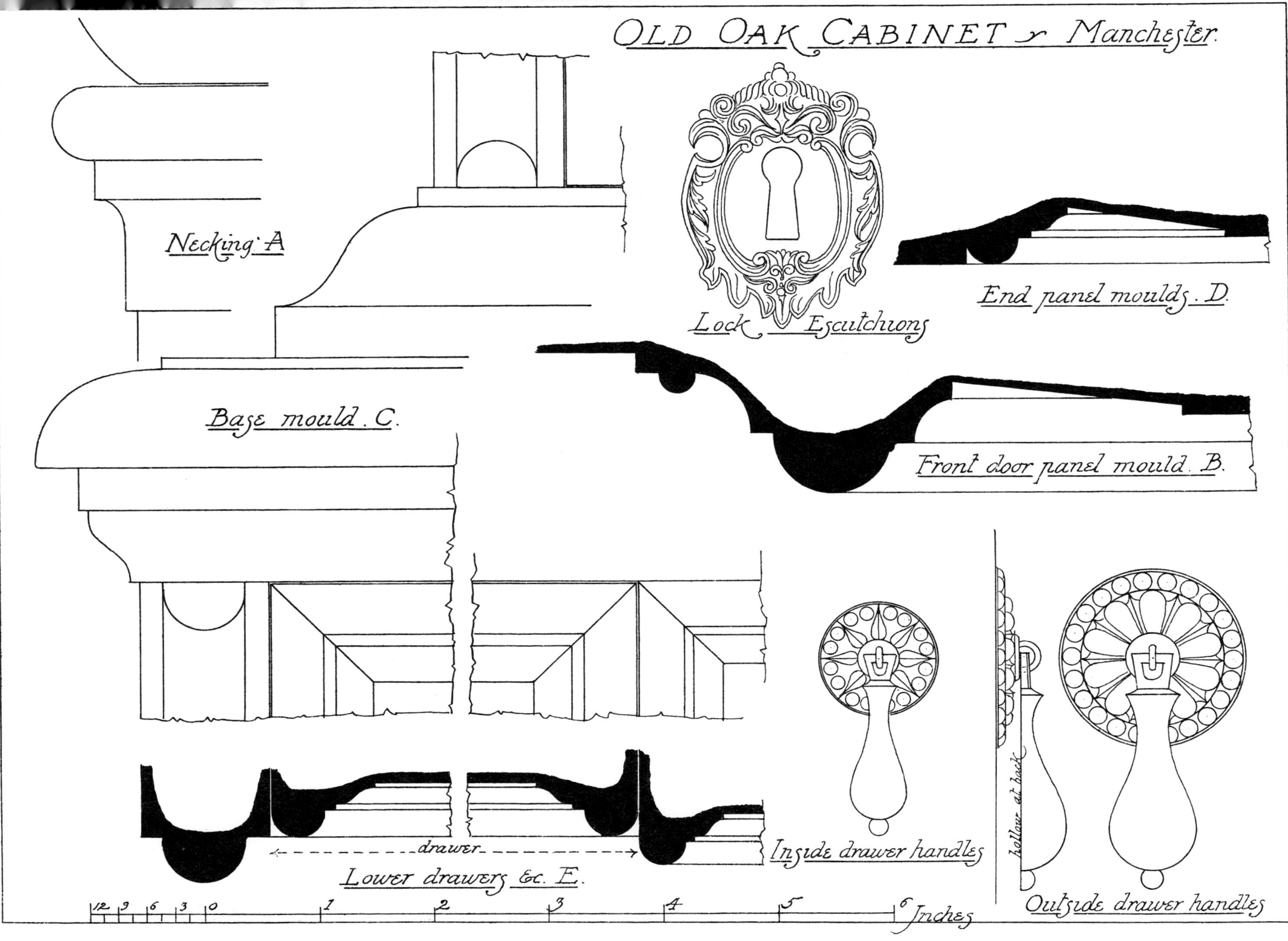
OLD OAK CABINET, Manchester.
Necking A
Lock Escutchions
End panel moulds. D.
Base mould. C.
Front door panel mould. B.
drawer
Lower drawers &c. E.
Inside drawer handles
hollow at back
Outside drawer handles
12 9 6 3 0 1 2 3 4 5 6 Inches

OLD OAK WARDROBE
Lancashire
Modern Cornice
Cupboard above.
Chest below
Chest lid
floor
Inches
feet

OLD OAK WARDROBE. Lancashire.

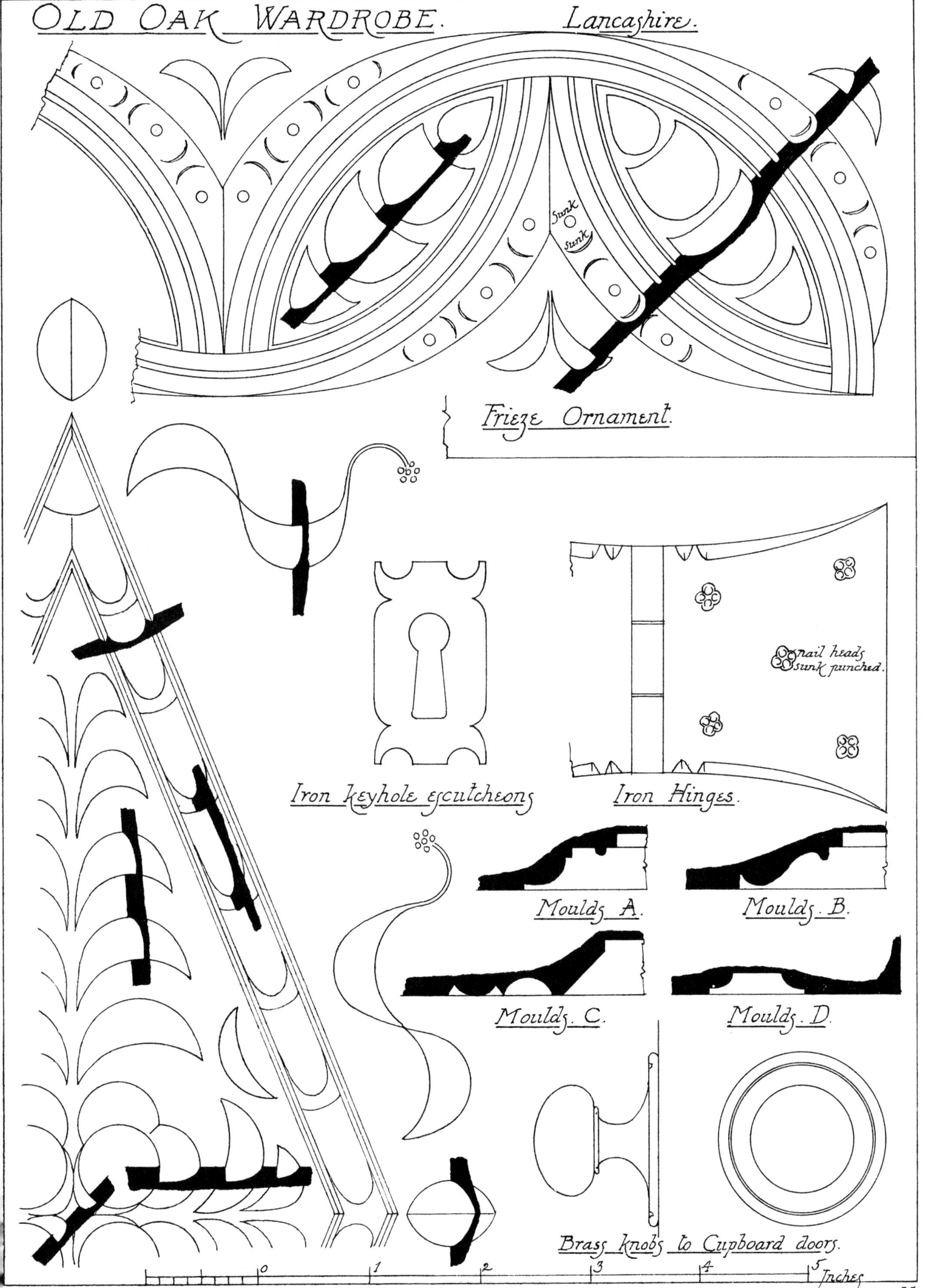

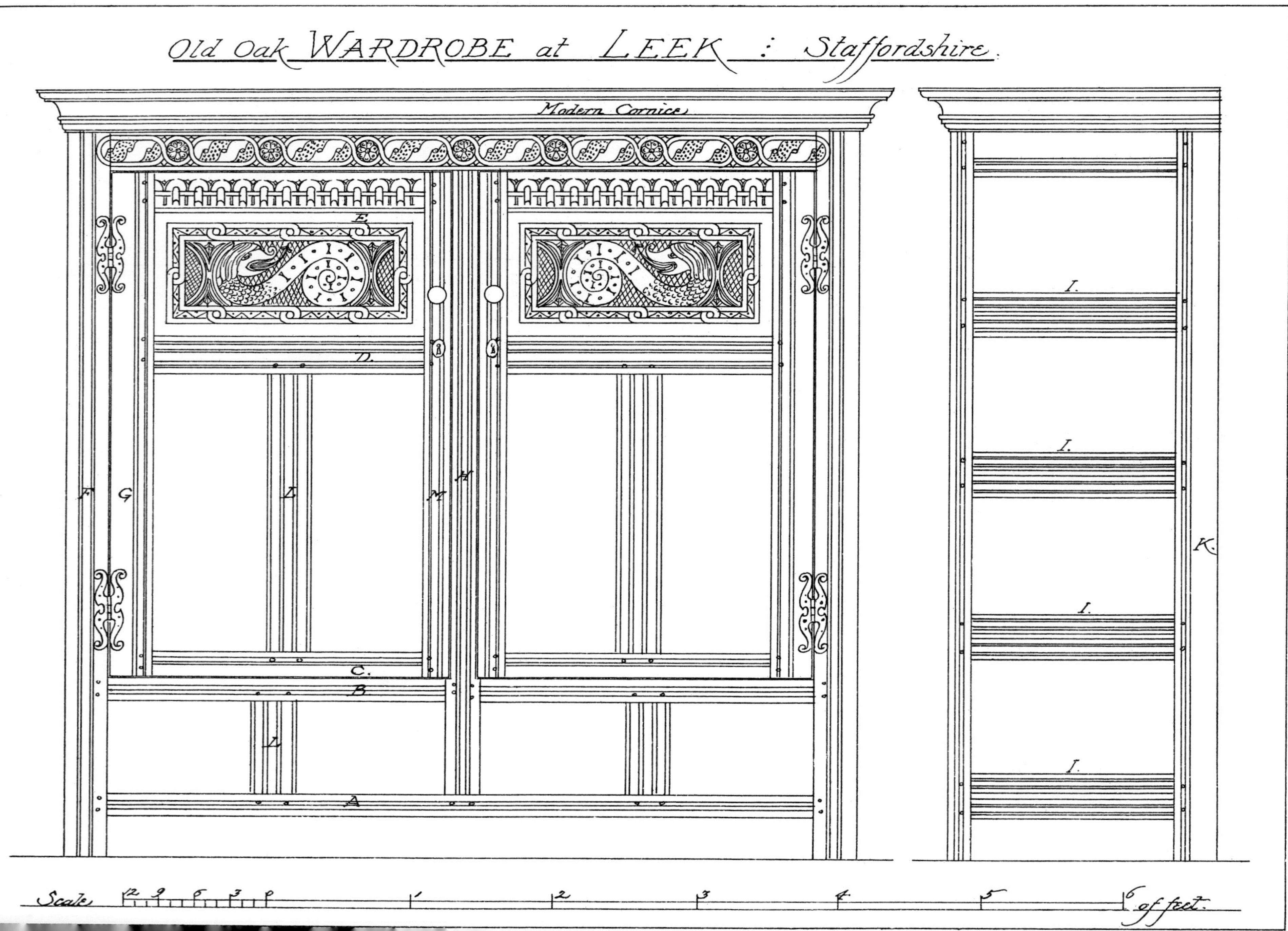
Old Oak WARDROBE at LEEK : Staffordshire.
Modern Cornice.
E.
D.
C.
B.
A.
F.
G.
L.
L.
M.
H.
I.
I.
I.
I.
K.
Scale 12 9 6 3 0 1 2 3 4 5 6 of feet.

Old Oak WARDROBE at LEEK : Details of Moldings &c.

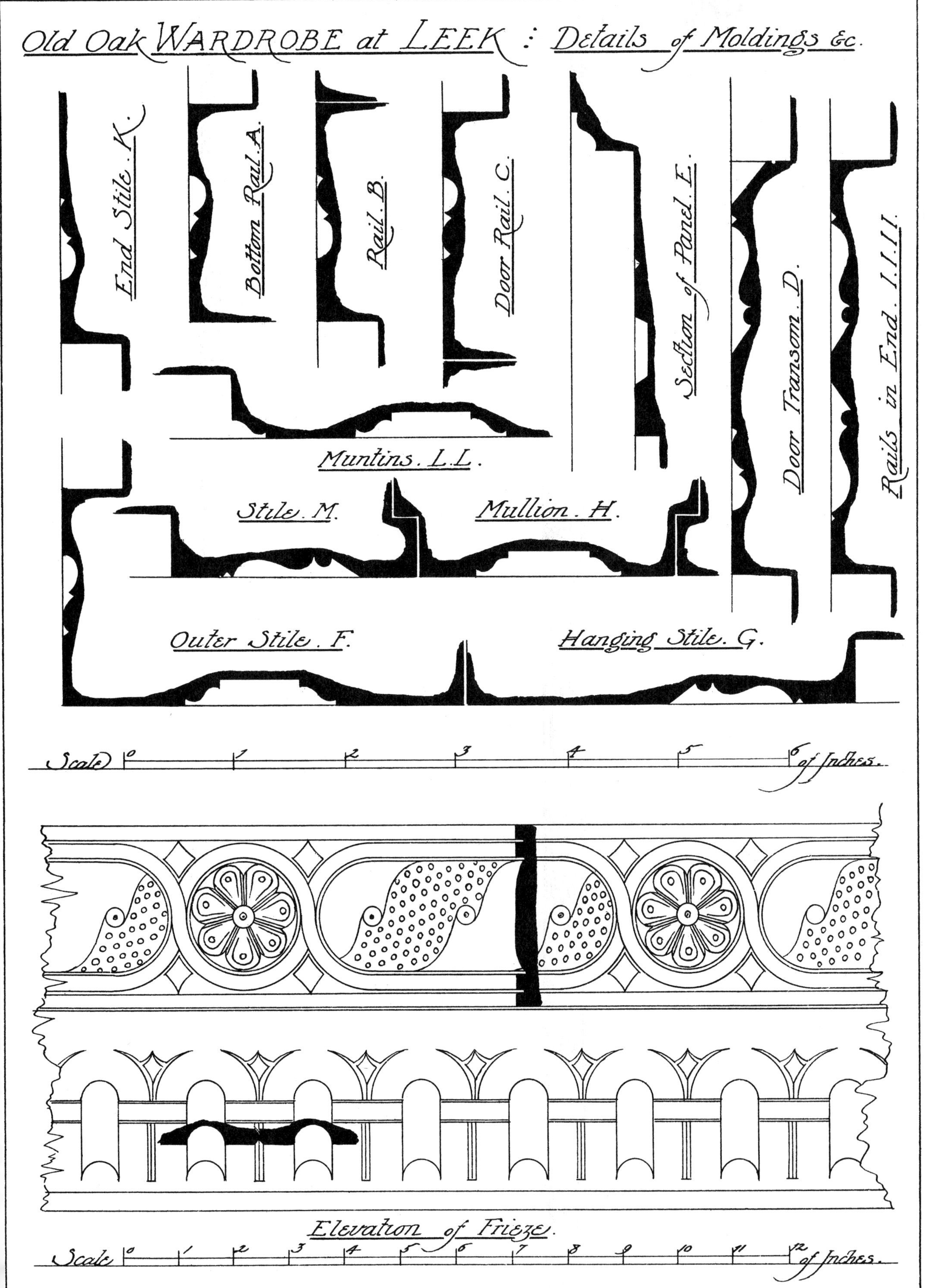

OLD · OAK · WARDROBE : from Tyldesley. Lancashire
Modern Cornice
A
B.
D
C
Panel.
Mould round Carved panels. A.
fixed.
Door Stile. B.
Rails in Ends. C.
Rails in Front. D.
Carved Panels.
Scale 0 1 2 3 4 5 of Inches
Scale 12 9 6 3 0 1 2 3 4 of Feet.

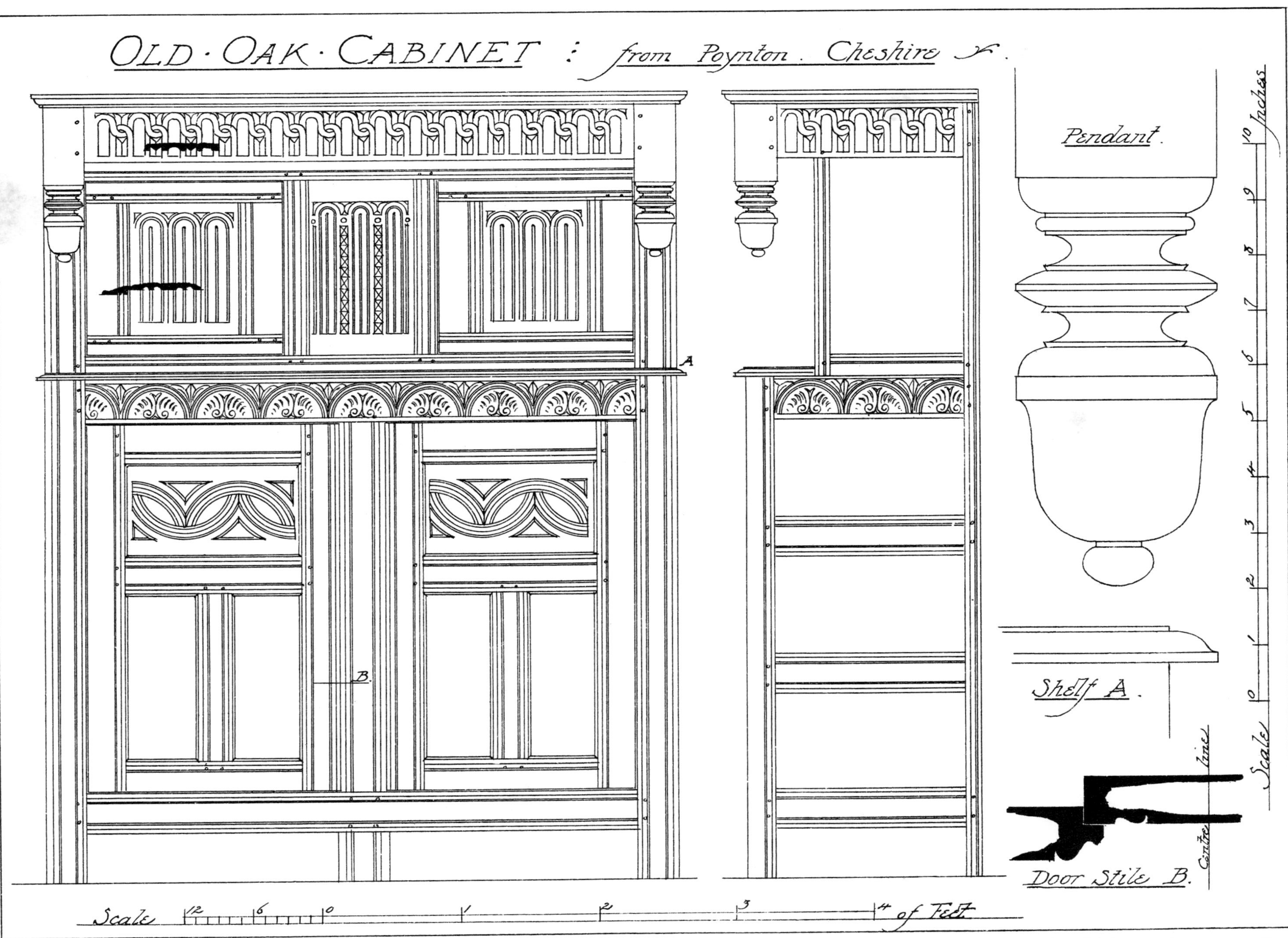
OLD·OAK·CABINET : from Poynton. Cheshire
A
B.
Pendant.
Shelf A.
Centre line
Door Stile B.
Scale 0 1 2 3 4 5 6 7 8 9 10 Inches
Scale 12 6 0 1 2 3 4 of Feet

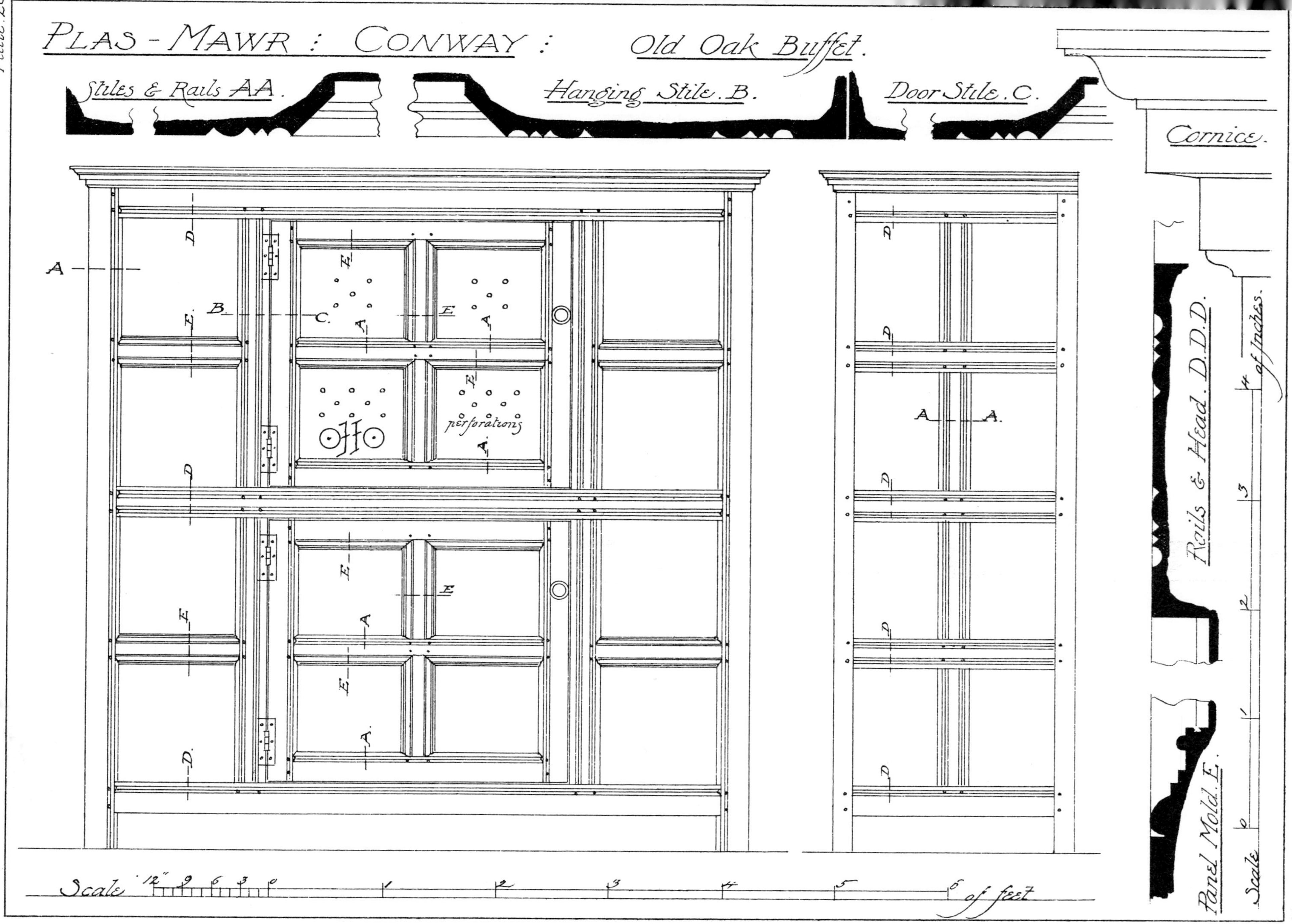
PLAS - MAWR : CONWAY : Old Oak Buffet.
Stiles & Rails AA.
Hanging Stile. B.
Door Stile. C.
Cornice.
Rails & Head. D.D.D.
Panel Mold. E.
Scale 0 1 2 3 4 of Inches.
perforations
Scale 12" 9 6 3 0 1 2 3 4 5 6 of feet

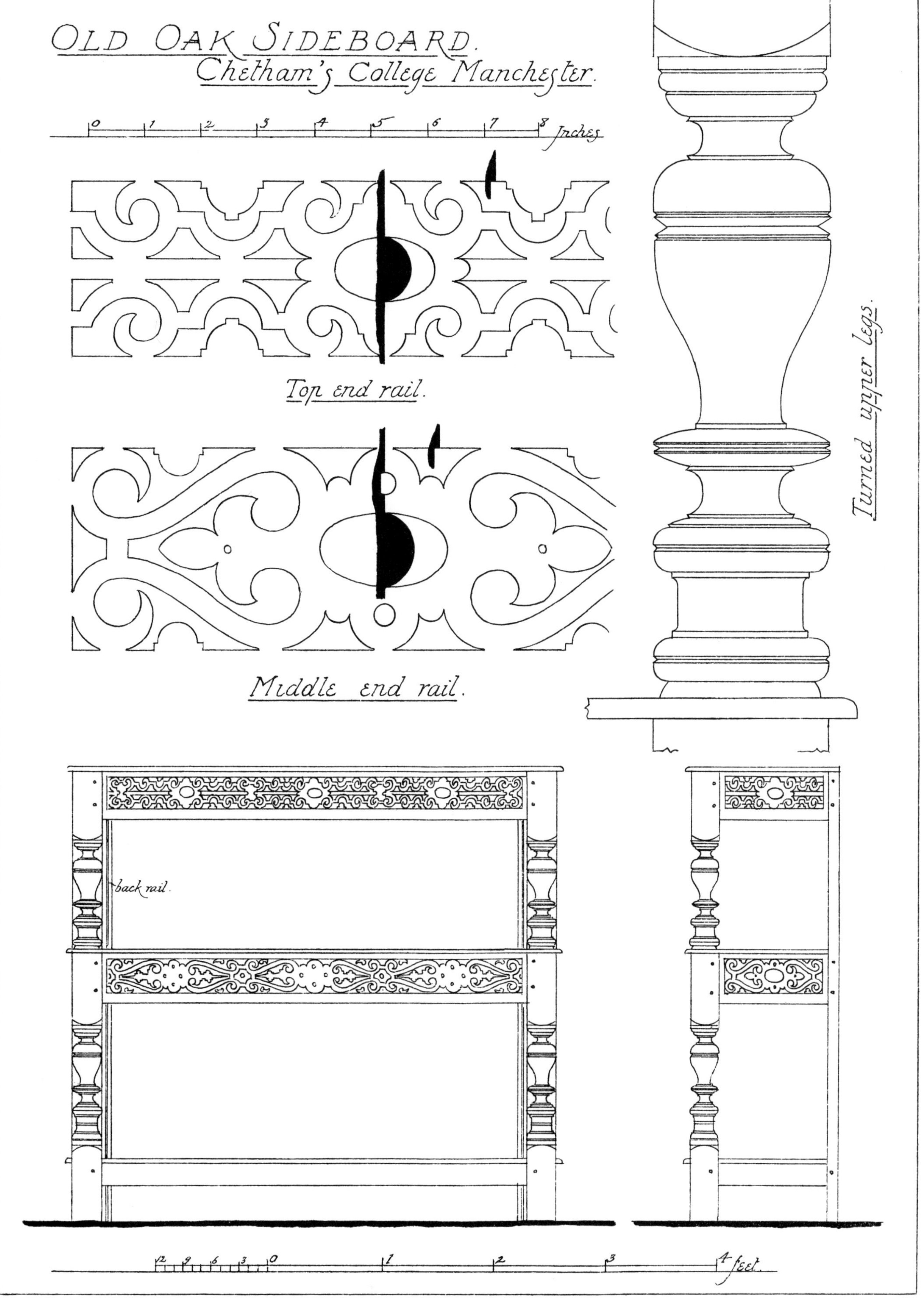
OLD OAK SIDEBOARD.
Chetham's College Manchester.
0 1 2 3 4 5 6 7 8 Inches
Top end rail.
Middle end rail.
Turned upper legs.
back rail.
12 9 6 3 0 1 2 3 4 feet.

OLD OAK DRESSER belonging to The Honourable Marshall Brooks. Rawtenstall.

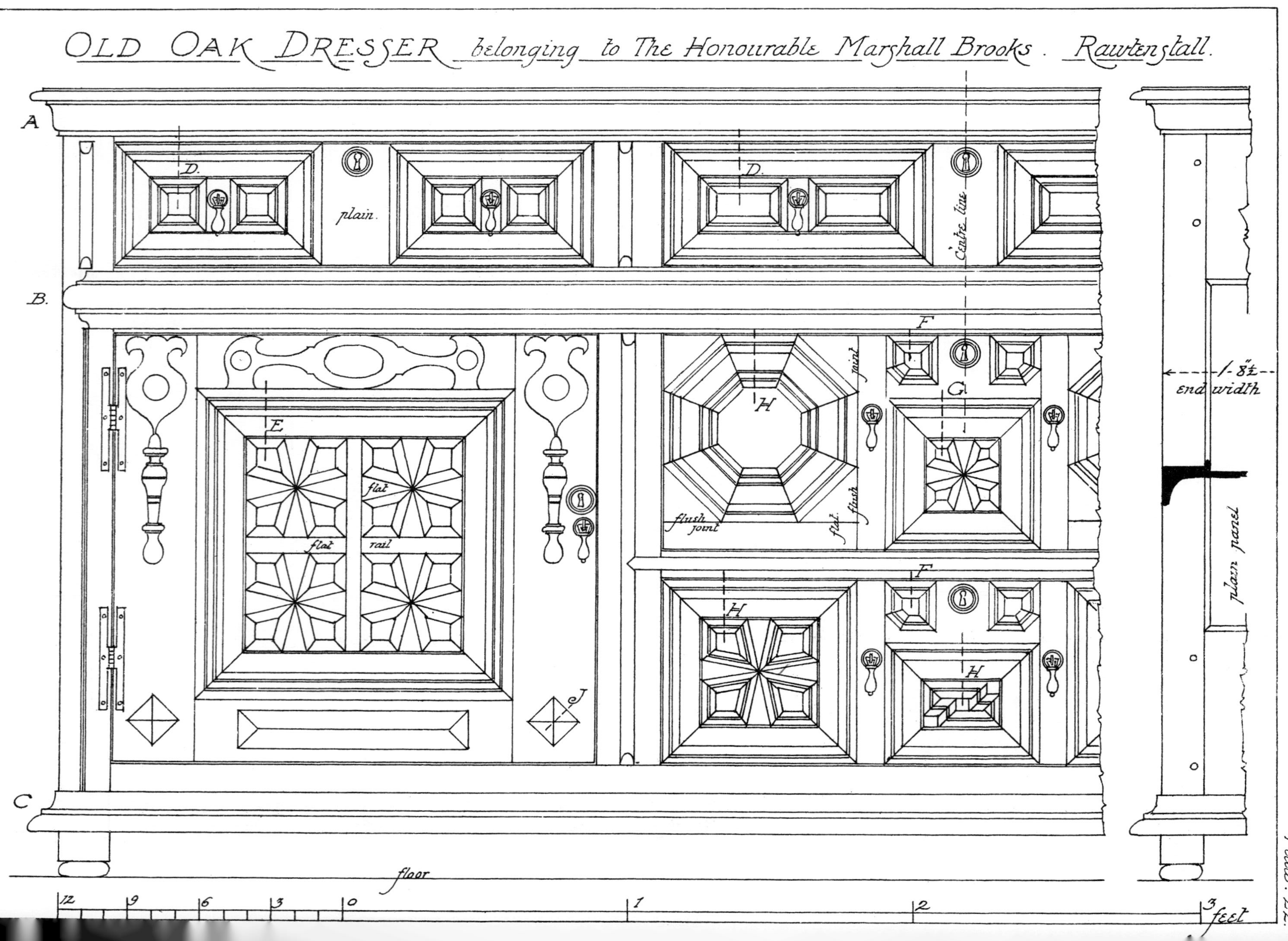

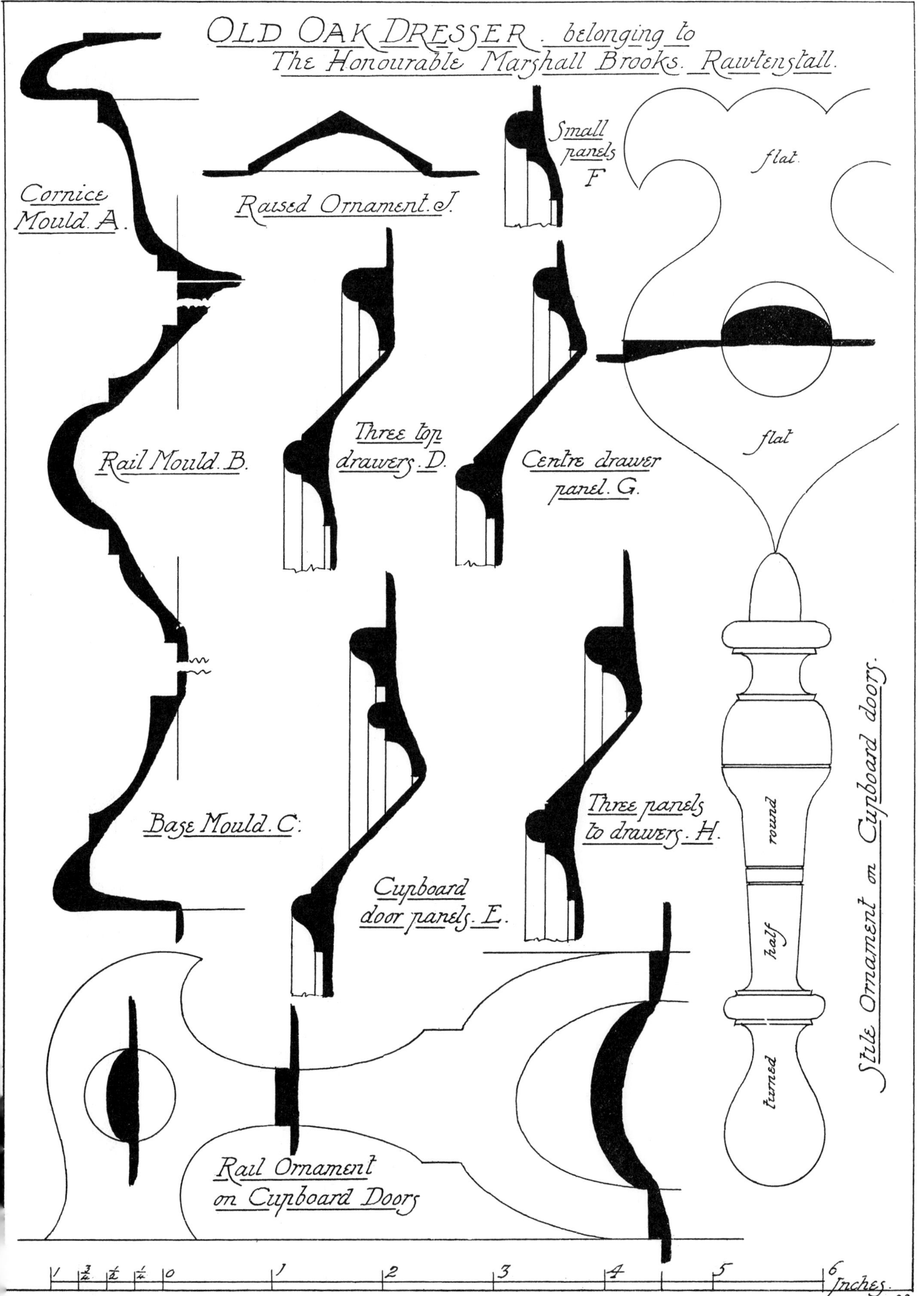
OLD OAK DRESSER. belonging to
The Honourable Marshall Brooks. Rawtenstall.
Cornice Mould. A.
Raised Ornament. J.
Small panels F
flat.
Rail Mould. B.
Three top drawers. D.
Centre drawer panel. G.
flat
Base Mould. C.
Three panels to drawers. H.
Cupboard door panels. E.
round
half
turned
Stile Ornament on Cupboard doors.
Rail Ornament on Cupboard Doors
1 3/4 1/2 1/4 0 1 2 3 4 5 6 Inches.

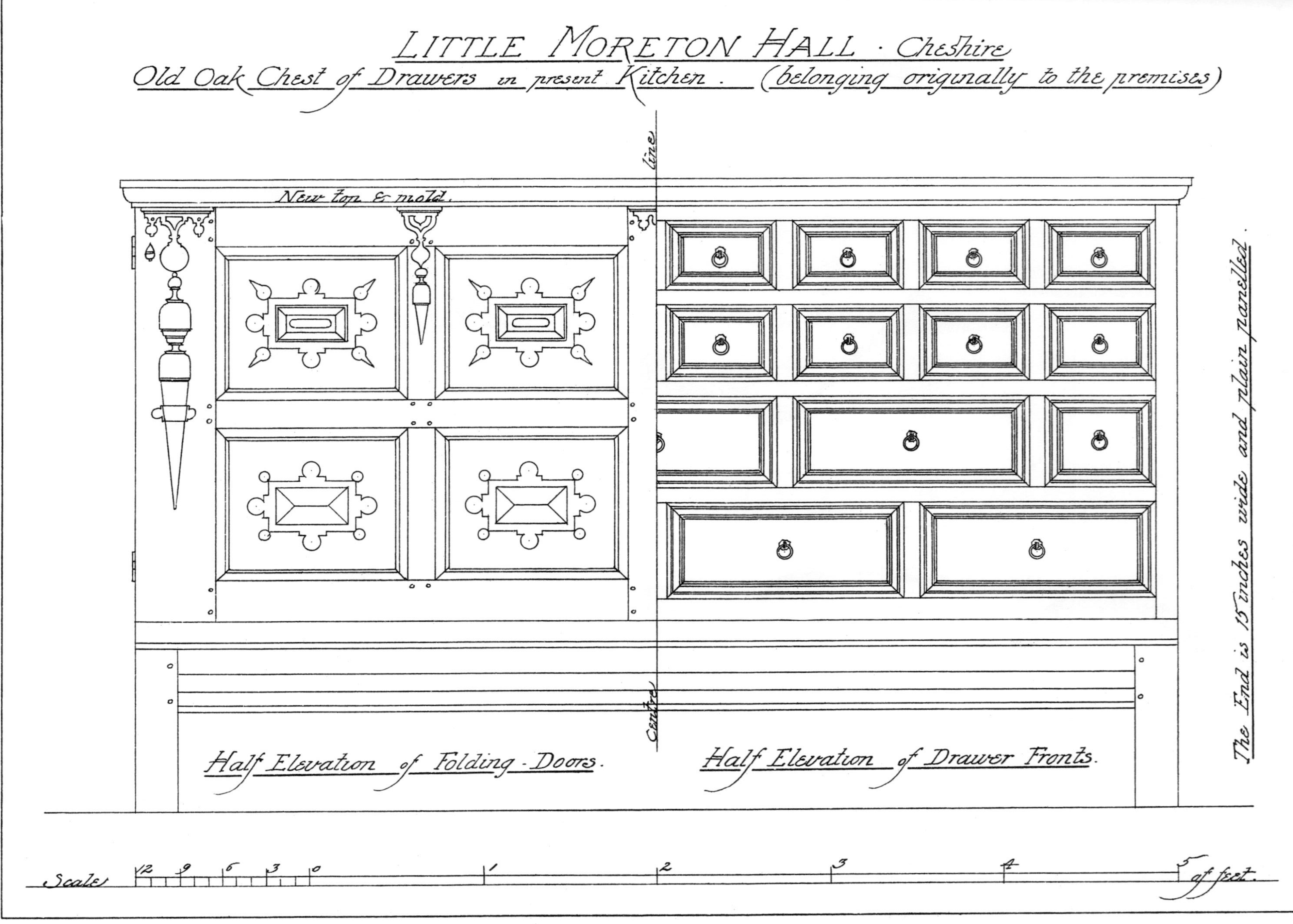
LITTLE MORETON HALL · Cheshire
Old Oak Chest of Drawers in present Kitchen. (belonging originally to the premises)
New top & mold.
Centre line
Half Elevation of Folding-Doors.
Half Elevation of Drawer Fronts.
The End is 15 inches wide and plain panelled.
Scale 12 9 6 3 0 1 2 3 4 5 of feet.

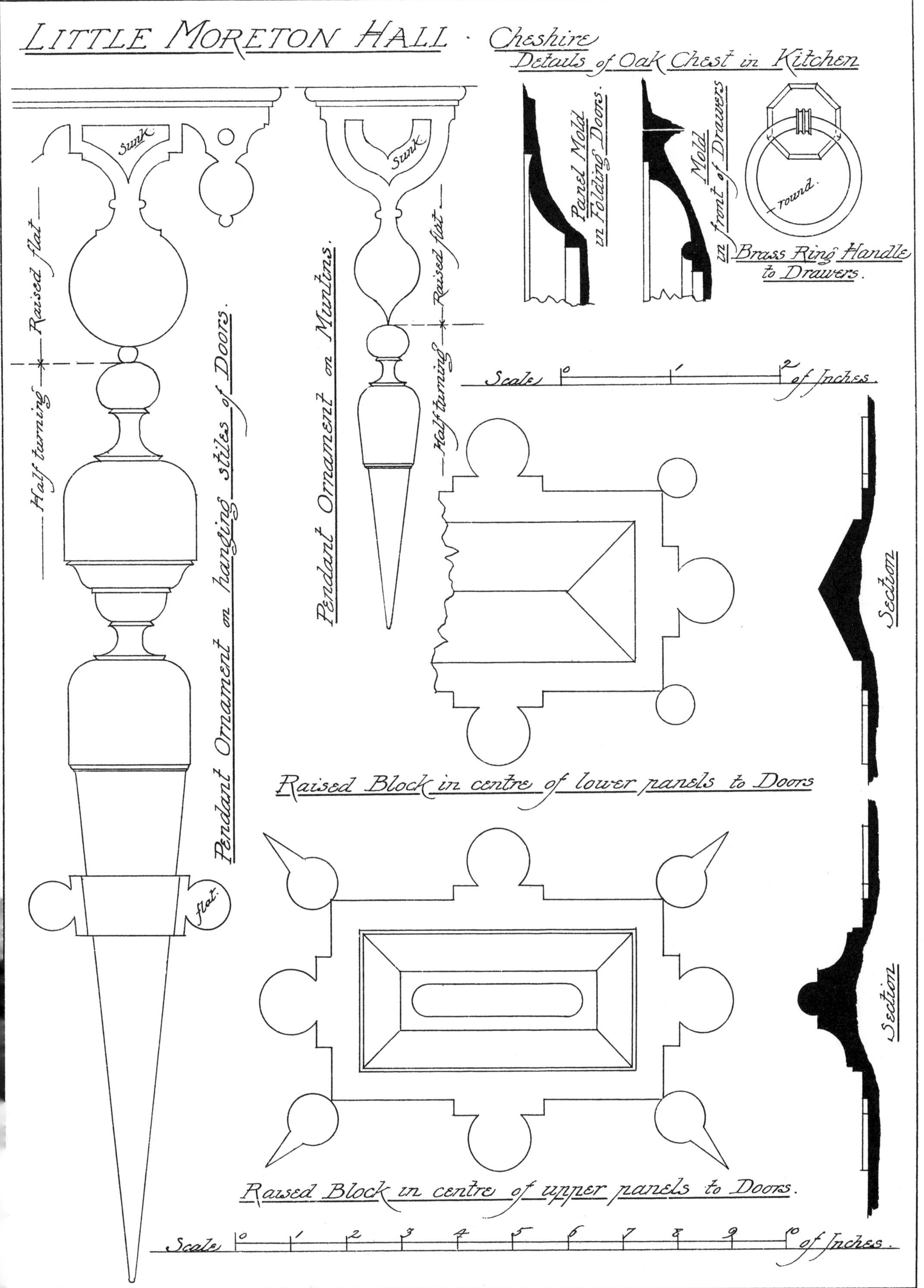
LITTLE MORETON HALL · Cheshire
Details of Oak Chest in Kitchen
sunk
sunk
Raised flat
Half turning
Raised flat
Half turning
Pendant Ornament on hanging stiles of Doors.
Pendant Ornament on Muntins.
flat.
Panel Mold in Folding Doors.
Mold in front of Drawers
round.
Brass Ring Handle to Drawers.
Scale 0 1 2 of Inches.
Section
Raised Block in centre of lower panels to Doors
Section
Raised Block in centre of upper panels to Doors.
Scale 0 1 2 3 4 5 6 7 8 9 10 of Inches.

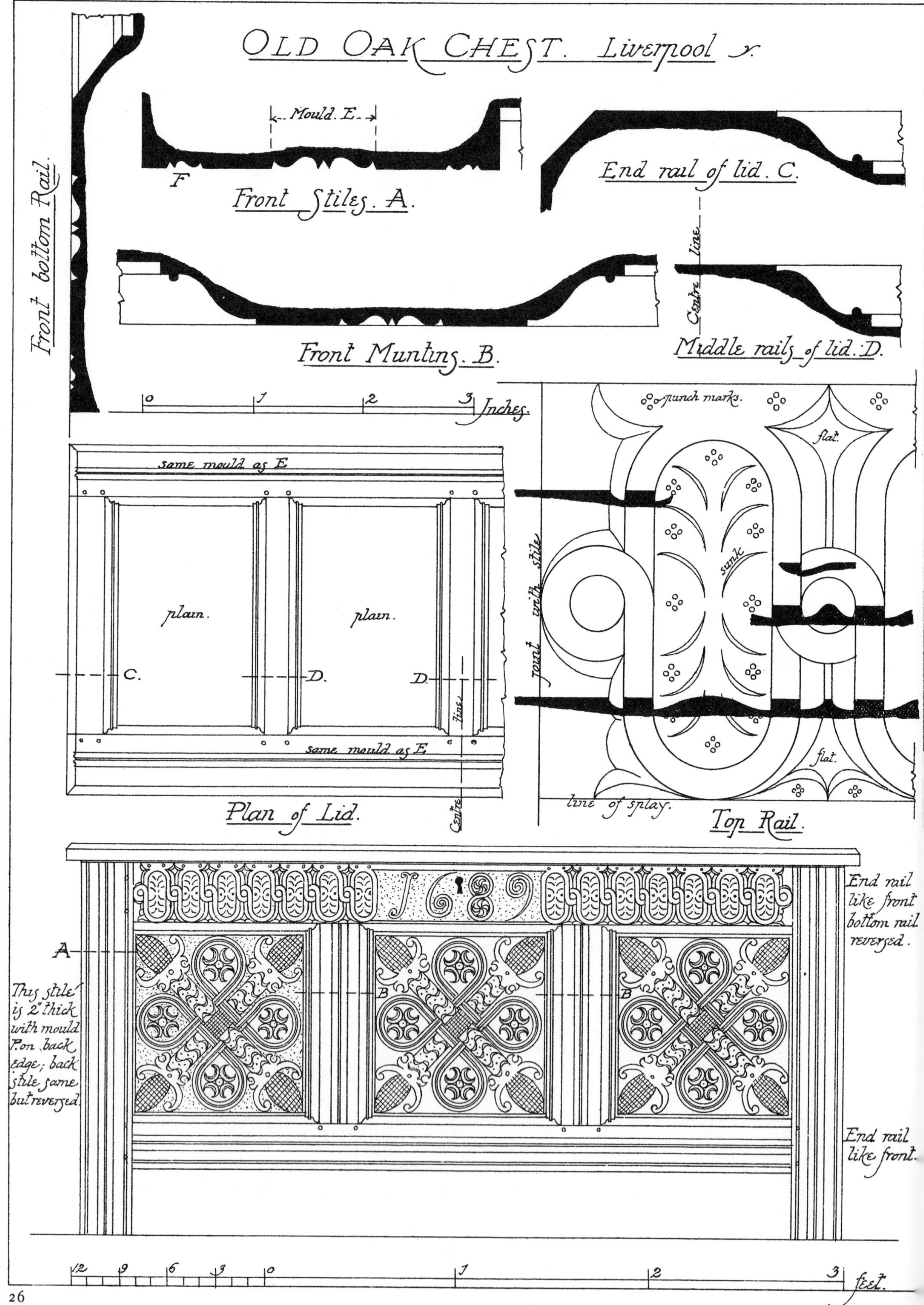

OLD OAK CHEST. Liverpool
Mould. E.
F
Front Stiles. A.
End rail of lid. C.
Front bottom Rail.
Centre line
Front Muntins. B.
Middle rails of lid. D.
0
1
2
3
Inches.
punch marks.
flat.
sunk
joint with stile
flat.
line of splay.
Top Rail.
same mould as E
plain.
plain.
C.
D.
D.
Centre line
same mould as E.
Plan of Lid.
1689
End rail like front bottom rail reversed.
A
B
B
This stile is 2" thick with mould F on back edge; back stile same but reversed.
End rail like front.
12
9
6
3
0
1
2
3
feet.

OLD OAK CHEST. Liverpool.
for correct spaces between the figures see general elevation.
incised lines
finely punched face
smooth.
smooth.
smooth face.
smooth.
incised lines
8 4 0 1 2 3 4 5 6 Inches.

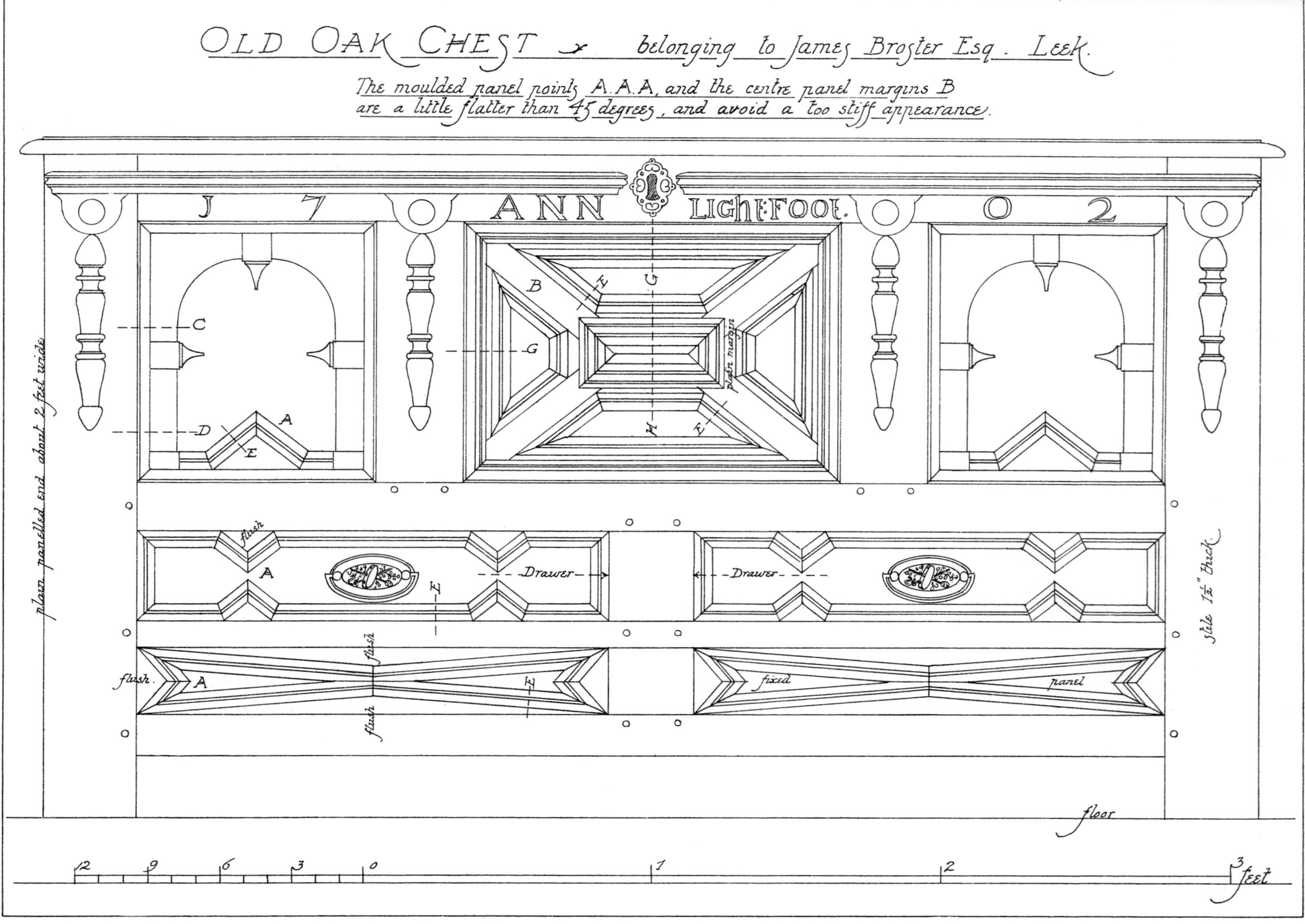

OLD OAK CHEST, belonging to James Broster Esq. Leek.
The moulded panel points A.A.A, and the centre panel margins B
are a little flatter than 45 degrees, and avoid a too stiff appearance.
J 7
ANN
LIGHTFOOT.
O 2
plain panelled end about 2 feet wide
stile 1½" thick
floor
flush
flush
flush
flush
fixed
panel
Drawer
Drawer
plain margin
A
B
C
D
E
F
G
H
12
9
6
3
0
1
2
3
feet

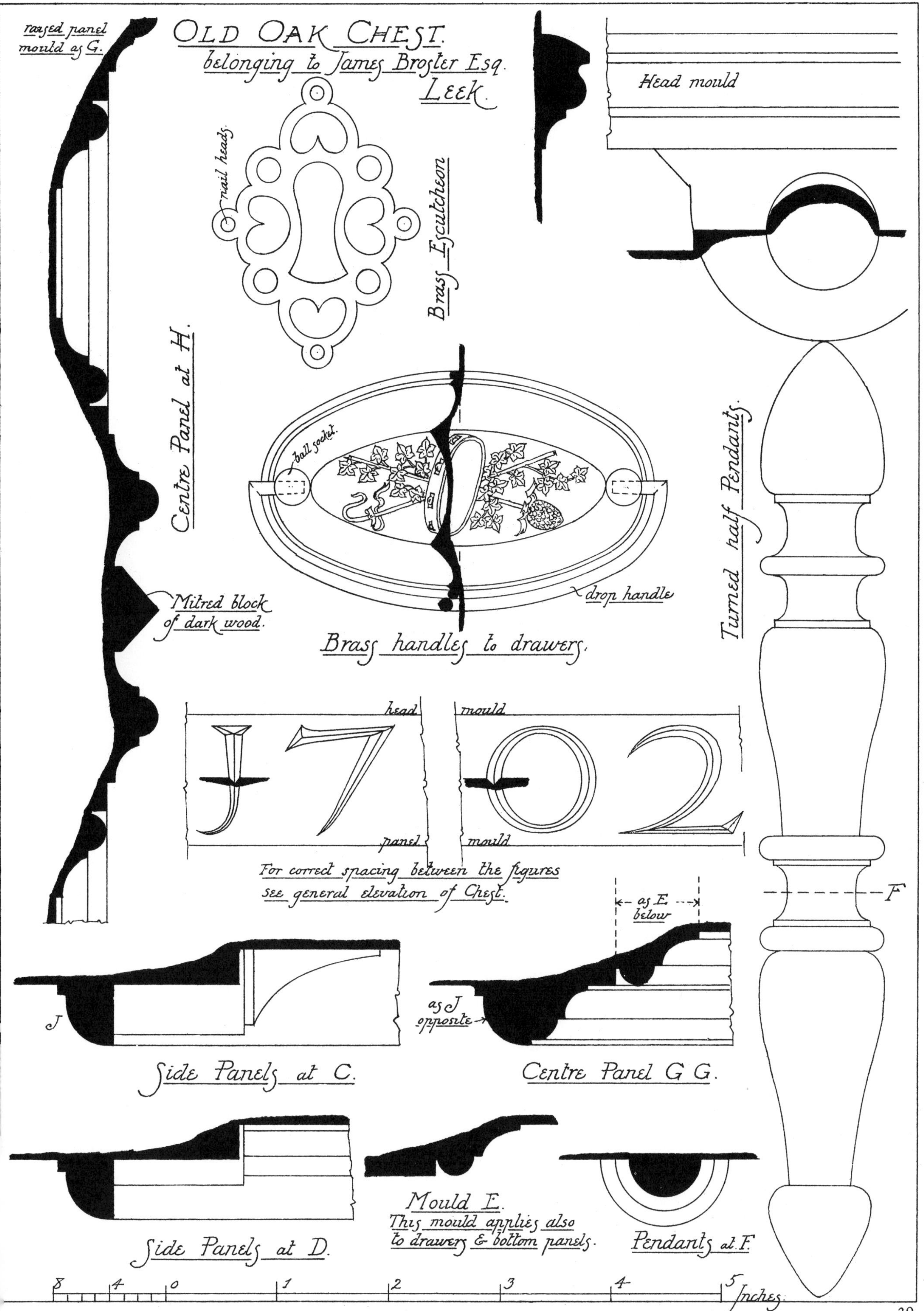

raised panel mould as G.
OLD OAK CHEST.
belonging to James Broster Esq.
LEEK.
nail heads.
Brass Escutcheon
Head mould
Centre Panel at H.
ball socket.
drop handle
Mitred block of dark wood.
Brass handles to drawers.
Turned half Pendants.
head
mould
panel
mould
1702
For correct spacing between the figures see general elevation of Chest.
as E below
F
J
as J opposite
Side Panels at C.
Centre Panel G G.
Side Panels at D.
Mould E.
This mould applies also to drawers & bottom panels.
Pendants at F.
8
4
0
1
2
3
4
5
Inches.

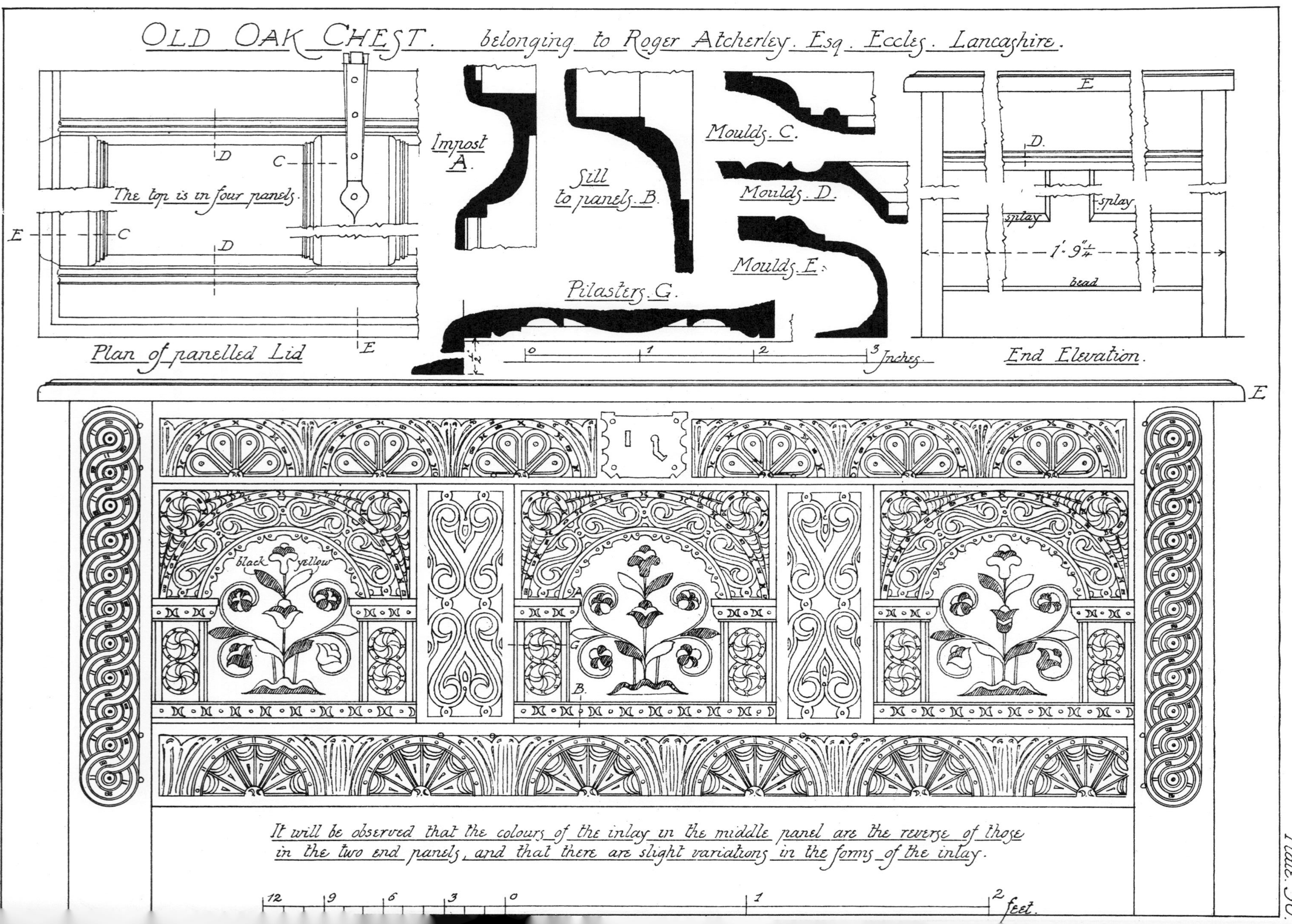
OLD OAK CHEST. belonging to Roger Atcherley. Esq. Eccles. Lancashire.
The top is in four panels.
Plan of panelled Lid
Impost A.
Sill to panels. B.
Moulds. C.
Moulds. D.
Moulds. E.
Pilasters. G.
0 1 2 3 Inches.
splay
splay
1' 9¼"
bead
End Elevation.
black
yellow
It will be observed that the colours of the inlay in the middle panel are the reverse of those in the two end panels, and that there are slight variations in the forms of the inlay.
12 9 6 3 0 1 2 feet.

OLD OAK CHEST: belonging to Roger Atcherley. Esq. Eccles. Lancashire.
Enlargement of Inlaid Panel & Carved Ornaments.
flat splay
punch marks
stem
black
yellow
face of panel
all flush inlay.
G
flat splay
0
2
4
6
8
10.
Inches

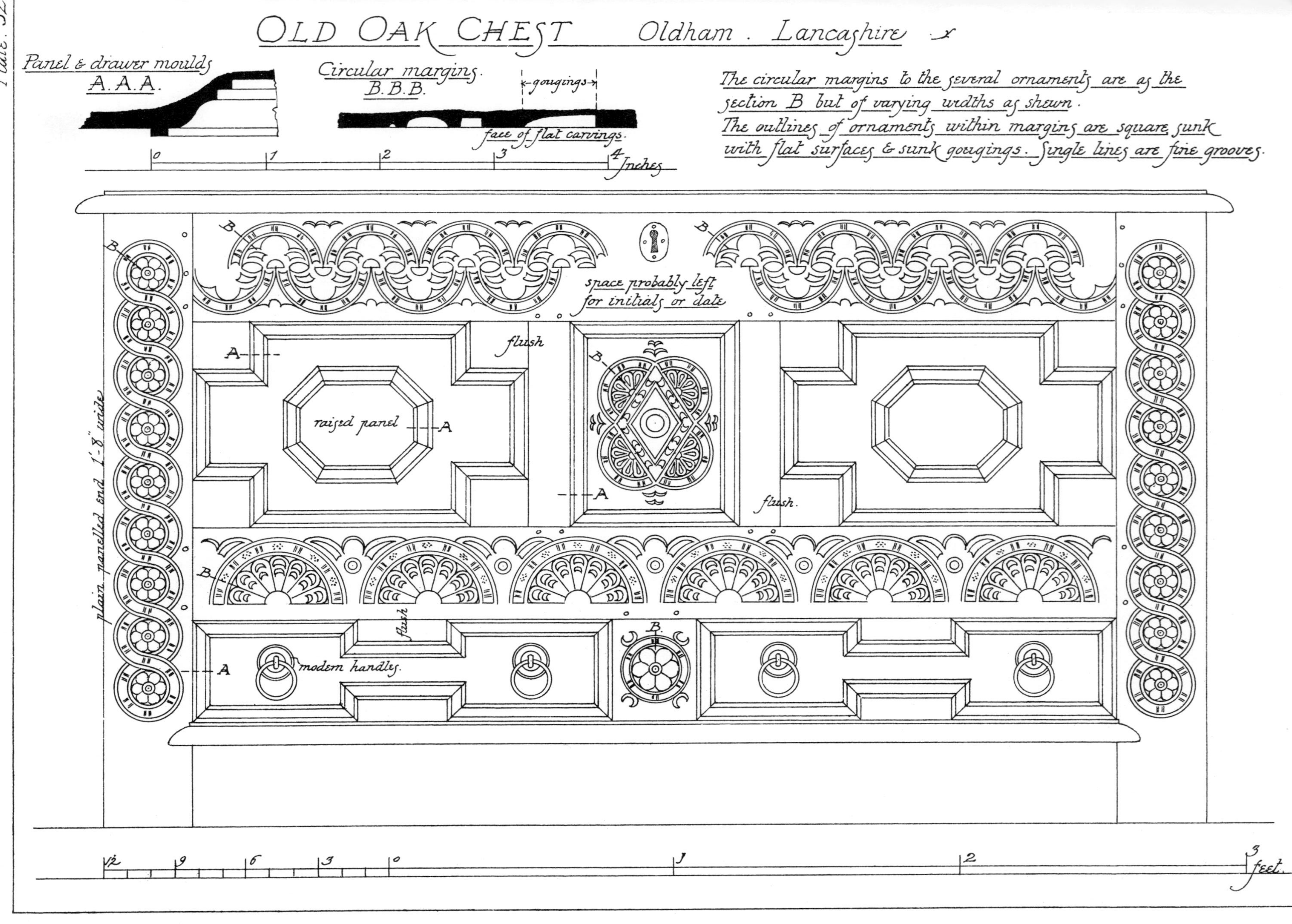
OLD OAK CHEST Oldham . Lancashire
Panel & drawer moulds
A.A.A.
Circular margins.
B.B.B.
gougings
face of flat carvings.
0
1
2
3
4 Inches
The circular margins to the several ornaments are as the section B but of varying widths as shewn.
The outlines of ornaments within margins are square sunk with flat surfaces & sunk gougings. Single lines are fine grooves.
space probably left for initials or date
flush
raised panel
flush.
modern handles.
plain panelled end 1'-8" wide
1/2
9
6
3
0
1
2
3 feet.

Old Oak CHEST at LEEK. Staffordshire
1/8" Sunk
Detail of Carved Top Rail.
Panel Ornament.
Section of Stiles.
Section of Muntins.
Scale 0 1 2 3 4 5 6 of Inches.
Front Elevation.
Scale 12 9 6 3 0 1 2 3 of feet.

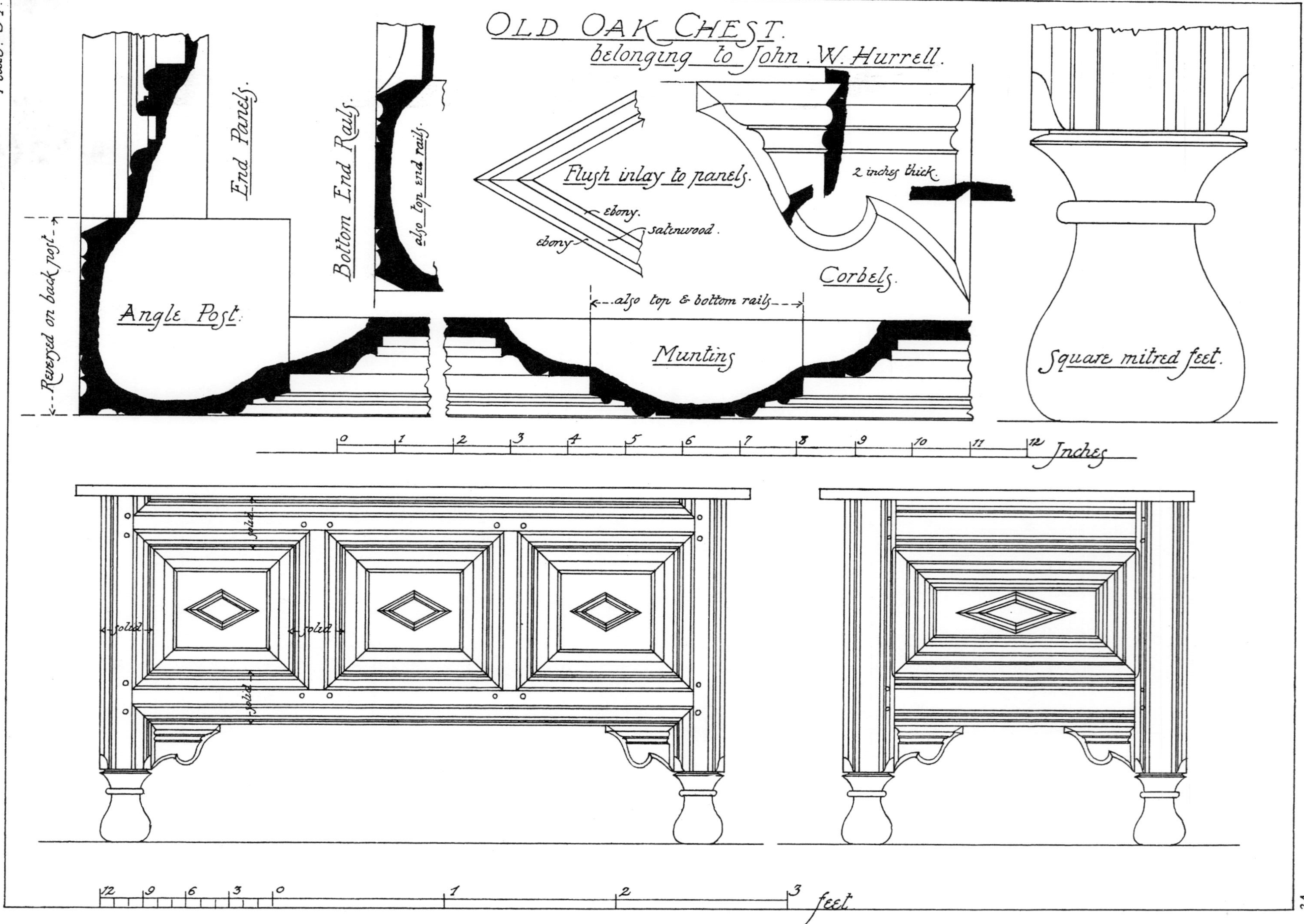
OLD OAK CHEST.
belonging to John. W. Hurrell.
End Panels.
Bottom End Rails.
also top end rails.
Reversed on back post
Angle Post.
Flush inlay to panels.
ebony.
ebony
satinwood.
2 inches thick.
Corbels.
also top & bottom rails
Muntins
Square mitred feet.
Inches
solid
solid
solid
solid
feet

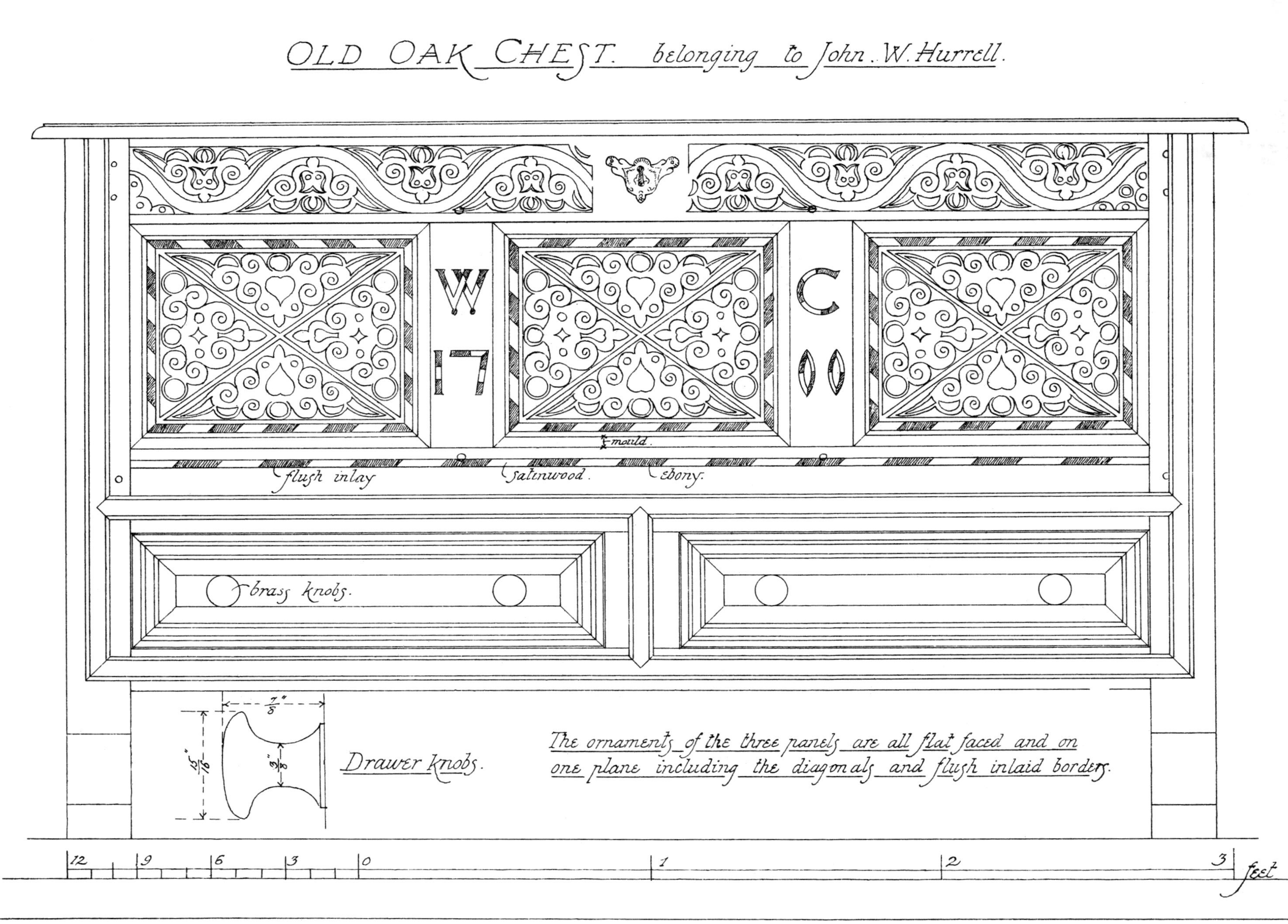
OLD OAK CHEST. belonging to John. W. Hurrell.
W C
17
mould.
flush inlay
satinwood.
ebony.
brass knobs.
Drawer knobs.
The ornaments of the three panels are all flat faced and on one plane including the diagonals and flush inlaid borders.
12 9 6 3 0 1 2 3 feet

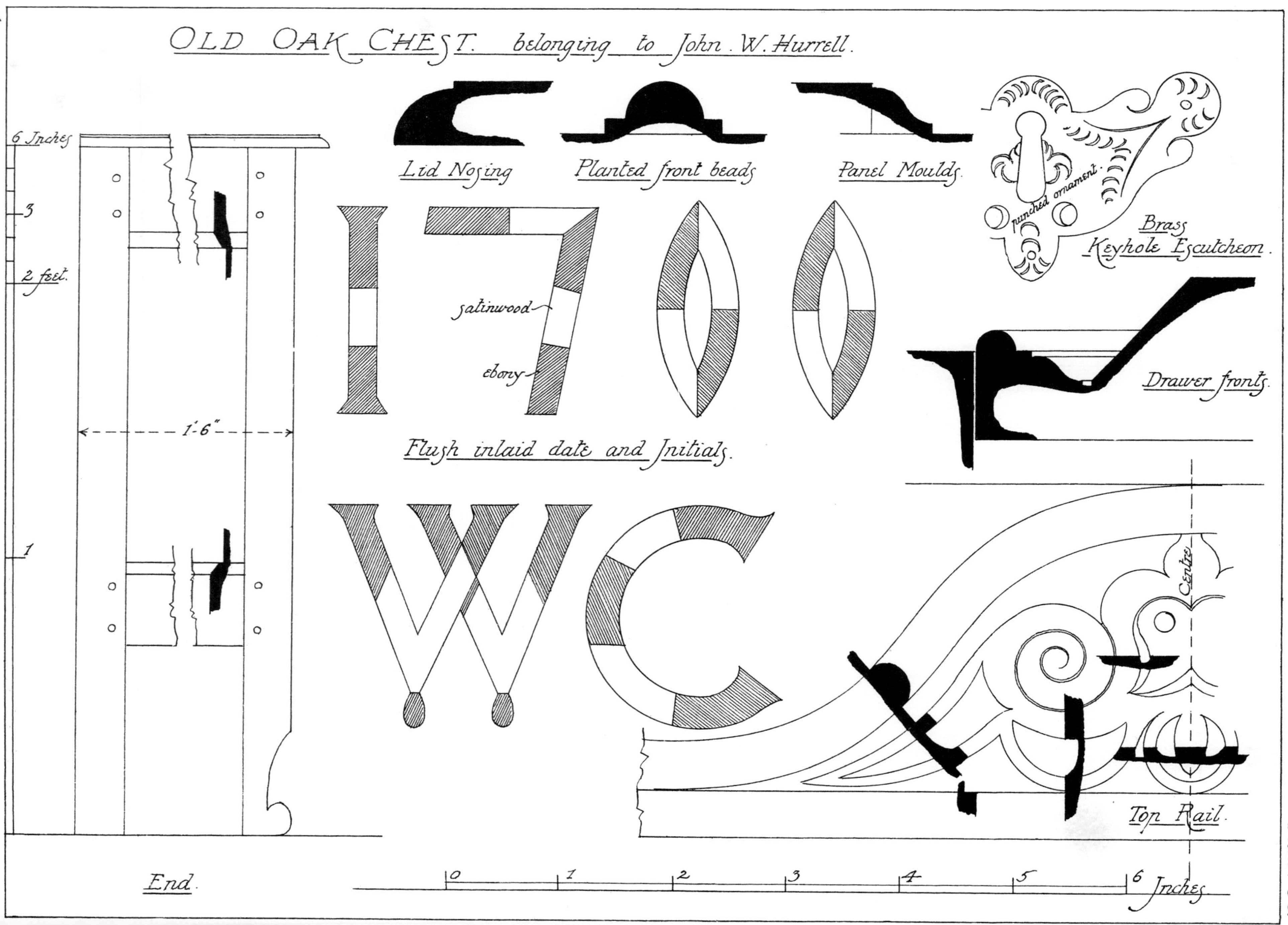
OLD OAK CHEST. belonging to John. W. Hurrell.
6 Inches
3
2 feet.
1
1'-6"
End.
Lid Nosing
Planted front beads
Panel Moulds.
punched ornament.
Brass
Keyhole Escutcheon.
satinwood
ebony
Flush inlaid date and Initials.
Drawer fronts.
Centre
Top Rail.
0 1 2 3 4 5 6 Inches

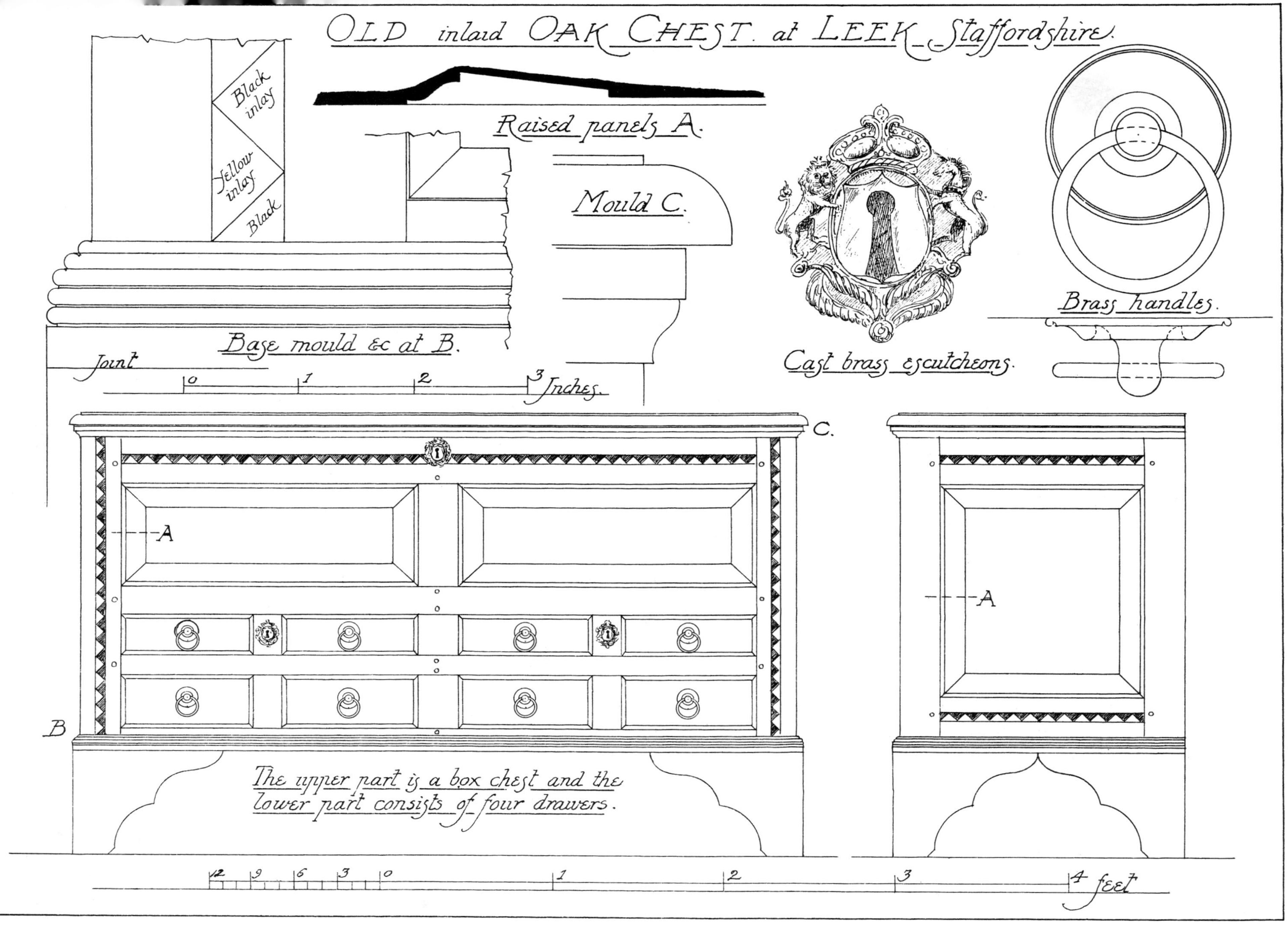
OLD inlaid OAK CHEST. at LEEK - Staffordshire.
Black inlay
Yellow inlay
Black
Raised panels A.
Mould C.
Base mould &c at B.
Joint
0 1 2 3 Inches.
Cast brass escutcheons.
Brass handles.
C.
A
A
B
The upper part is a box chest and the lower part consists of four drawers.
12 9 6 3 0 1 2 3 4 feet

OLD OAK CHESTS. r.
Top end rails
also stiles A
Bottom front rail D.
Muntin mould B.
flat
flat
Inches
Panel C.
plain end 1'6" wide
Bottom end rails
Chest belonging to the author.
feet.
Lid A.
Panel moulds B.
flat face
Raised panels and stiles C.
Inches.
Square soffit.
1'-8"
plain panel
Chest belonging to William Broster Esq. Leek r.
End.
feet.

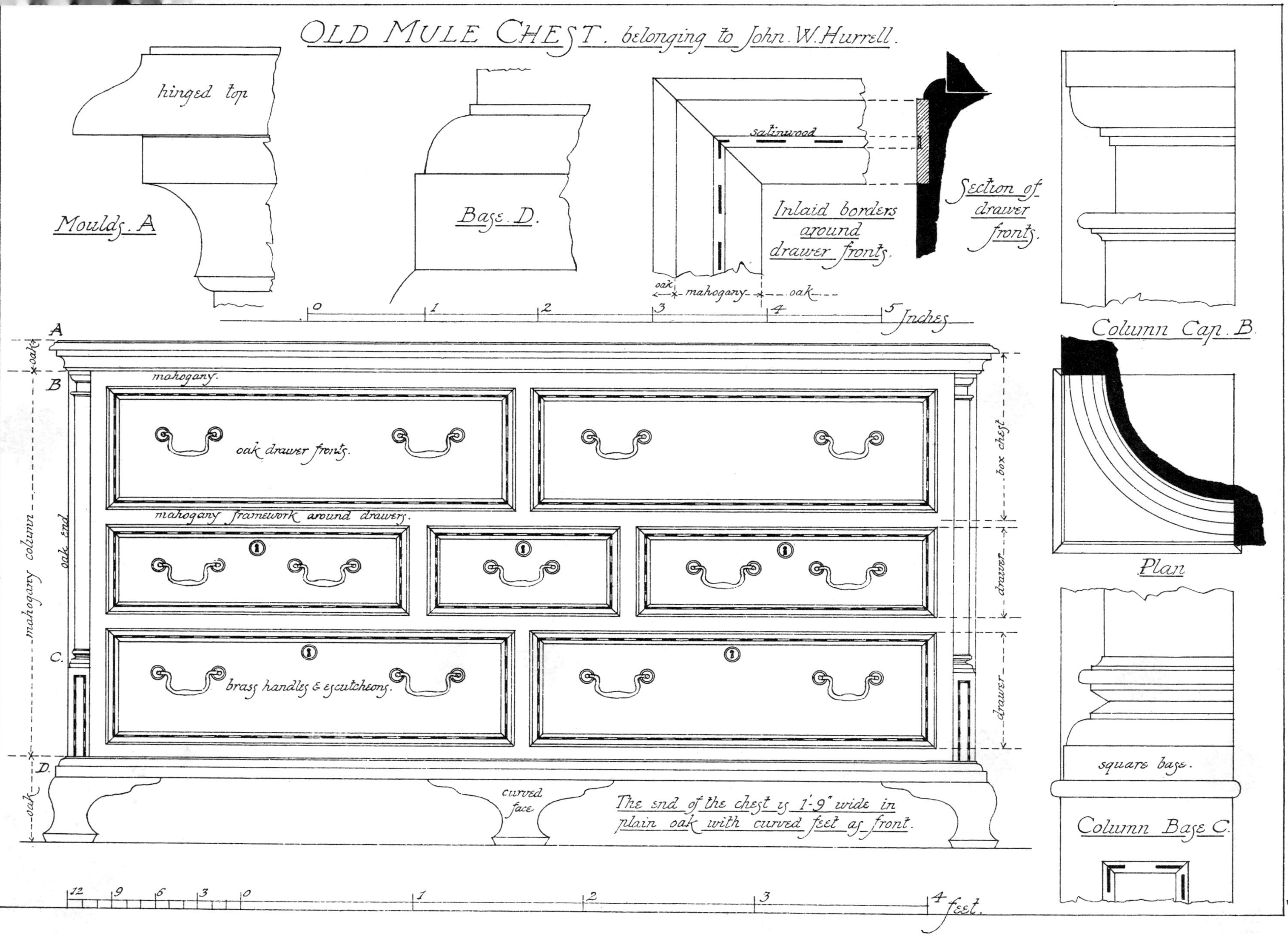
OLD MULE CHEST. belonging to John. W. Hurrell.
hinged top
Moulds. A
Base. D.
satinwood
Inlaid borders around drawer fronts.
Section of drawer fronts.
oak
mahogany
oak
0
1
2
3
4
5 Inches
Column Cap. B
Plan
square base.
Column Base C.
A
B
C.
D.
oak
mahogany column
oak end
oak
mahogany.
oak drawer fronts.
mahogany framework around drawers.
brass handles & escutcheons.
box chest
drawer
drawer
curved face
The end of the chest is 1'-9" wide in plain oak with curved feet as front.
12
9
6
3
0
1
2
3
4 feet.

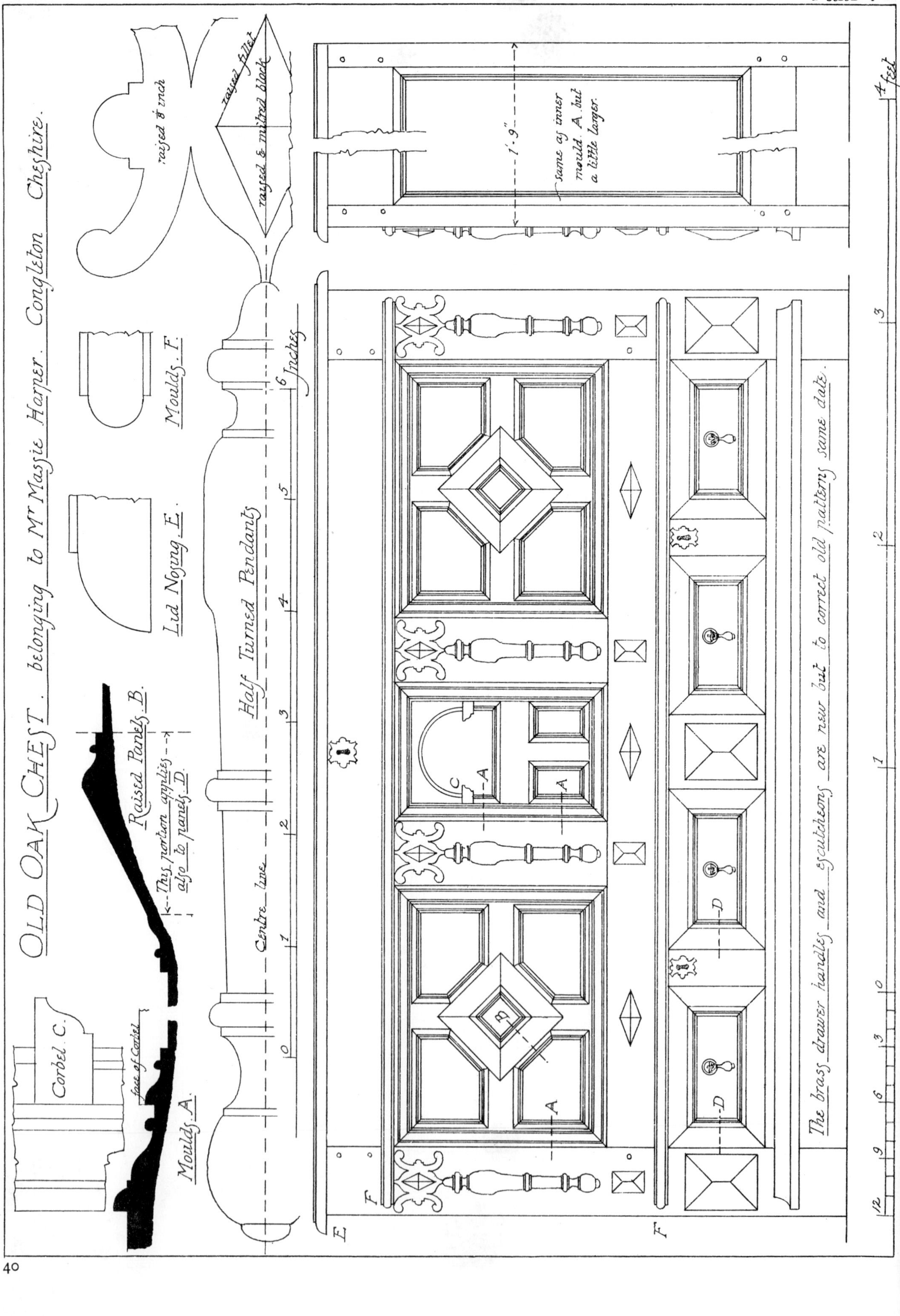

Old Oak Chest. belonging to Mr Massie Harper. Congleton Cheshire.

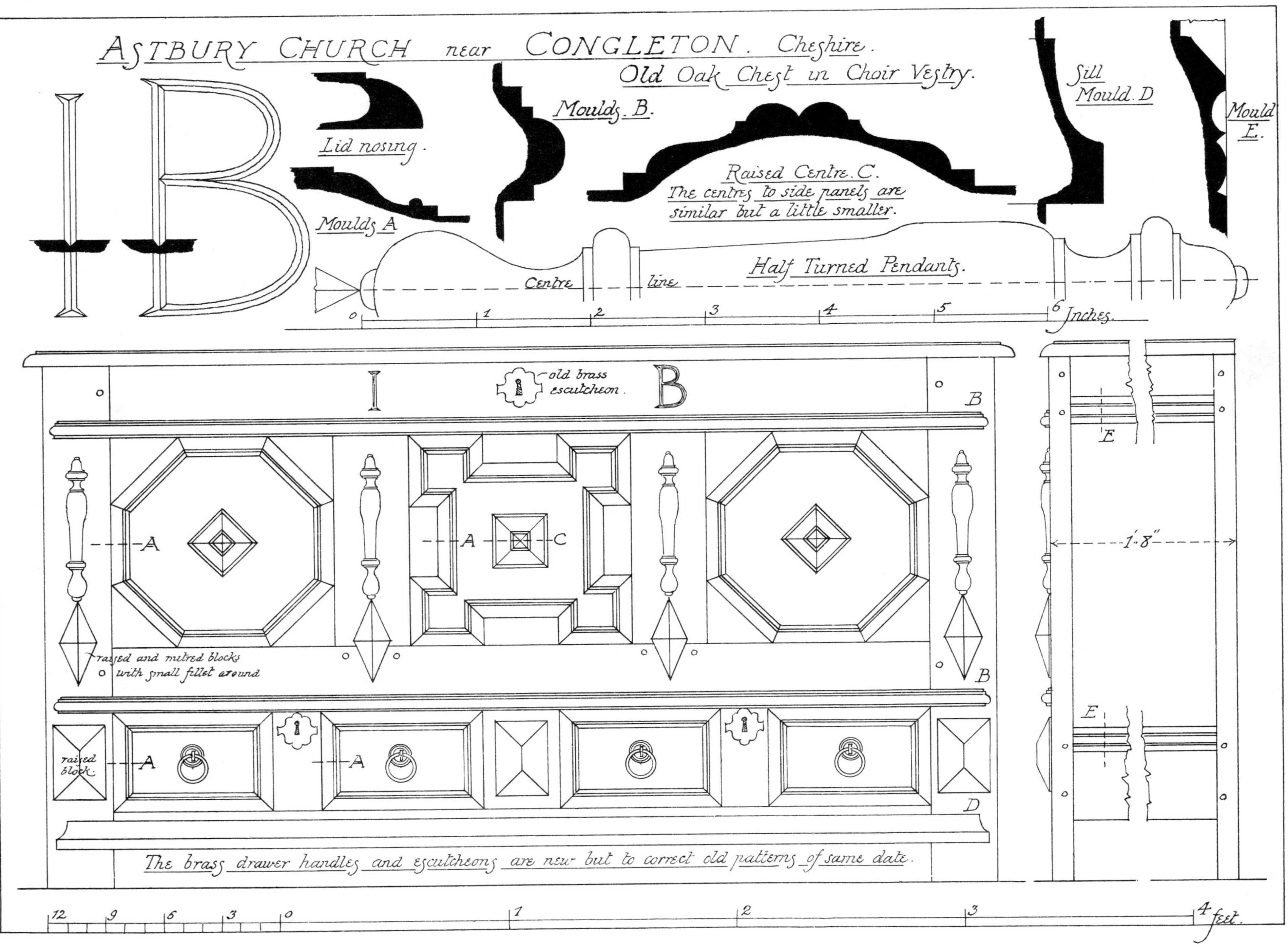

ASTBURY CHURCH near CONGLETON. Cheshire.
Old Oak Chest in Choir Vestry.
Lid nosing.
Moulds A
Moulds B.
Raised Centre C.
The centres to side panels are similar but a little smaller.
Sill Mould D
Mould E.
Half Turned Pendants.
Centre line
Inches.
old brass escutcheon.
raised and mitred blocks with small fillet around
raised block.
1'8"
The brass drawer handles and escutcheons are new but to correct old patterns of same date.
feet.

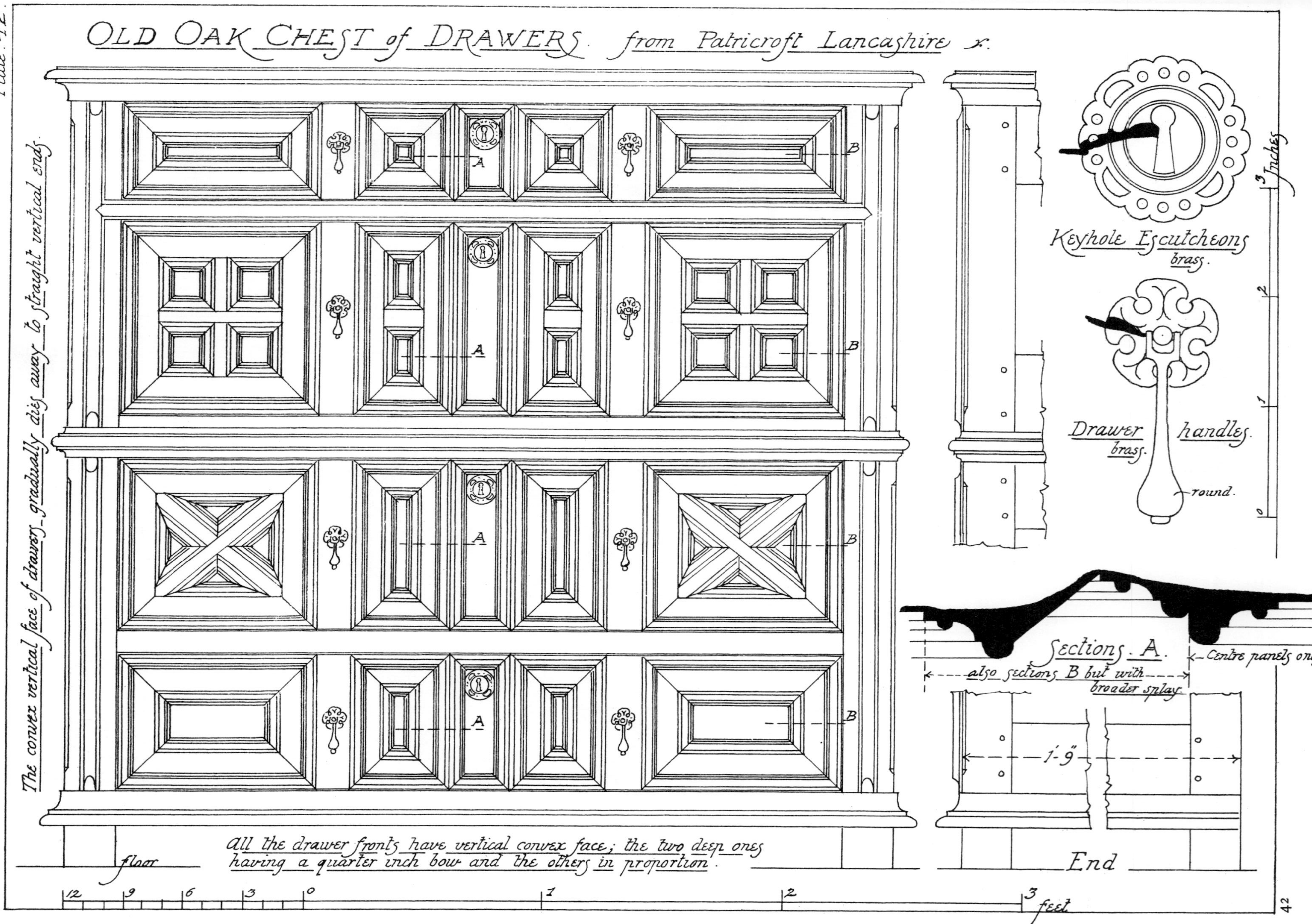
OLD OAK CHEST of DRAWERS. from Patricroft Lancashire.
The convex vertical face of drawers gradually dies away to straight vertical ends.
A
B
Keyhole Escutcheons brass.
Drawer handles. brass.
round.
0 1 2 3 Inches
Sections. A.
Centre panels only
also sections B but with broader splay.
1'-9"
All the drawer fronts have vertical convex face; the two deep ones having a quarter inch bow and the others in proportion.
floor
End
12 9 6 3 0 1 2 3 feet

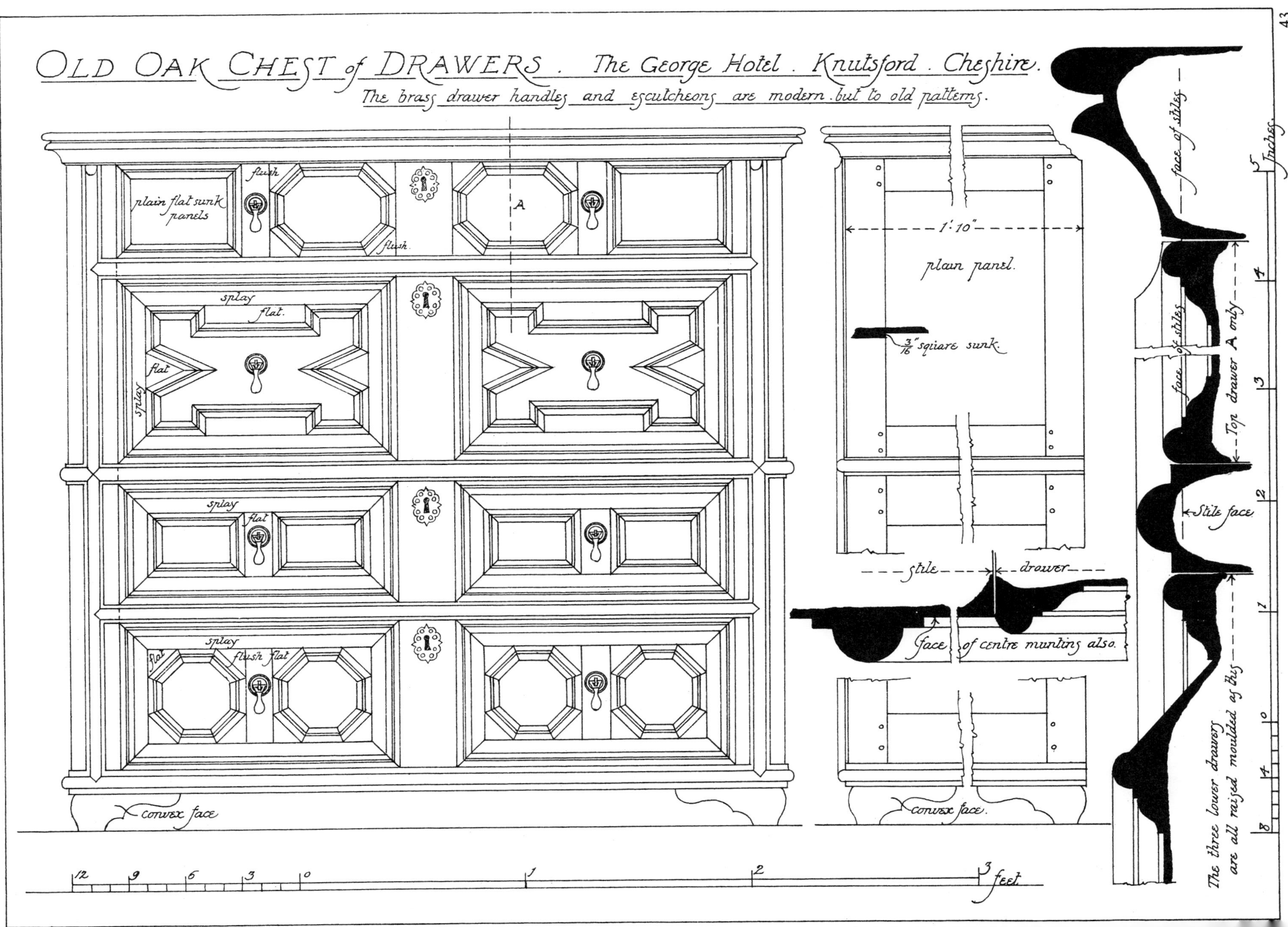
OLD OAK CHEST of DRAWERS. The George Hotel. Knutsford. Cheshire.
The brass drawer handles and escutcheons are modern but to old patterns.
plain flat sunk panels
flush
A
splay
flat.
flat
splay
flush flat
convex face
1'10"
plain panel.
3/16" square sunk.
stile
drawer
face of centre muntins also.
face of stiles
Top drawer A only
Stile face
The three lower drawers are all raised moulded as this
Inches.
feet.

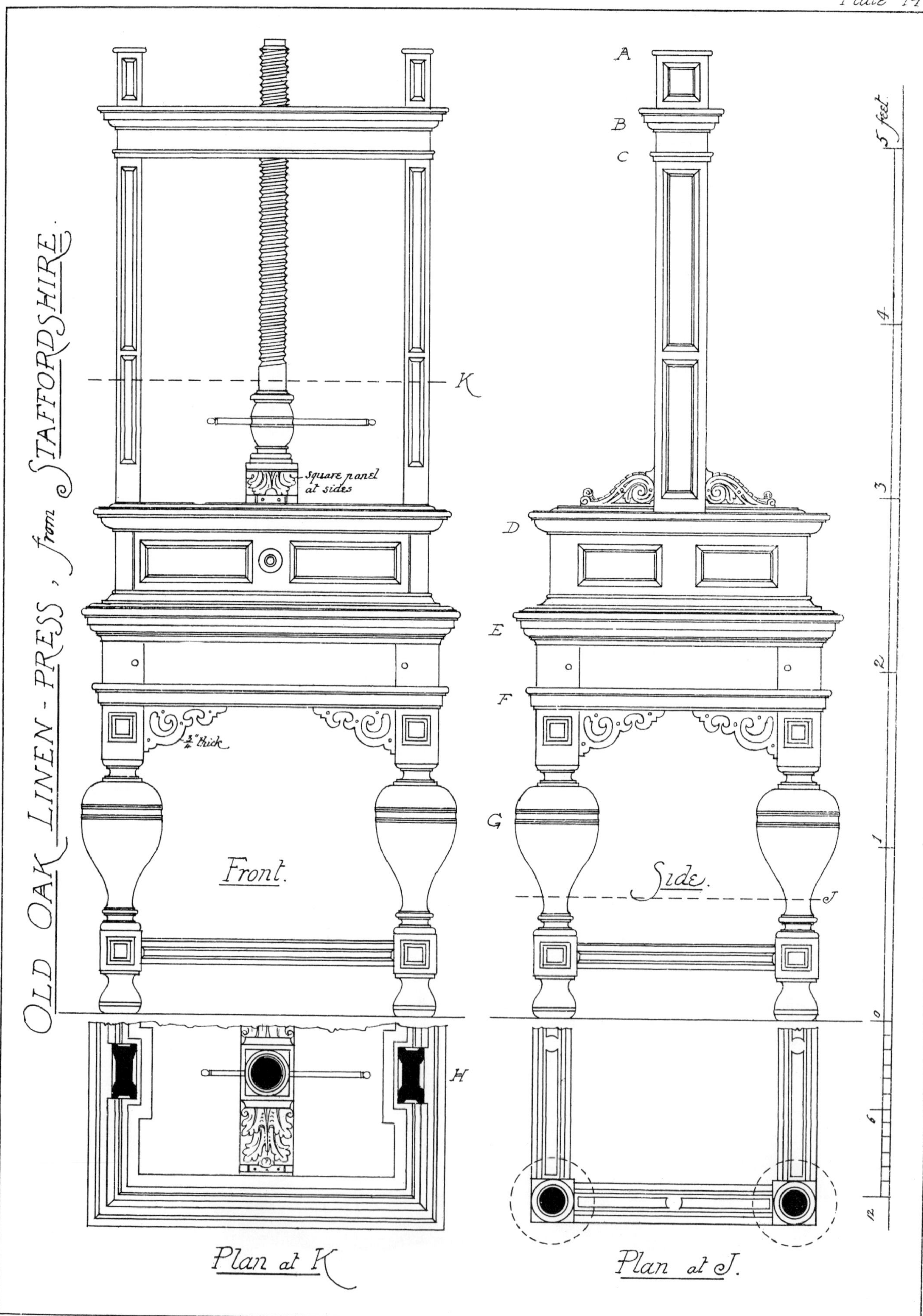
OLD OAK LINEN-PRESS, from STAFFORDSHIRE.
A
B
C
D
E
F
G
H
J
K
square panel at sides
3/4" thick
Front.
Side.
Plan at K
Plan at J.
5 feet
4
3
2
1
0
6
12

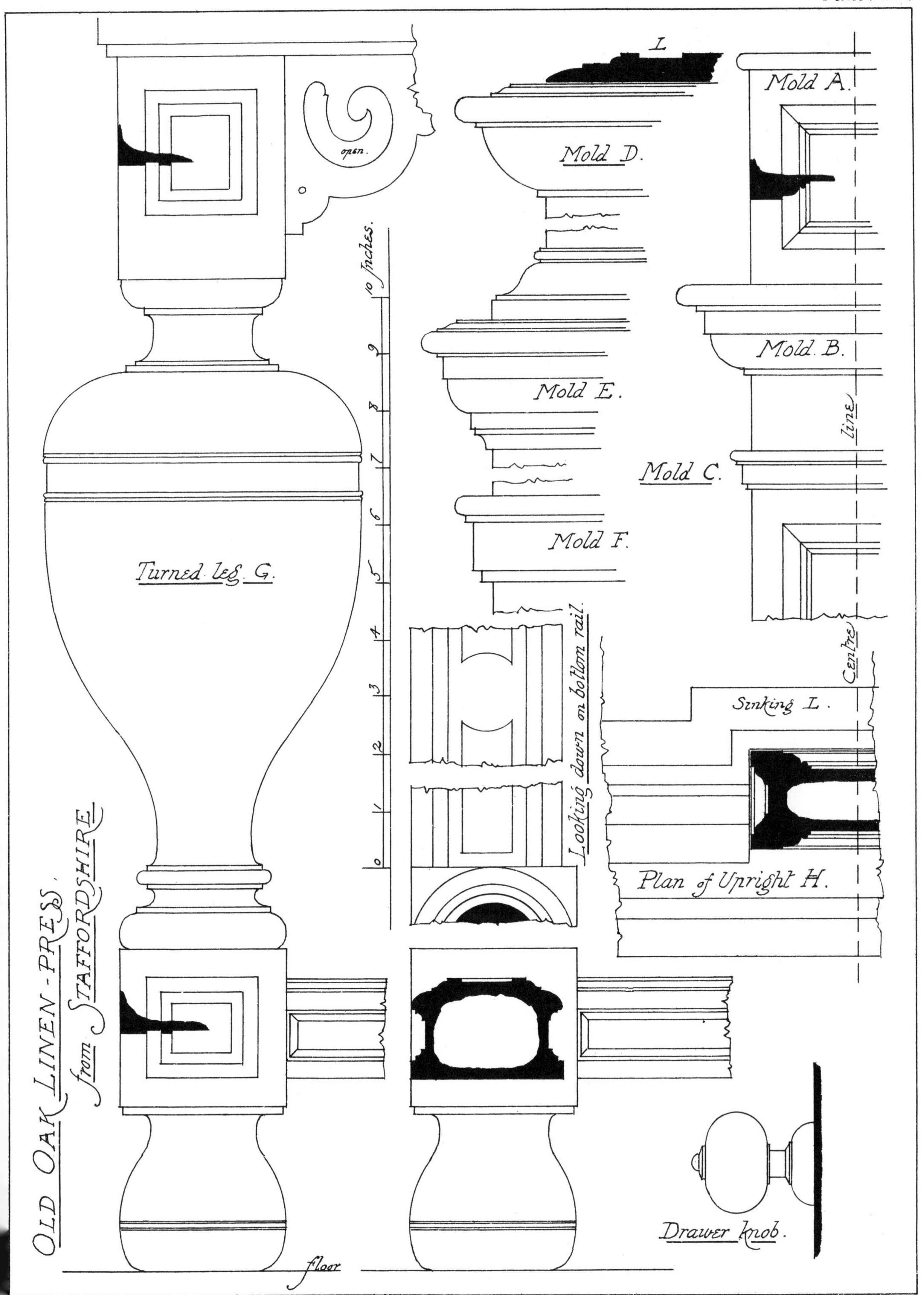
OLD OAK LINEN-PRESS, from STAFFORDSHIRE
L
open.
Mold A.
Mold D.
Mold B.
Mold E.
Mold C.
Mold F.
line
Centre
10 Inches.
9
8
7
6
5
4
3
2
1
0
Turned leg. G.
Looking down on bottom rail.
Sinking L.
Plan of Upright H.
Drawer knob.
floor

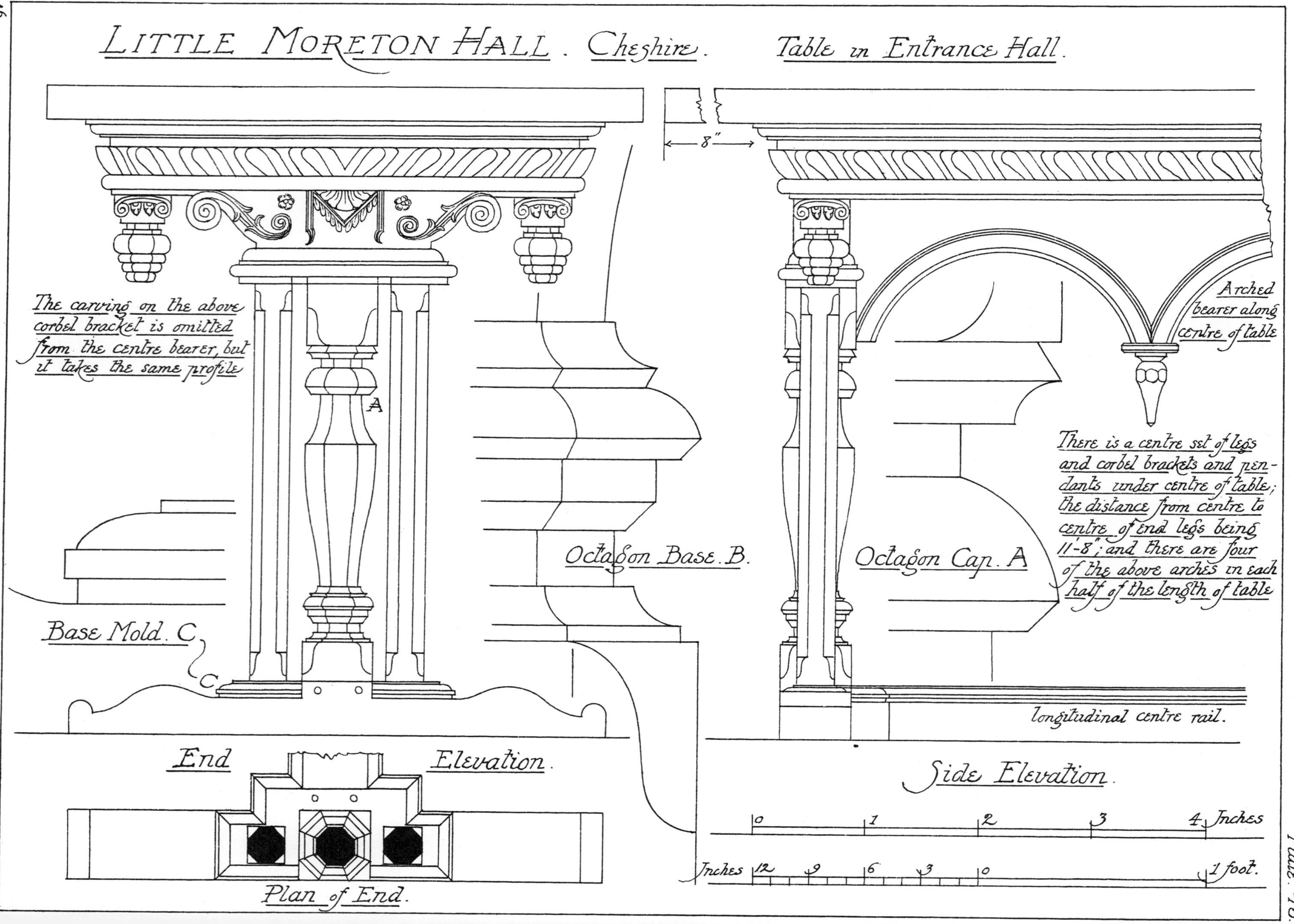
LITTLE MORETON HALL. Cheshire.
Table in Entrance Hall.
8"
The carving on the above corbel bracket is omitted from the centre bearer, but it takes the same profile
A
Arched bearer along centre of table
There is a centre set of legs and corbel brackets and pendants under centre of table; the distance from centre to centre of end legs being 11'-8"; and there are four of the above arches in each half of the length of table
Octagon Base. B.
Octagon Cap. A
Base Mold. C.
C
longitudinal centre rail.
End Elevation.
Side Elevation.
Plan of End.
0
1
2
3
4 Inches
Inches 12
9
6
3
0
1 foot.

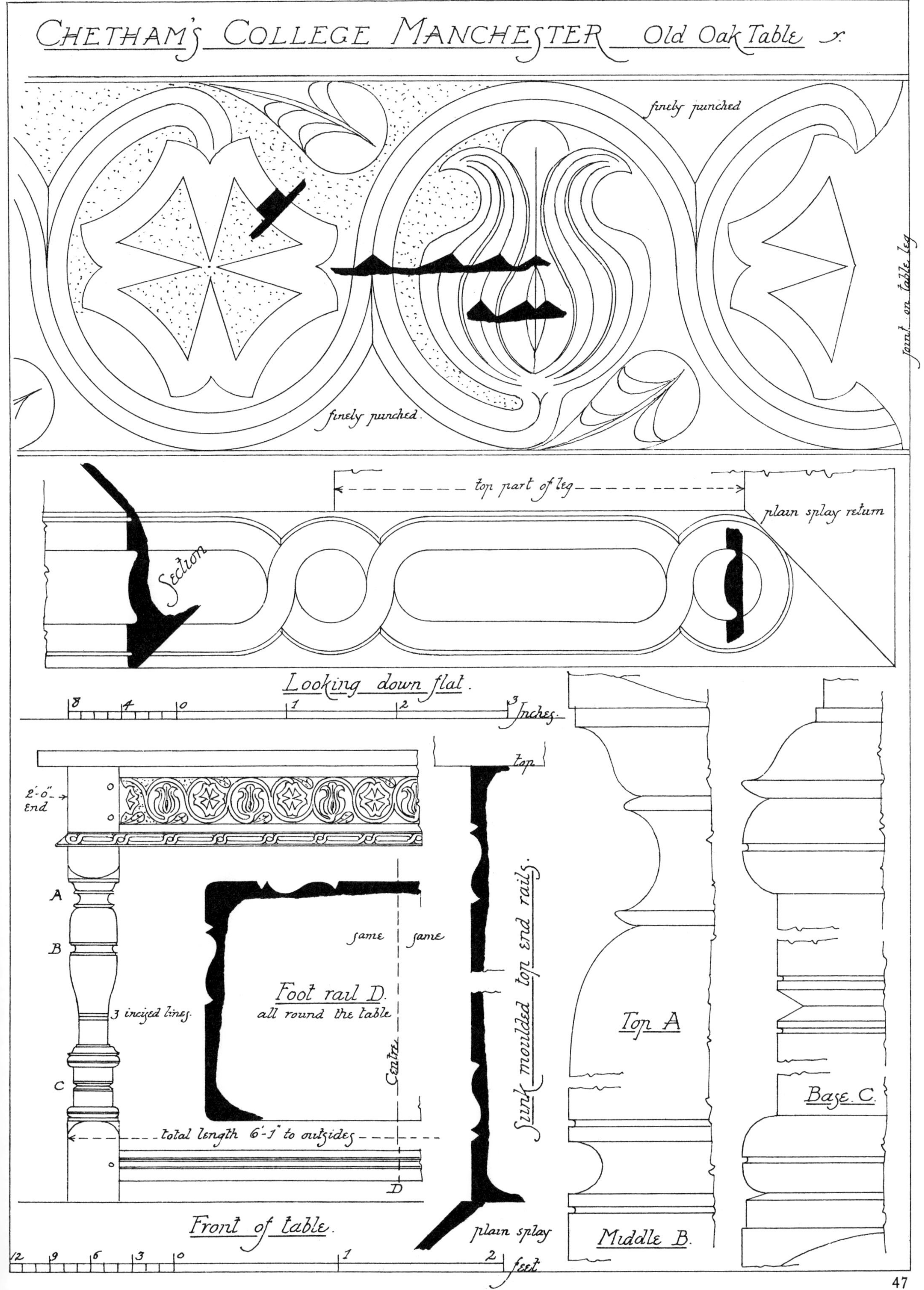
CHETHAM'S COLLEGE MANCHESTER Old Oak Table x.
finely punched
finely punched
joint on table leg
top part of leg
plain splay return
Section
Looking down flat.
8 4 0 1 2 3 Inches.
top
2'-0" End
A
B
C
3 incised lines.
same same
Foot rail D. all round the table
Centre
Sunk moulded top end rails.
total length 6'-1" to outsides
D
Front of table.
plain splay
12 9 6 3 0 1 2 feet
Top A
Middle B.
Base. C.

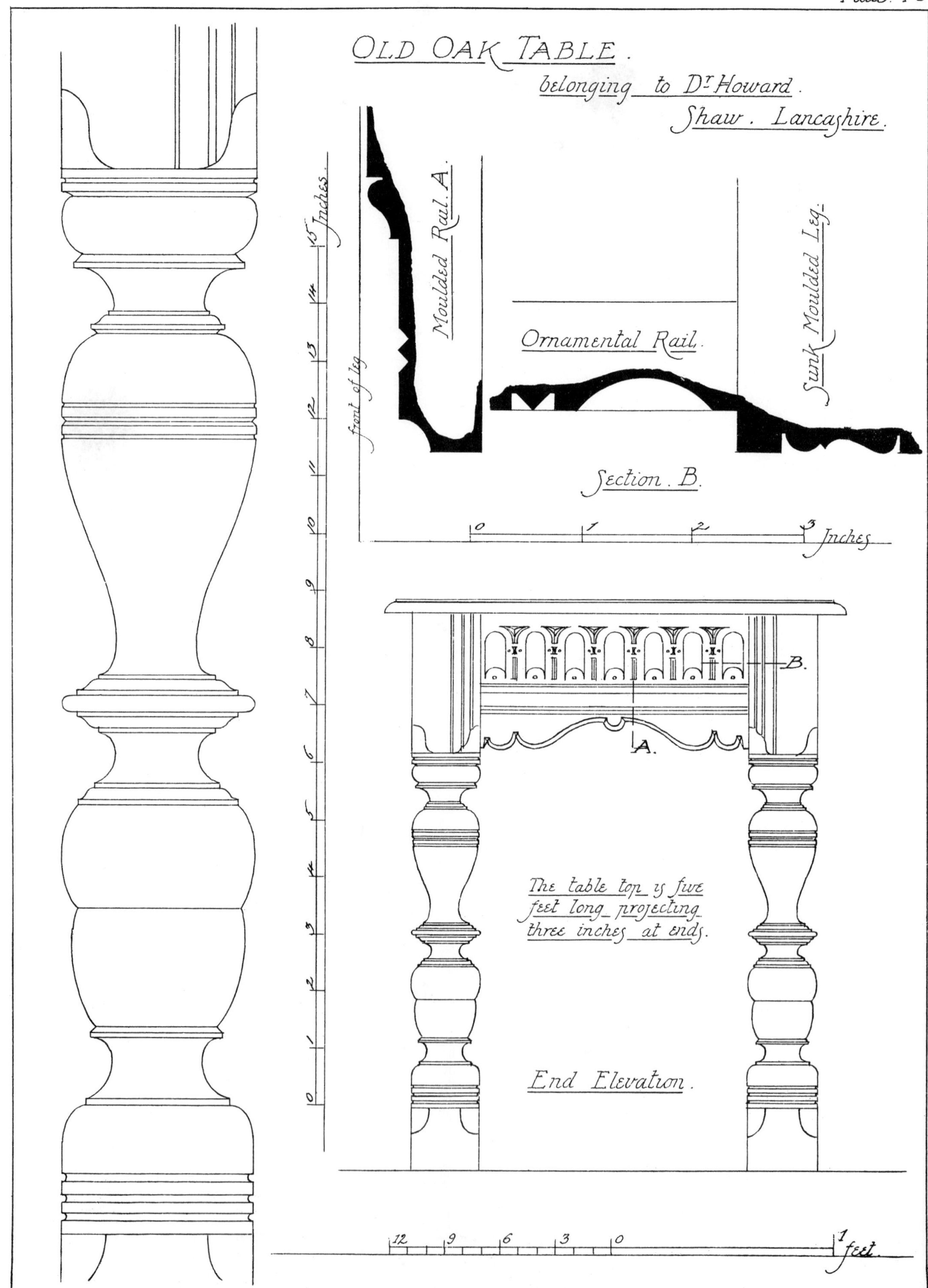
Old Oak Table.
belonging to Dr Howard.
Shaw. Lancashire.
Inches.
0 1 2 3 4 5 6 7 8 9 10 11 12 13 14 15
front of leg
Moulded Rail. A.
Ornamental Rail.
Sunk Moulded Leg.
Section. B.
0 1 2 3 Inches.
B.
A.
The table top is five feet long projecting three inches at ends.
End Elevation.
12 9 6 3 0 1 feet.

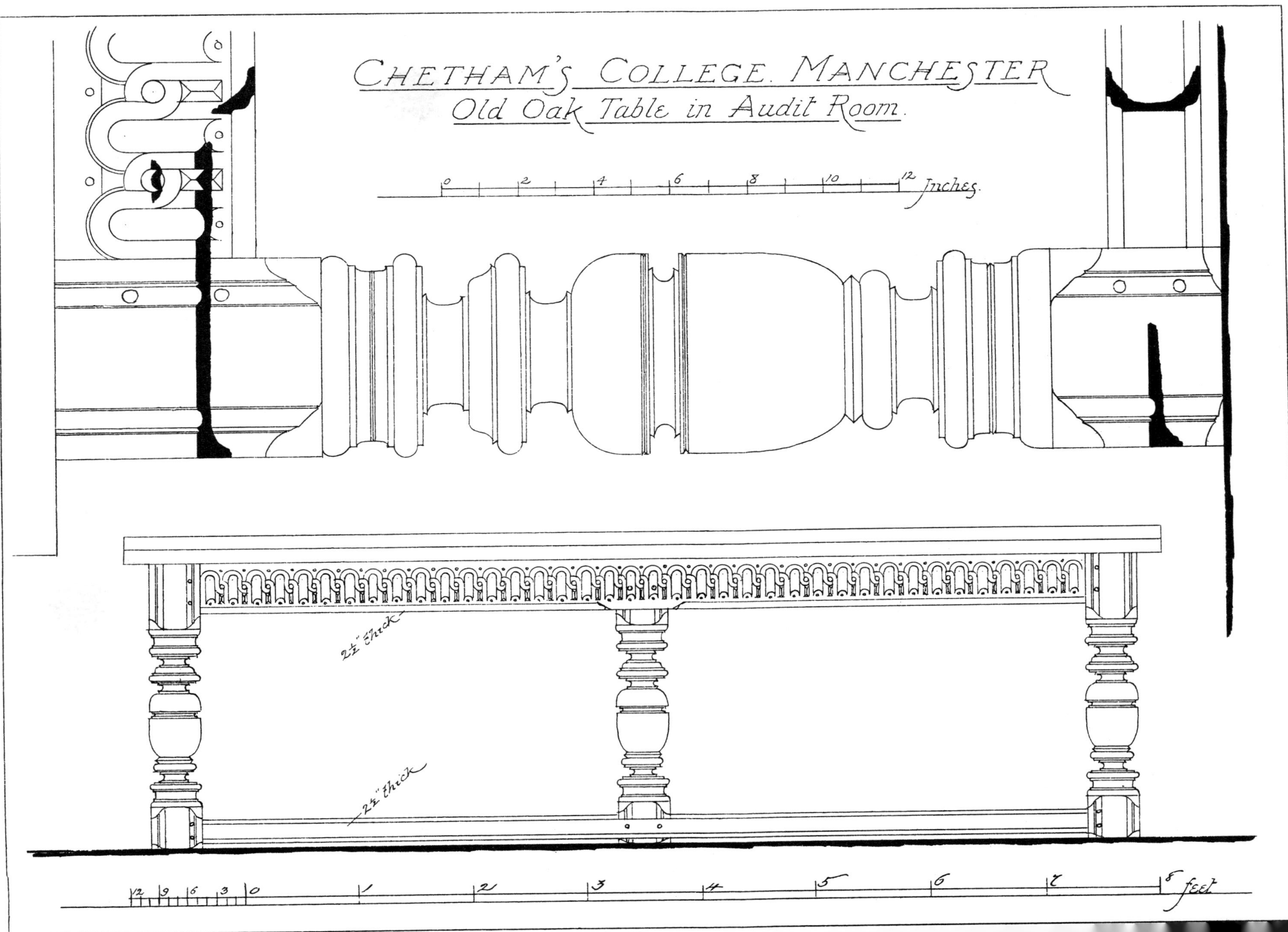
CHETHAM'S COLLEGE. MANCHESTER
Old Oak Table in Audit Room.
0 2 4 6 8 10 12 Inches.
2½" thick
2½" thick
12 9 6 3 0 1 2 3 4 5 6 7 8 feet

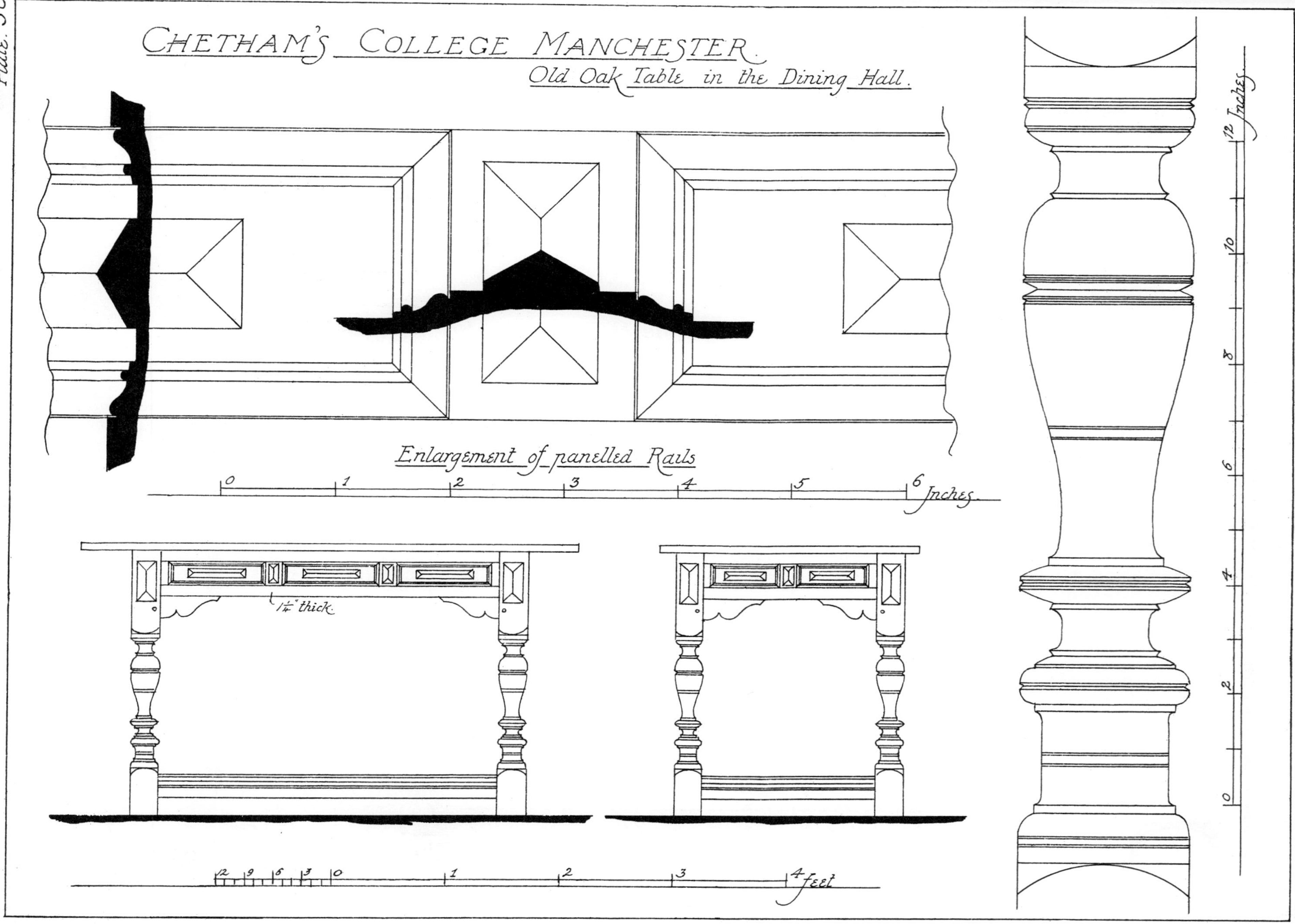
Chetham's College Manchester.
Old Oak Table in the Dining Hall.
Enlargement of panelled Rails
0 1 2 3 4 5 6 Inches.
1 1/4" thick.
12 9 6 3 0 1 2 3 4 feet
0 2 4 6 8 10 12 Inches.

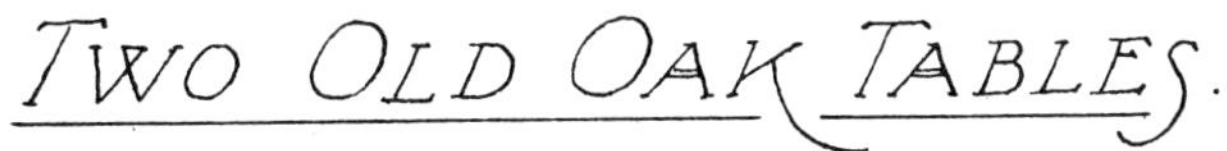

Two Old Oak Tables.

Tables belonging to Mr. Mayhew, Dealer in Antiques, New Bailey Street, Manchester.

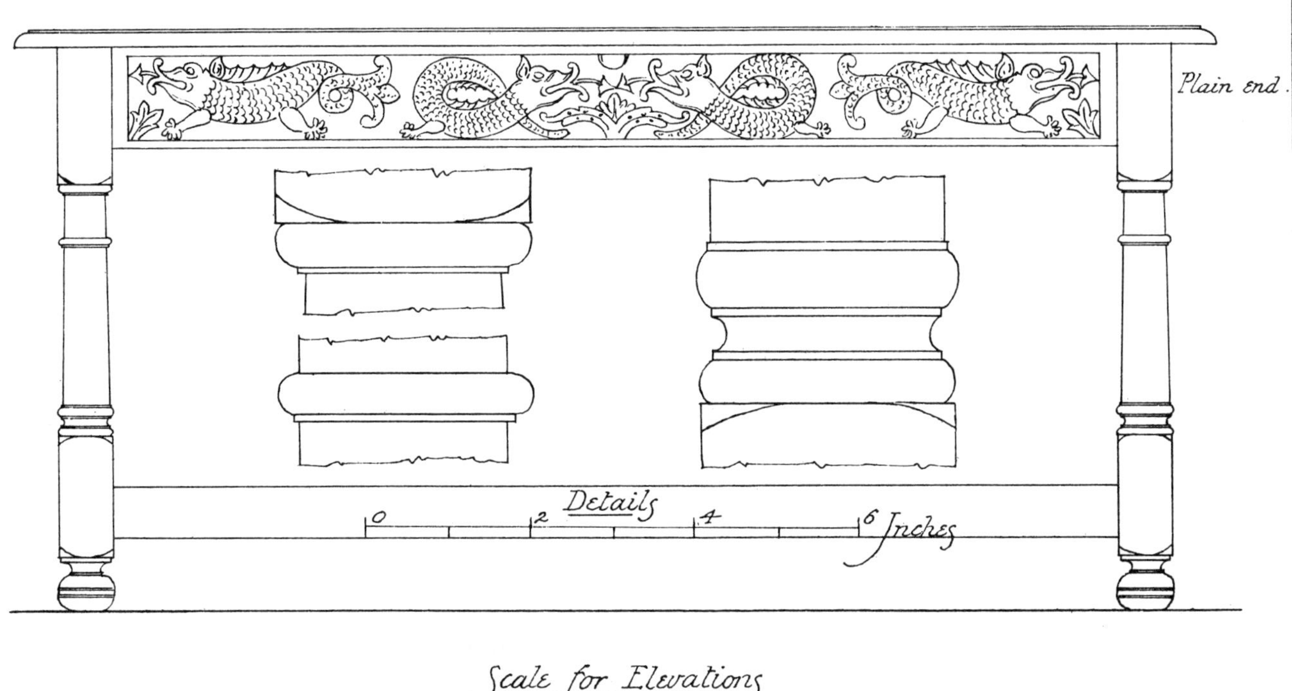

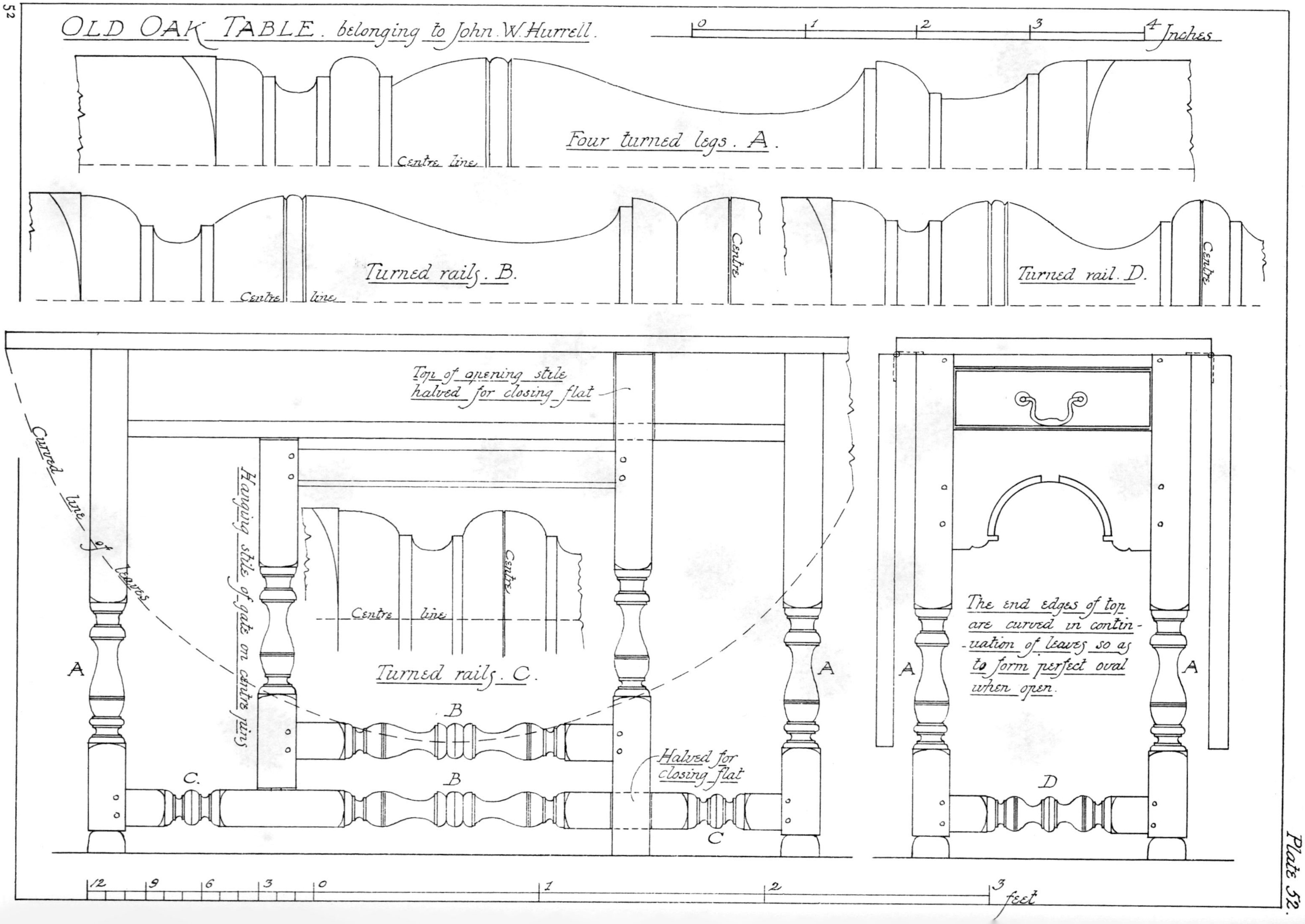
OLD OAK TABLE. belonging to John. W. Hurrell.
0 1 2 3 4 Inches
Four turned legs. A.
Centre line
Turned rails. B.
Centre line
Centre
Turned rail. D.
Centre
Top of opening stile halved for closing flat
Curved line of leaves
Hanging stile of gate on centre pins
Centre
Centre line
Turned rails. C.
A
B
B
C.
C
A
Halved for closing flat
A
A
D
The end edges of top are curved in continuation of leaves so as to form perfect oval when open.
12 9 6 3 0 1 2 3 feet

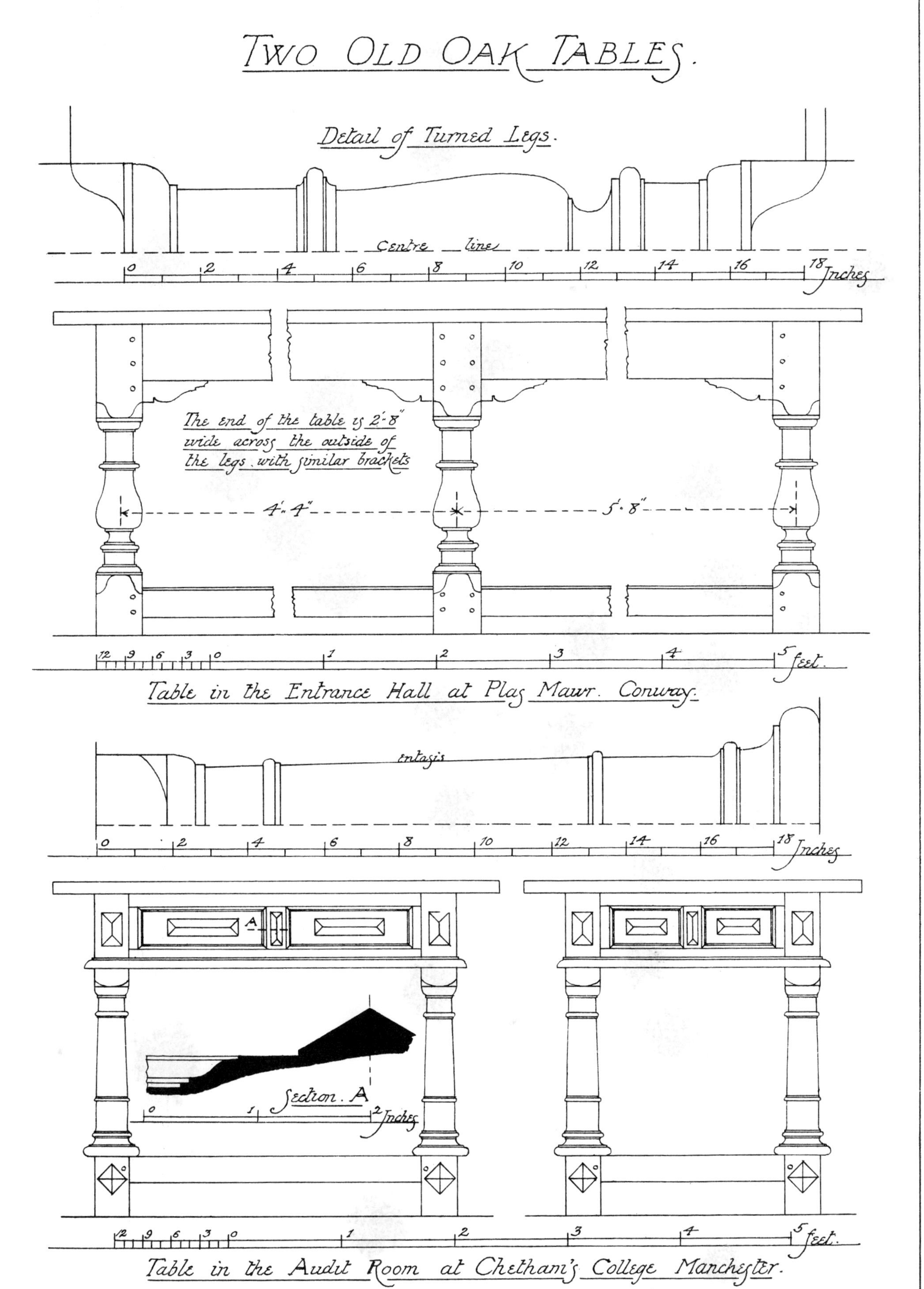
TWO OLD OAK TABLES.
Detail of Turned Legs.
Centre line
0 2 4 6 8 10 12 14 16 18 Inches
The end of the table is 2'-8" wide across the outside of the legs with similar brackets
4'-4"
5'-8"
12 9 6 3 0 1 2 3 4 5 feet.
Table in the Entrance Hall at Plas Mawr. Conway.
entasis
0 2 4 6 8 10 12 14 16 18 Inches
A
Section. A
0 1 2 Inches
12 9 6 3 0 1 2 3 4 5 feet.
Table in the Audit Room at Chetham's College Manchester.

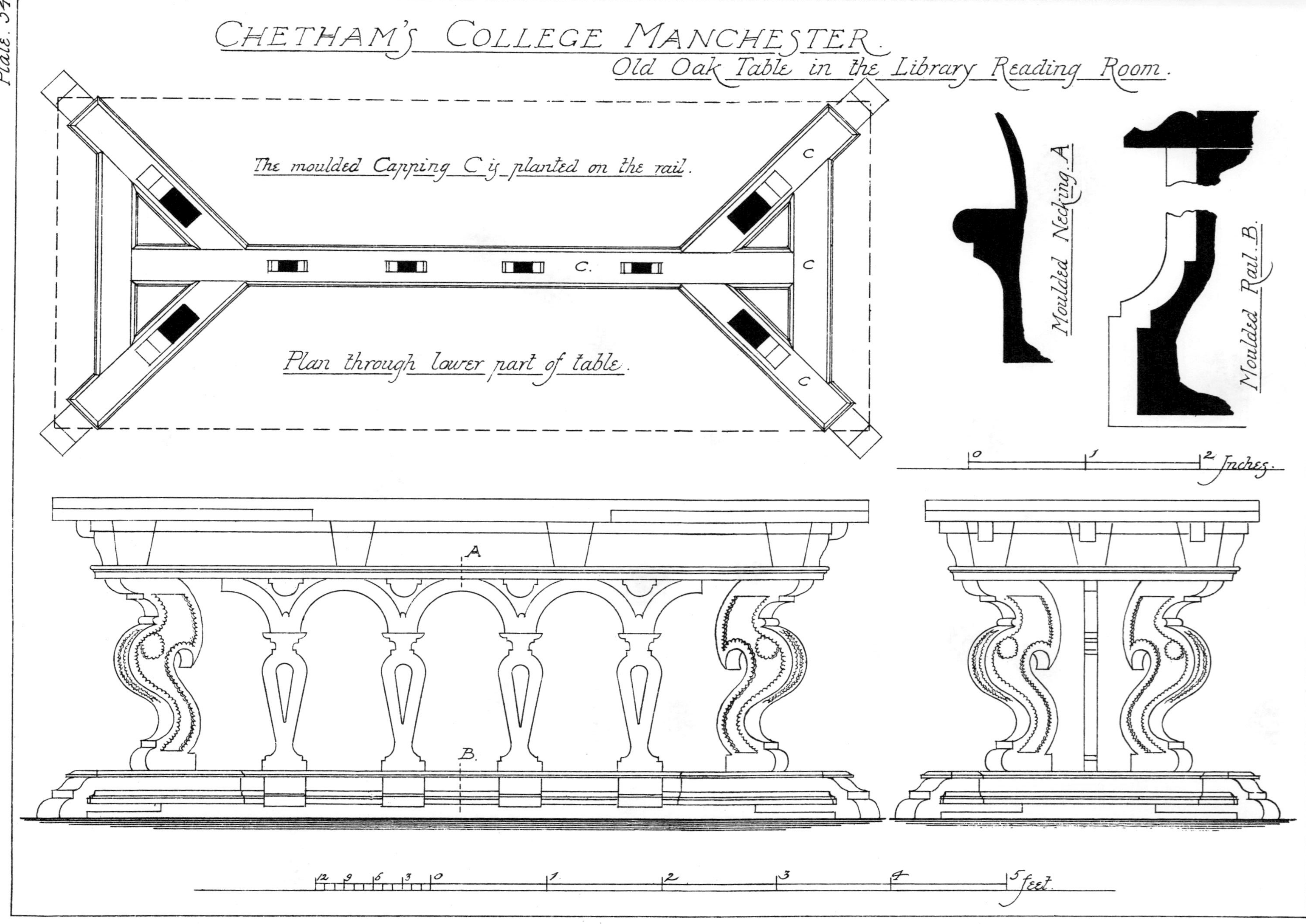
CHETHAM'S COLLEGE MANCHESTER.
Old Oak Table in the Library Reading Room.
The moulded Capping C is planted on the rail.
Plan through lower part of table.
C.
C
C
C
Moulded Necking. A
Moulded Rail. B.
0
1
2 Inches.
A
B.
12
9
6
3
0
1
2
3
4
5 feet.

LITTLE MORETON HALL. Cheshire
0 1 2 3 4 5 Inches
Note
These corbels with heads and wallposts were fixed probably about 150 years ago to support the older oak ceiling beams.
Oak Corbels under Ceiling Beams
12 9 6 3 0 1 2 3 feet.
1" thick
Table top out of one inch thick in boards about 8 inches wide
Centre line
Legs. A.
A
Scale 4 times the elevation
plain footrail.
Half Plan.
Scale one-half the elevation.
Original oak table in Kitchen.
12 9 6 3 0 1 2 Feet.

OLD OAK CHAIR. belonging to Alfred Darbyshire Esq. F.S.A. Manchester.
E
splay
A
splay.
carving
D
C.
B.
Section through Rail. A.
line
Centre
Knobs.
Ornament. D.
Curved Top E
carving
Modern upholstered seat
plain sinking
Modern leather band and nails
line
carving
splay.
Centre
Section through Muntin. C.
Section of Rail. B.
Scale for Details
Inches
4
3
2
1
0
6
3
0
1
2 feet.

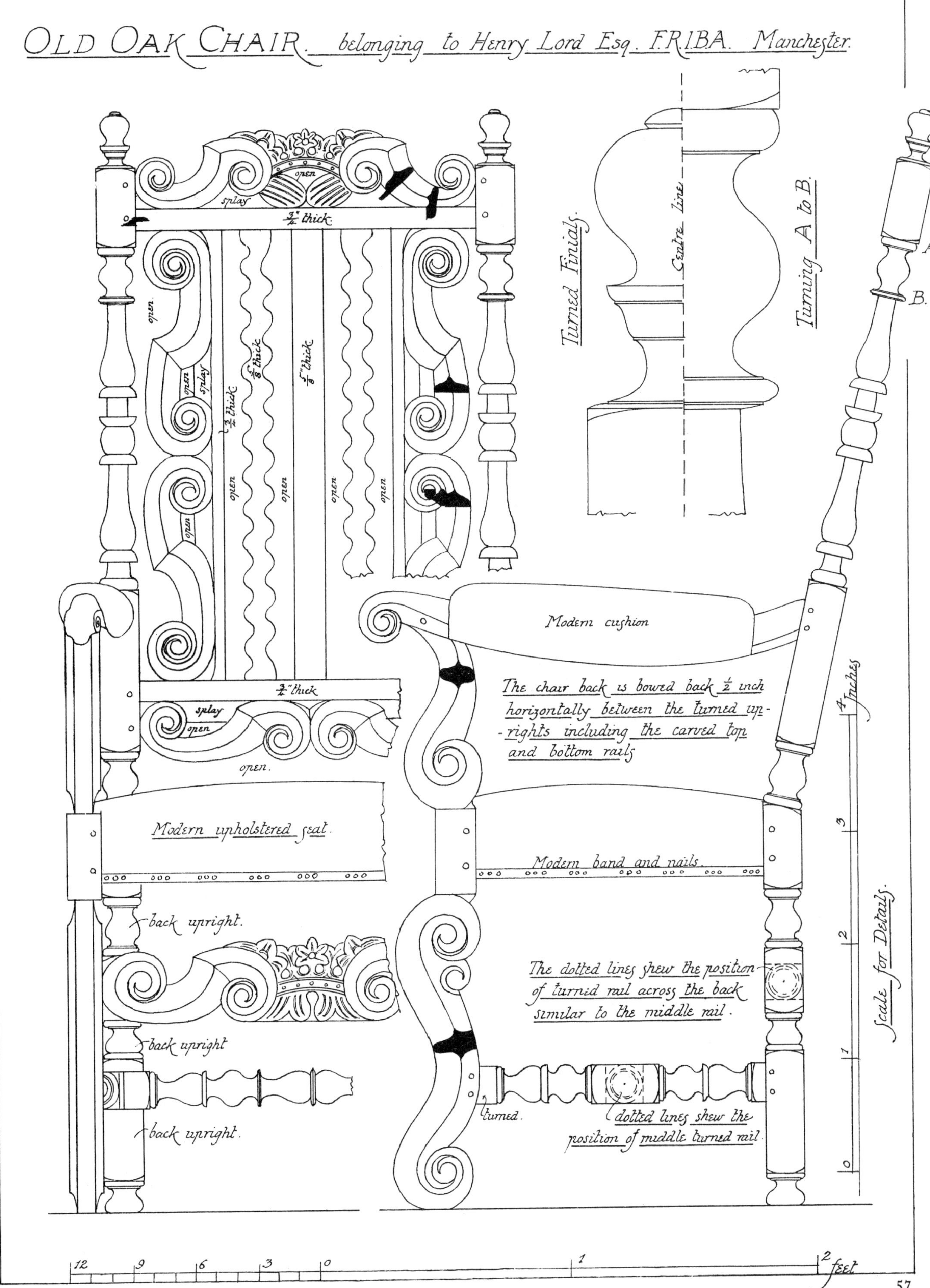
OLD OAK CHAIR. belonging to Henry Lord Esq. F.R.I.B.A. Manchester.
open
splay
3/4" thick
open
open
splay
3/4" thick
5/8" thick
5/8" thick
open
open
open
open
open
Turned Finials.
Centre line
Turning A to B.
A
B.
3/4" thick
splay
open
open.
Modern cushion
The chair back is bowed back 1/2 inch horizontally between the turned up-rights including the carved top and bottom rails
Modern upholstered seat.
Modern band and nails.
back upright.
back upright
back upright.
The dotted lines shew the position of turned rail across the back similar to the middle rail.
turned.
dotted lines shew the position of middle turned rail.
Scale for Details.
4 Inches
3
2
1
0
12
9
6
3
0
1
2 feet

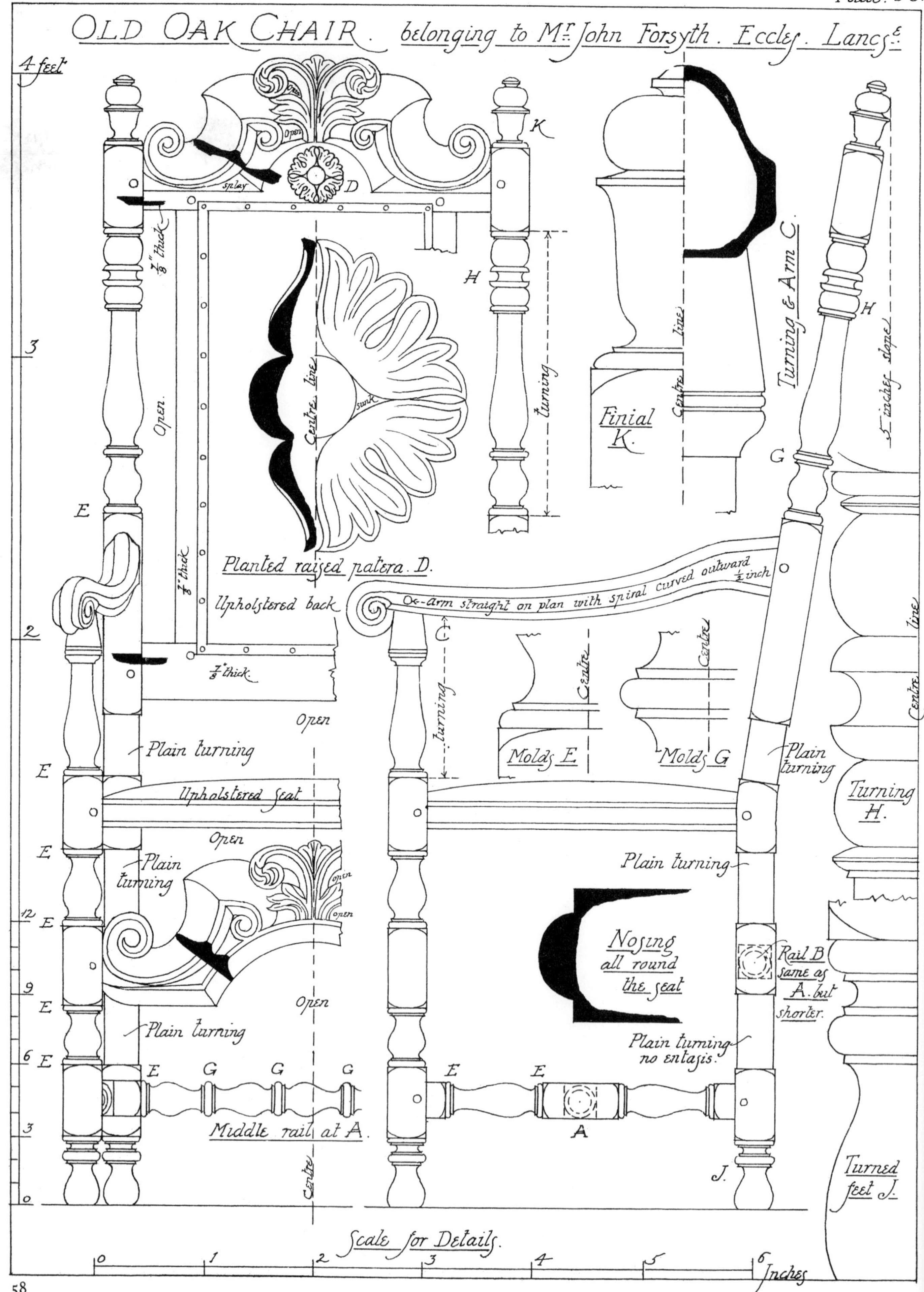
OLD OAK CHAIR. belonging to Mr. John Forsyth. Eccles. Lancs.
4 feet
3
2
12
9
6
3
0
K
H
E
D
splay
Open
7/8" thick
Open.
Centre line
sunk
turning
Finial K.
Centre line
Turning & Arm C.
H
5 inches slope
G
Planted raised patera. D.
Upholstered back
C - Arm straight on plan with spiral curved outward 1/2 inch
turning
Centre
Molds E
Centre
Molds G
Centre line
Plain turning
Turning H.
Open
Upholstered seat
Open
Plain turning
open
Nosing all round the seat
Rail B same as A. but shorter.
Open
Plain turning no entasis.
E
G
G
G
E
E
Middle rail at A.
A
J.
Turned feet J.
Centre
Scale for Details.
0
1
2
3
4
5
6
Inches

OLD OAK CHAIR. belonging to Mr. Massey Harper. Congleton.
Section of Arch. C.
A.
gougings
B.
Incised
Elevation
Section of Lozenge. D.
plain face
C.
D.
plain face
plain face
E
E
Section at E.E.
Rails. F.F.
Inches
4
3
2
1
0
Scale for Details
F
F
G
H
slight entasis
line
Centre
line
Centre
Cap. G.
Base. H
Section. B.
Section. A.
12
9
6
3
0
1
2
feet

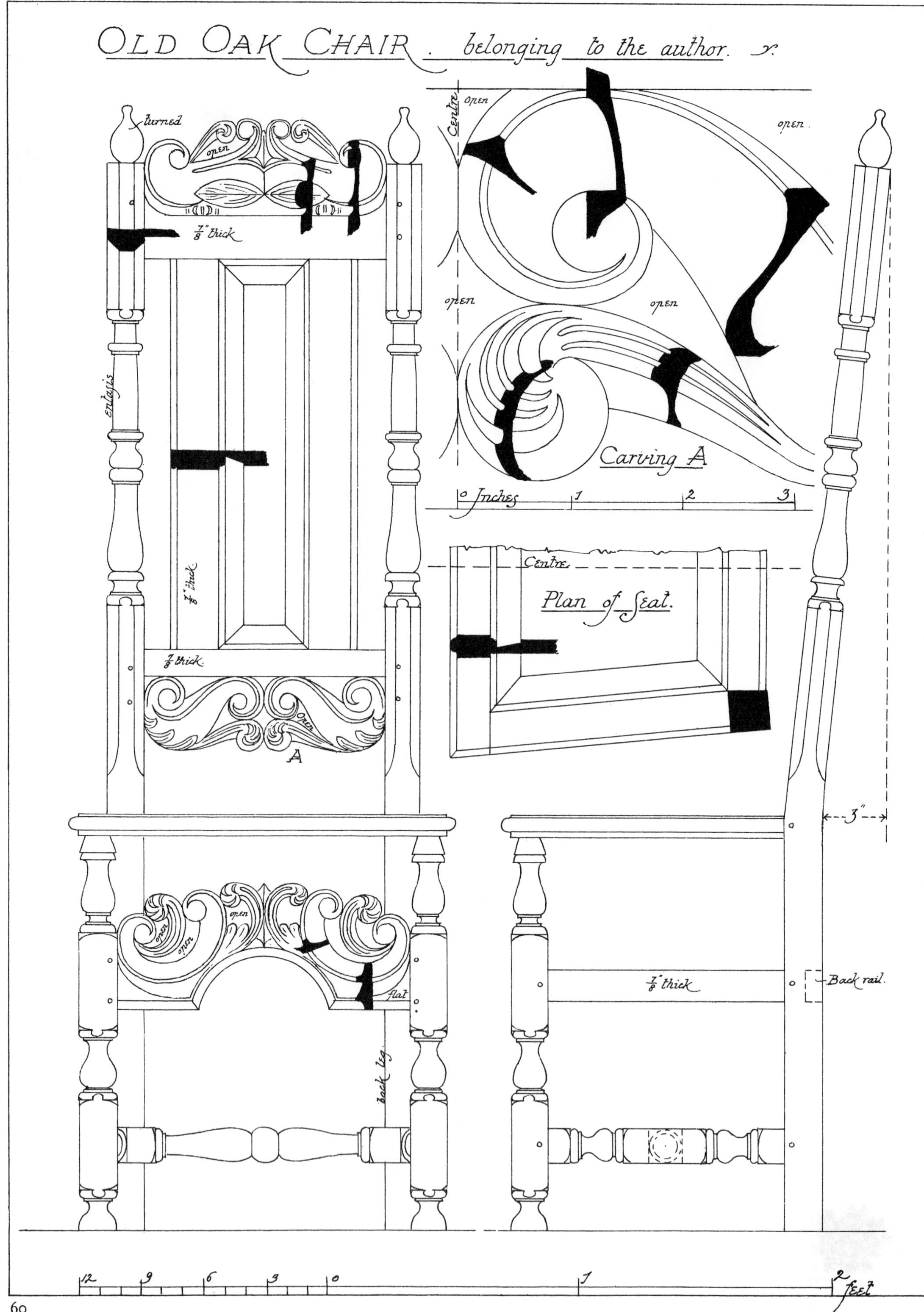
Old Oak Chair . belonging to the author .
turned
open
7/8" thick
entasis
7/8" thick
7/8 thick
open
A
Centre
open
open .
open
open
Carving A
0 Inches 1 2 3
Centre
Plan of Seat.
open
open
open
open
flat
back leg
7/8" thick
Back rail.
3"
12 9 6 3 0 1 2 feet

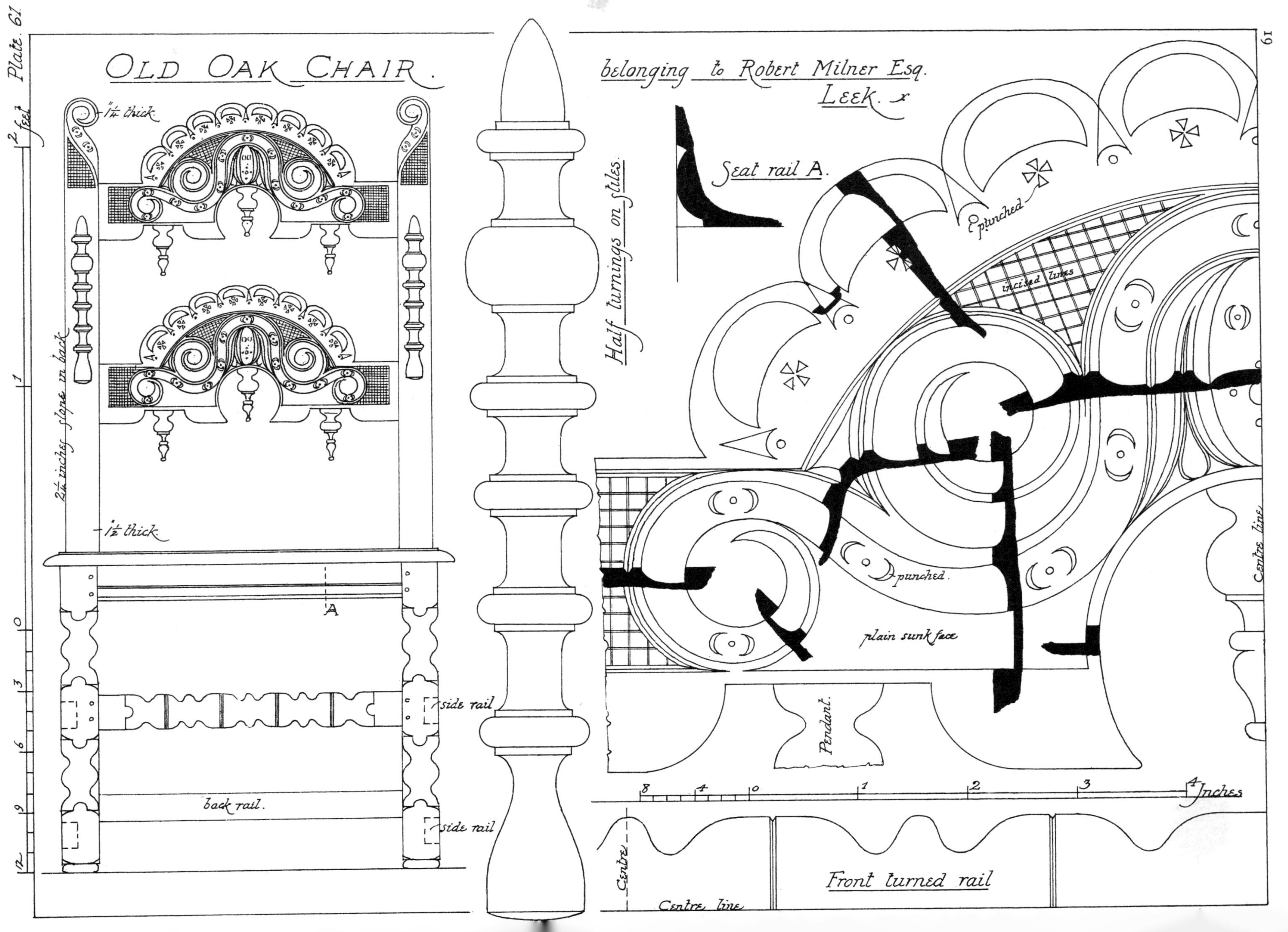

OLD OAK CHAIR.
belonging to Robert Milner Esq.
Leek.
¼" thick
2¼ inches slope in back
½" thick
A
side rail
back rail.
side rail
Half turnings on stiles.
Seat rail A.
punched
incised lines
punched.
plain sunk face
Pendant.
Centre line
Inches
Centre
Centre line
Front turned rail
feet

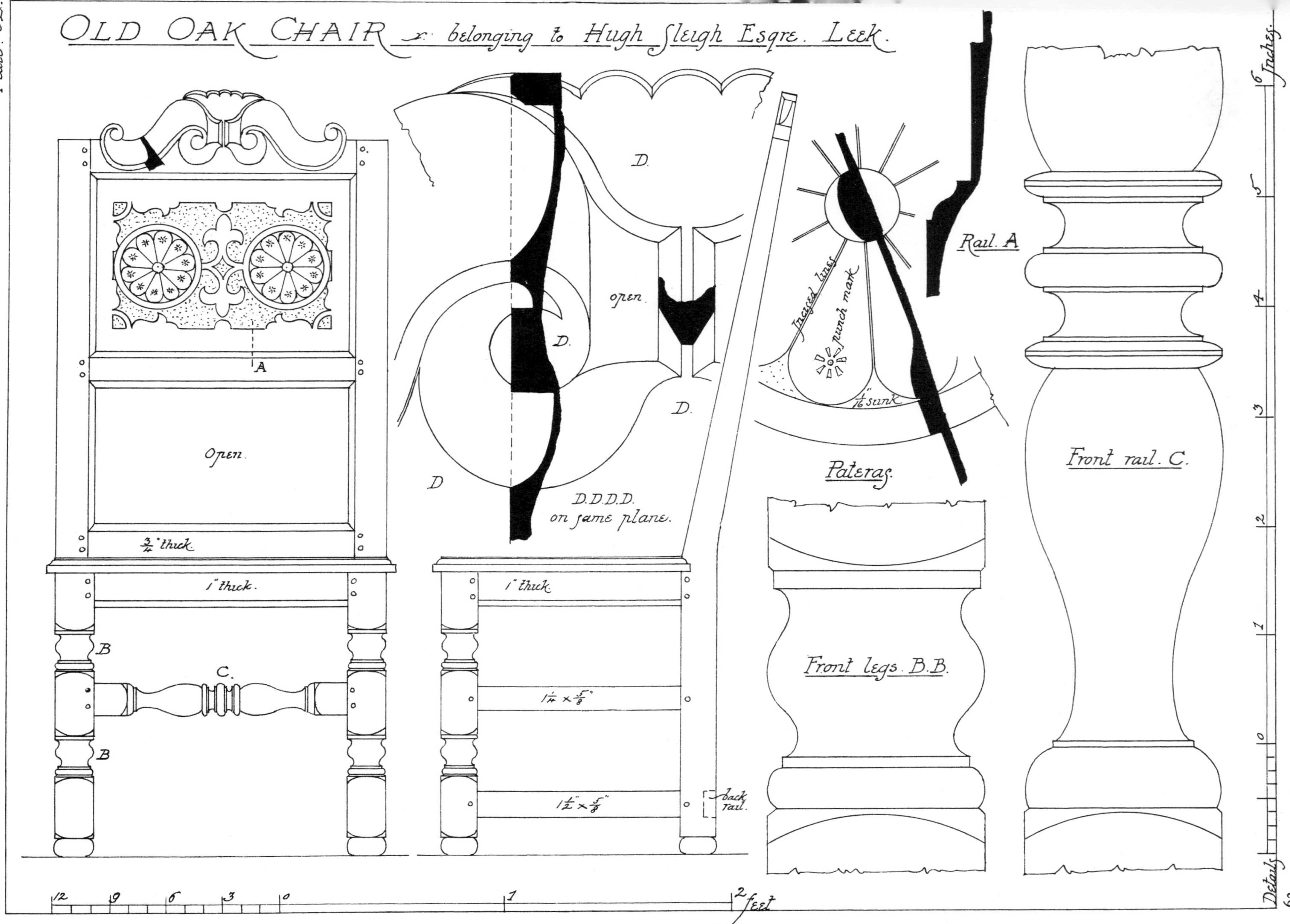
OLD OAK CHAIR x: belonging to Hugh Sleigh Esqre. Leek.
A
Open.
3/4" thick.
1" thick.
B
C.
B
1" thick
1 1/4" × 5/8"
1 1/2" × 5/8"
back rail.
D.
D.
D.
D
D.D.D.D.
on same plane.
open.
Incised lines
punch mark
1/16" sunk
Pateras.
Rail. A
Front legs. B.B.
Front rail. C.
12 9 6 3 0 1 2 feet
Details 0 1 2 3 4 5 6 Inches.

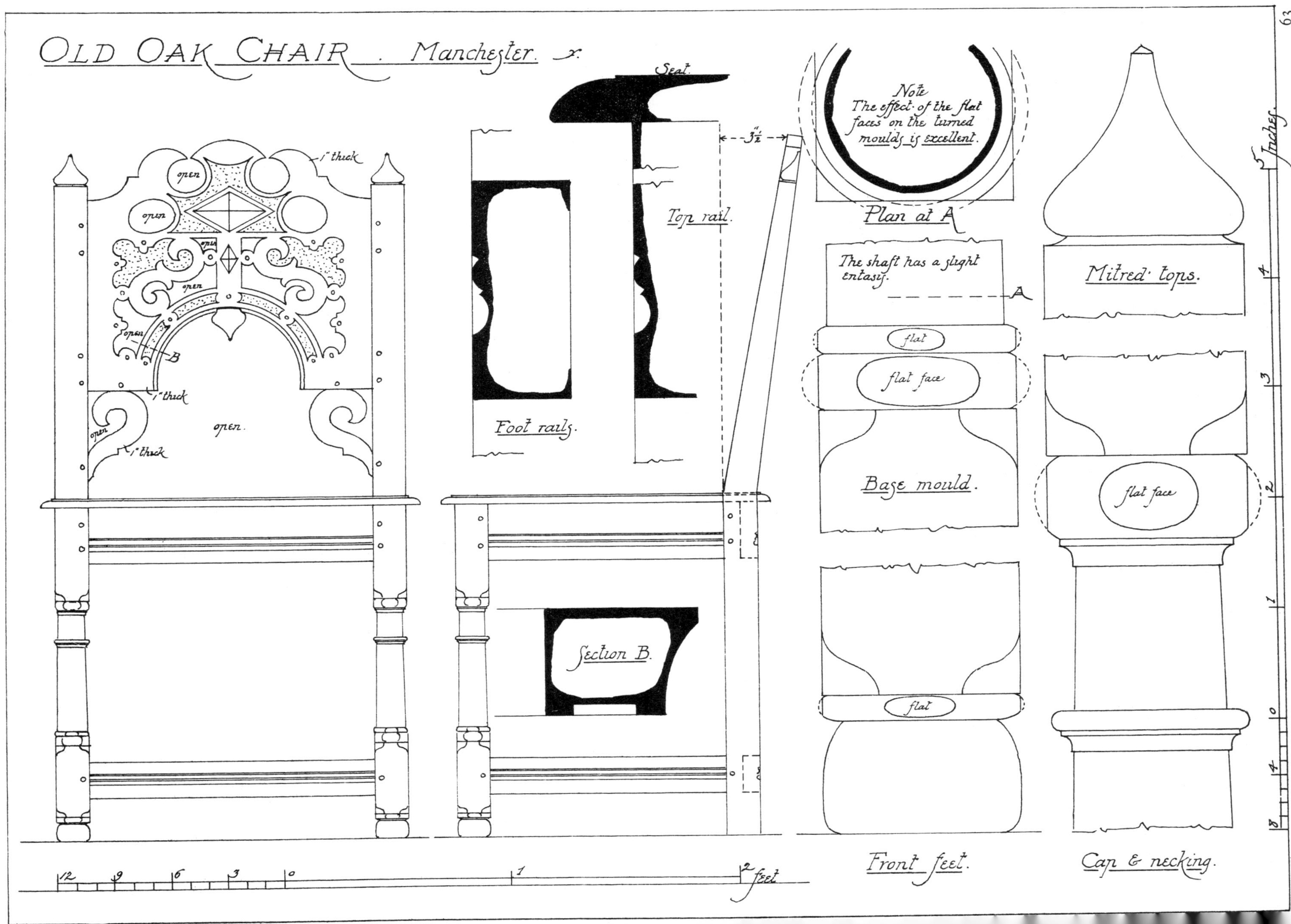
OLD OAK CHAIR. Manchester. x.
1" thick
open
B
Seat.
Top rail.
Foot rails.
3½"
Note
The effect of the flat faces on the turned moulds is excellent.
Plan at A
The shaft has a slight entasis.
A
flat
flat face
Base mould.
Section B.
Mitred tops.
Front feet.
Cap & necking.
feet
Inches

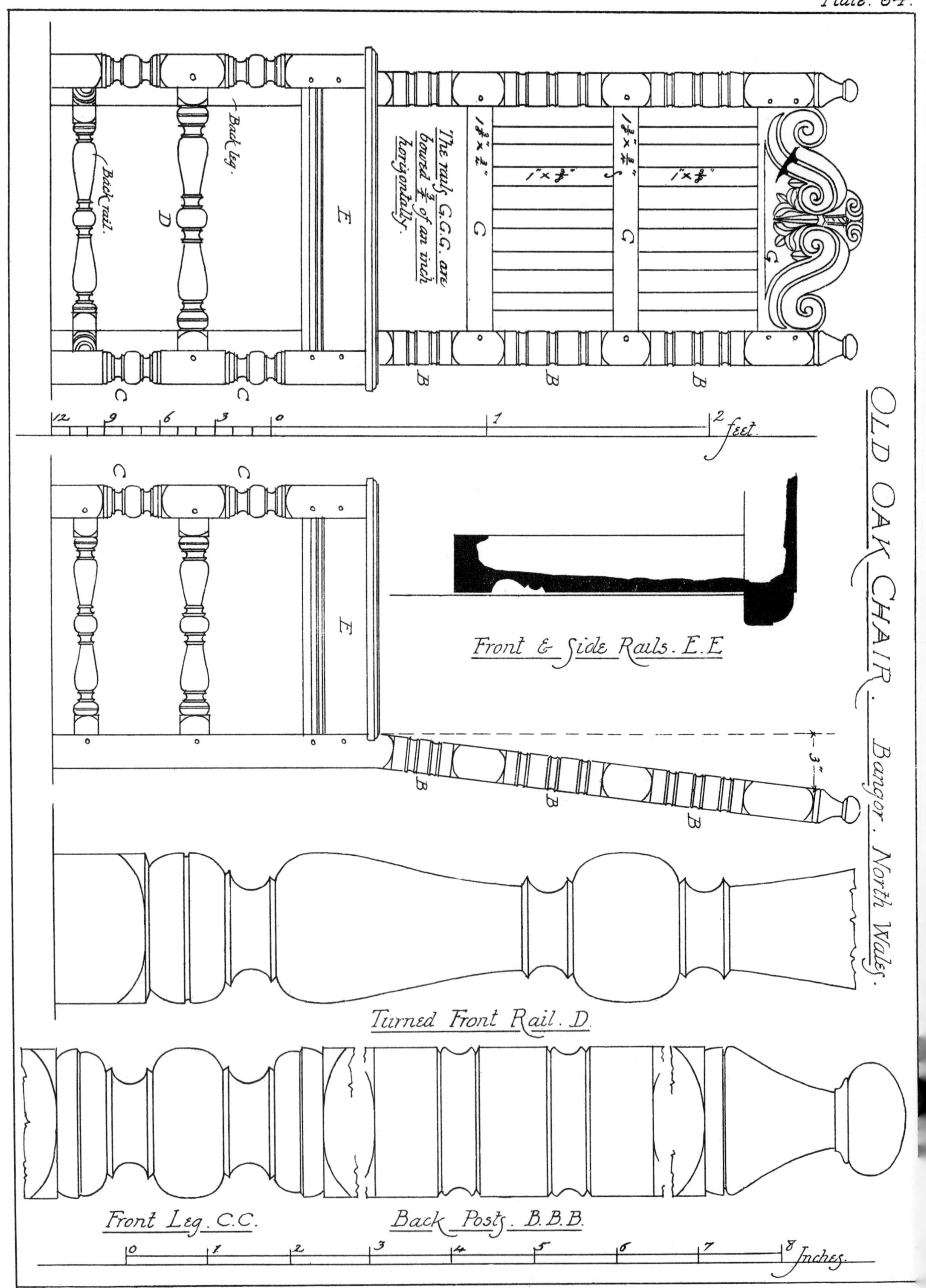
OLD OAK CHAIR. Bangor. North Wales.
The rails G.G.G. are bowed 3/4 of an inch horizontally.
Back leg.
Back rail.
D
E
G
G
G
B
B
B
C
C
12 9 6 3 0 1 2 feet.
Front & Side Rails. E.E
Turned Front Rail. D
Front Leg. C.C.
Back Posts. B.B.B.
0 1 2 3 4 5 6 7 8 Inches.

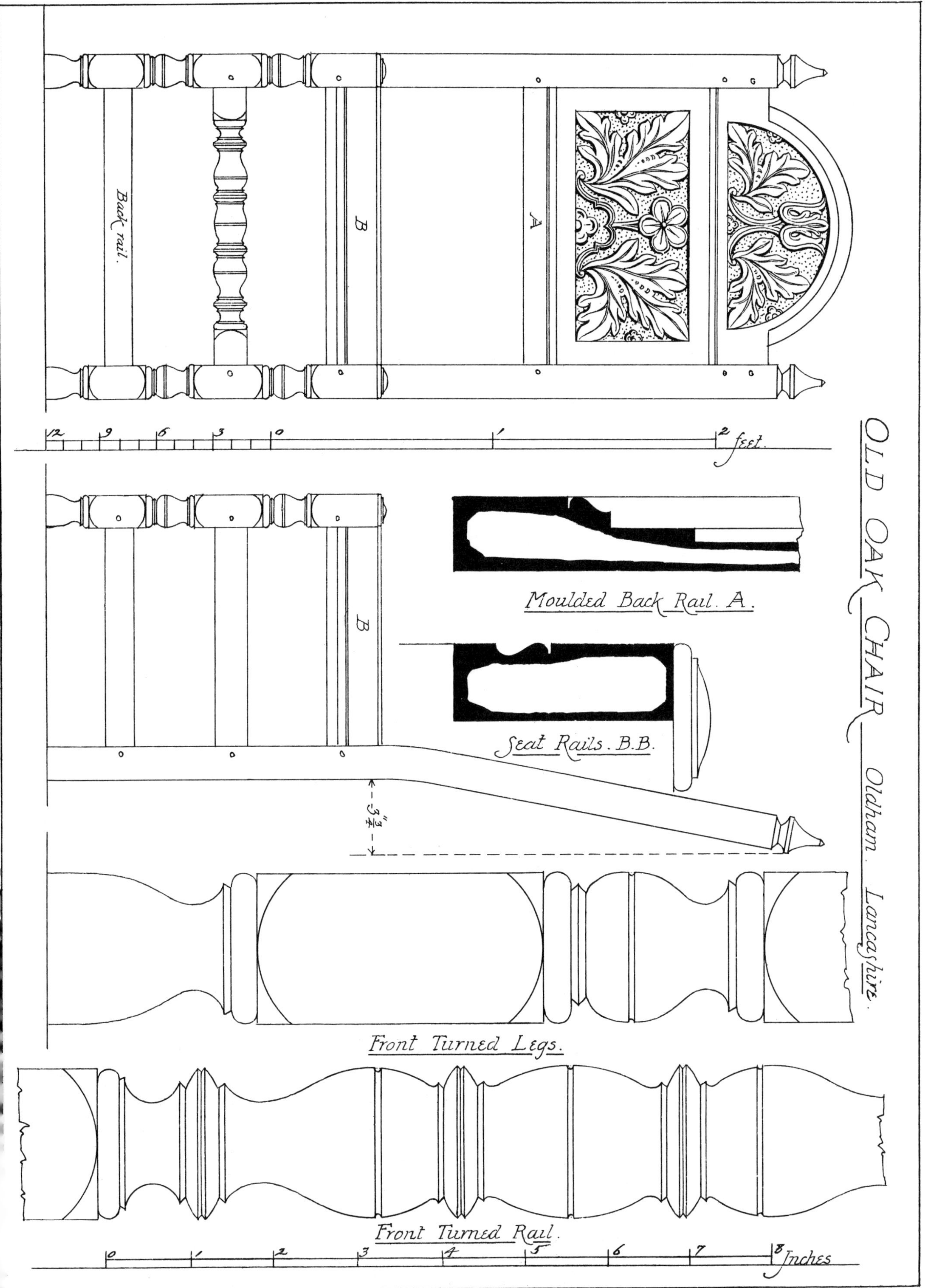
Back rail.
B
A
12 9 6 3 0 1 2 feet.
OLD OAK CHAIR Oldham. Lancashire.
B
Moulded Back Rail. A.
Seat Rails. B.B.
3¾"
Front Turned Legs.
Front Turned Rail.
0 1 2 3 4 5 6 7 8 Inches

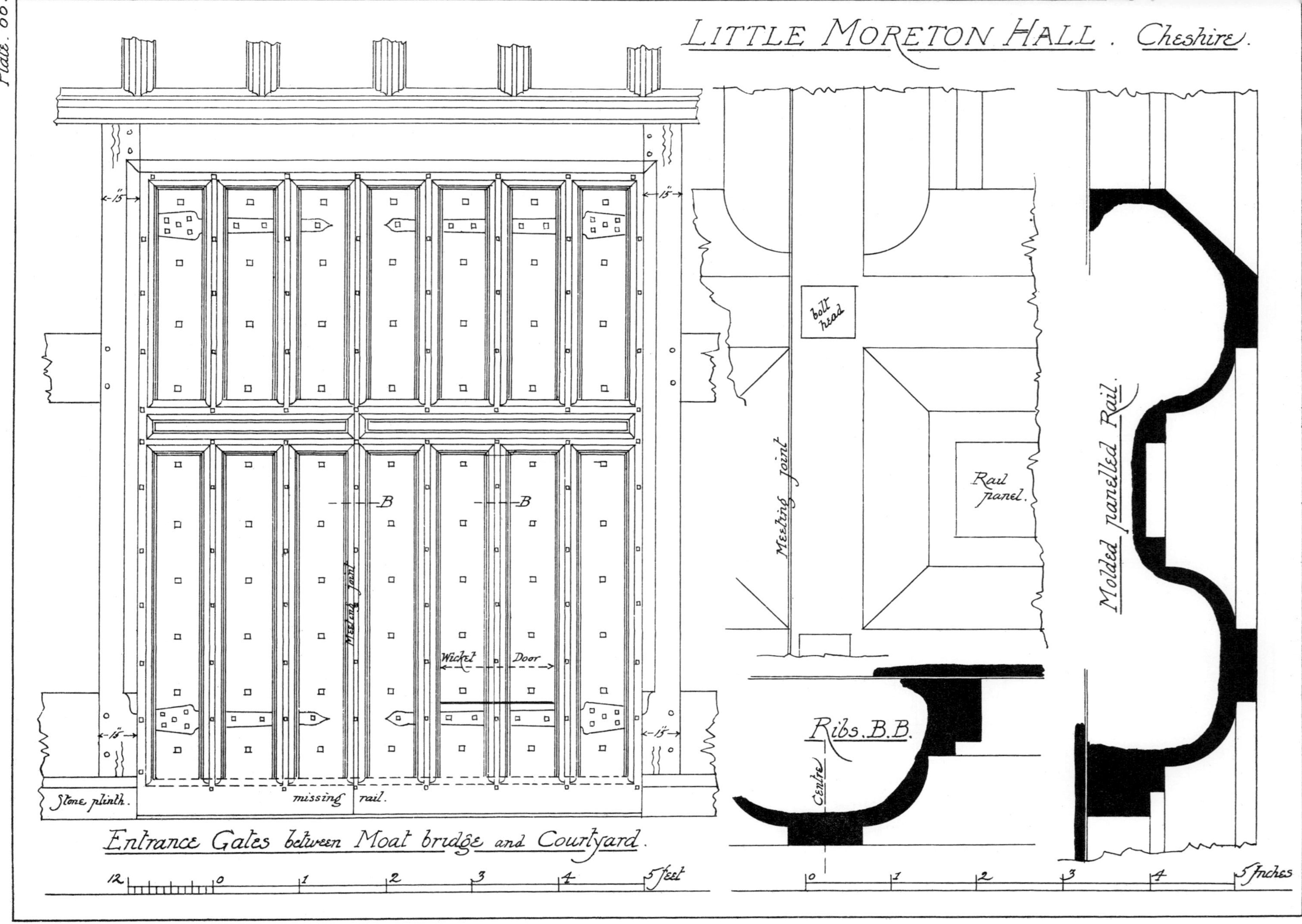
LITTLE MORETON HALL . Cheshire.
15"
15"
B
B
Meeting joint
Wicket Door
15"
15"
Stone plinth.
missing rail.
Entrance Gates between Moat bridge and Courtyard.
12 0 1 2 3 4 5 feet
bolt head
Meeting joint
Rail panel.
Molded panelled Rail.
Ribs. B.B.
Centre
0 1 2 3 4 5 Inches

BRAMHALL HALL. CHESHIRE.
Old Oak Door in Entrance Hall.

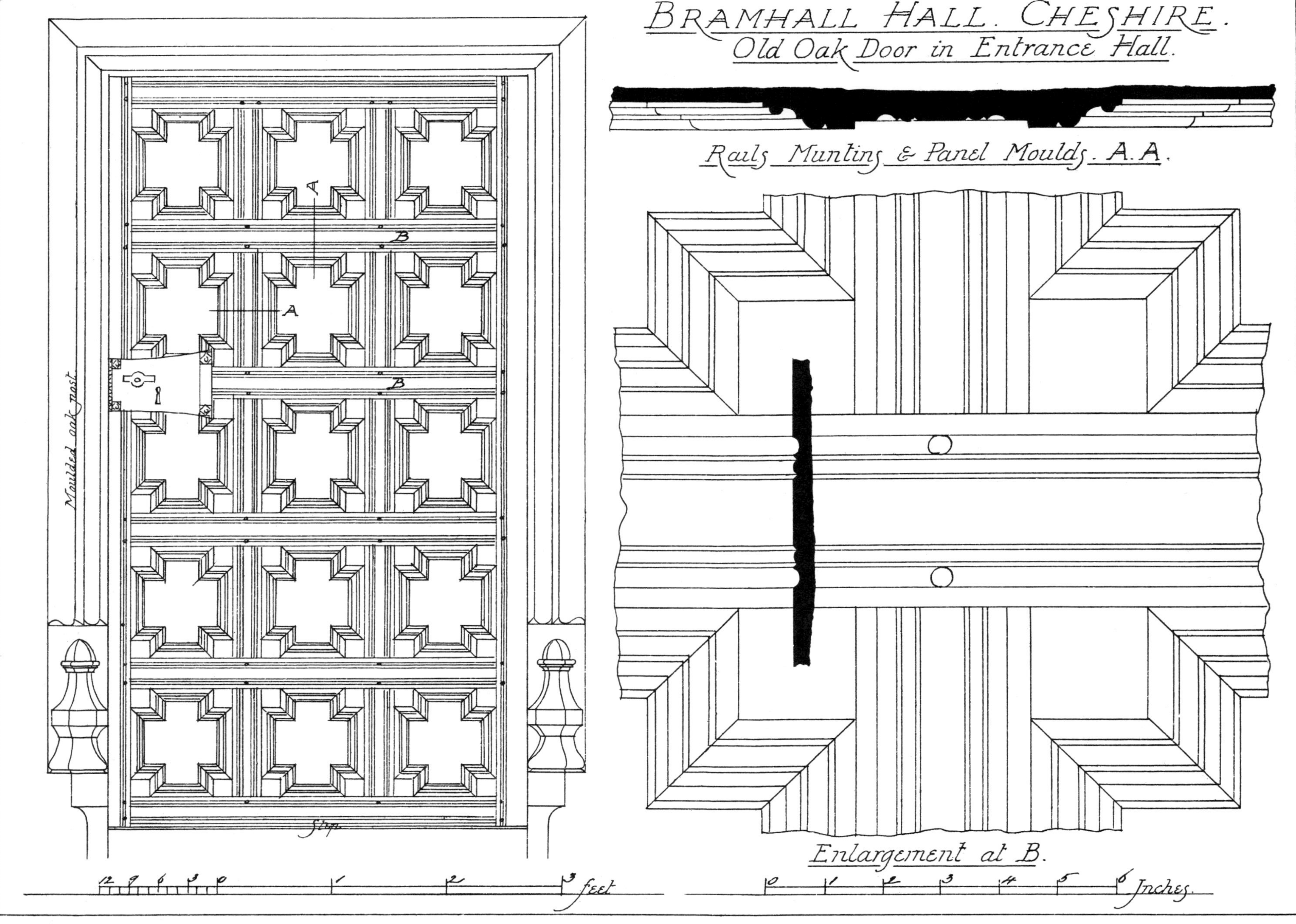

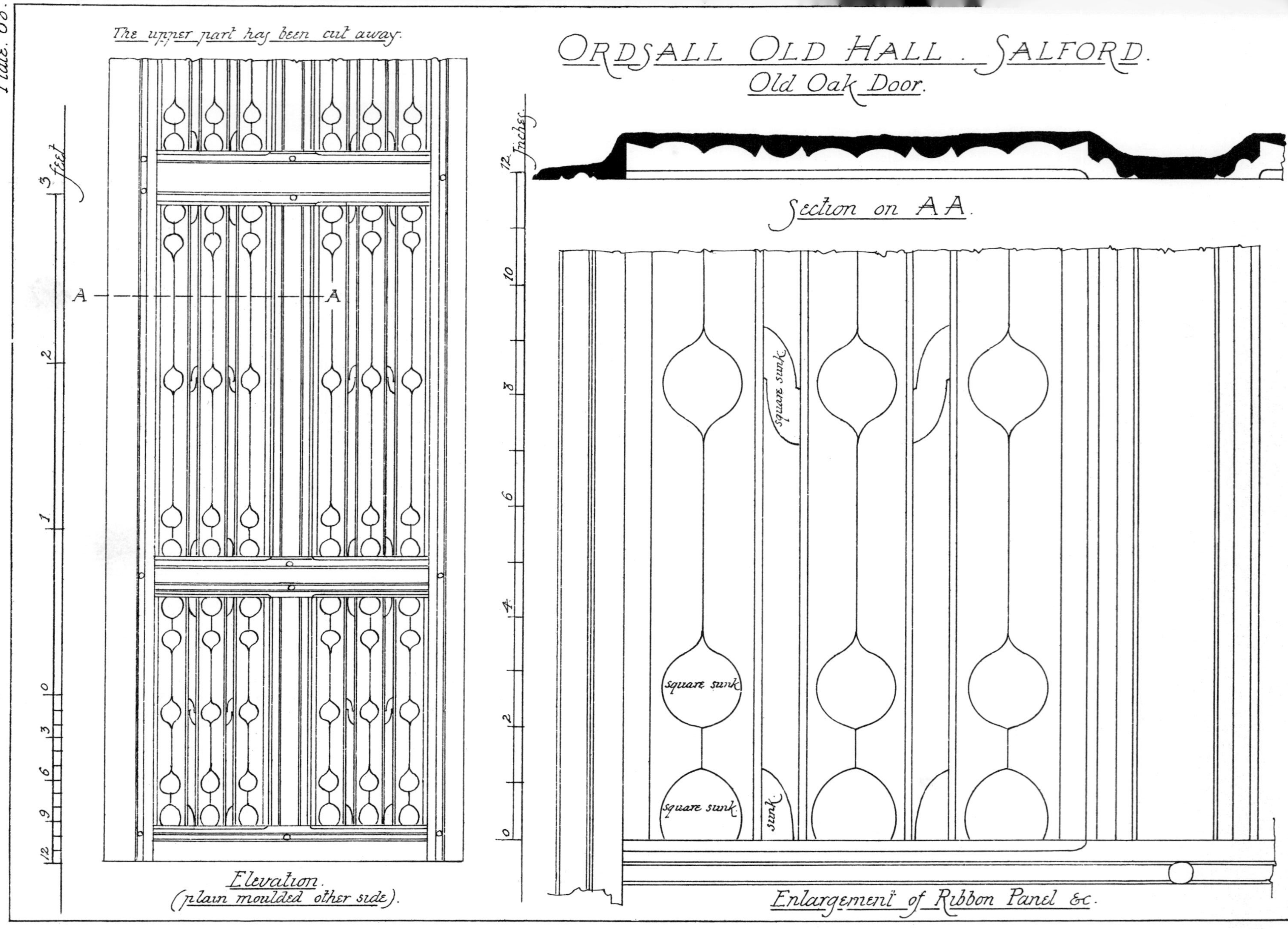

ORDSALL OLD HALL. SALFORD.
Old Oak Door.
The upper part has been cut away.
12 9 6 3 0 1 2 3 feet
A
A
Elevation.
(plain moulded other side).
0 2 4 6 8 10 12 Inches.
Section on AA.
square sunk
square sunk
square sunk
sunk.
Enlargement of Ribbon Panel &c.

BRAMHALL HALL. CHESHIRE. Oak Door to Billiard-Room.

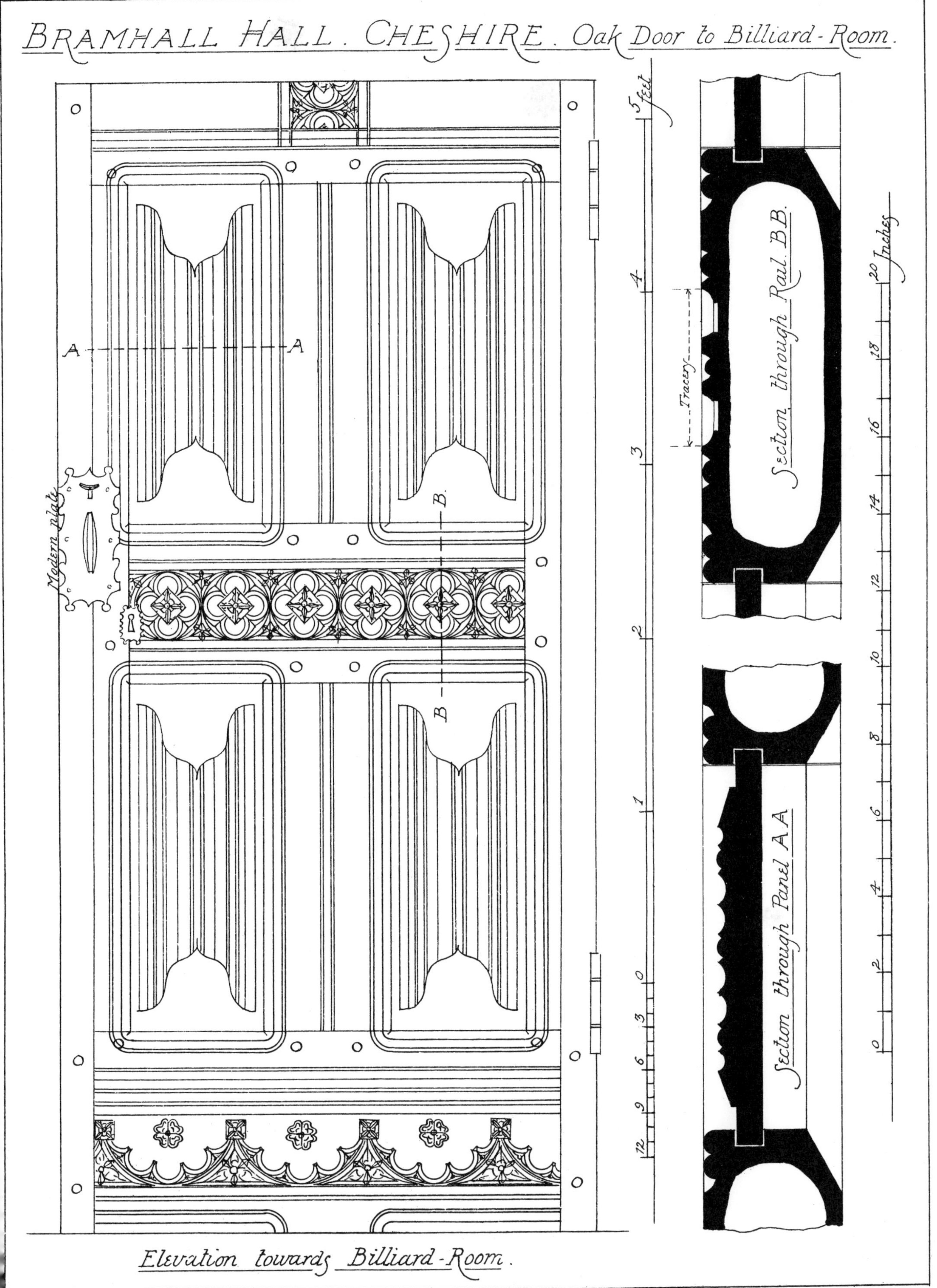

Elevation towards Billiard-Room.

Kersal Cell near Higher Broughton. Manchester.

Old Oak Door.

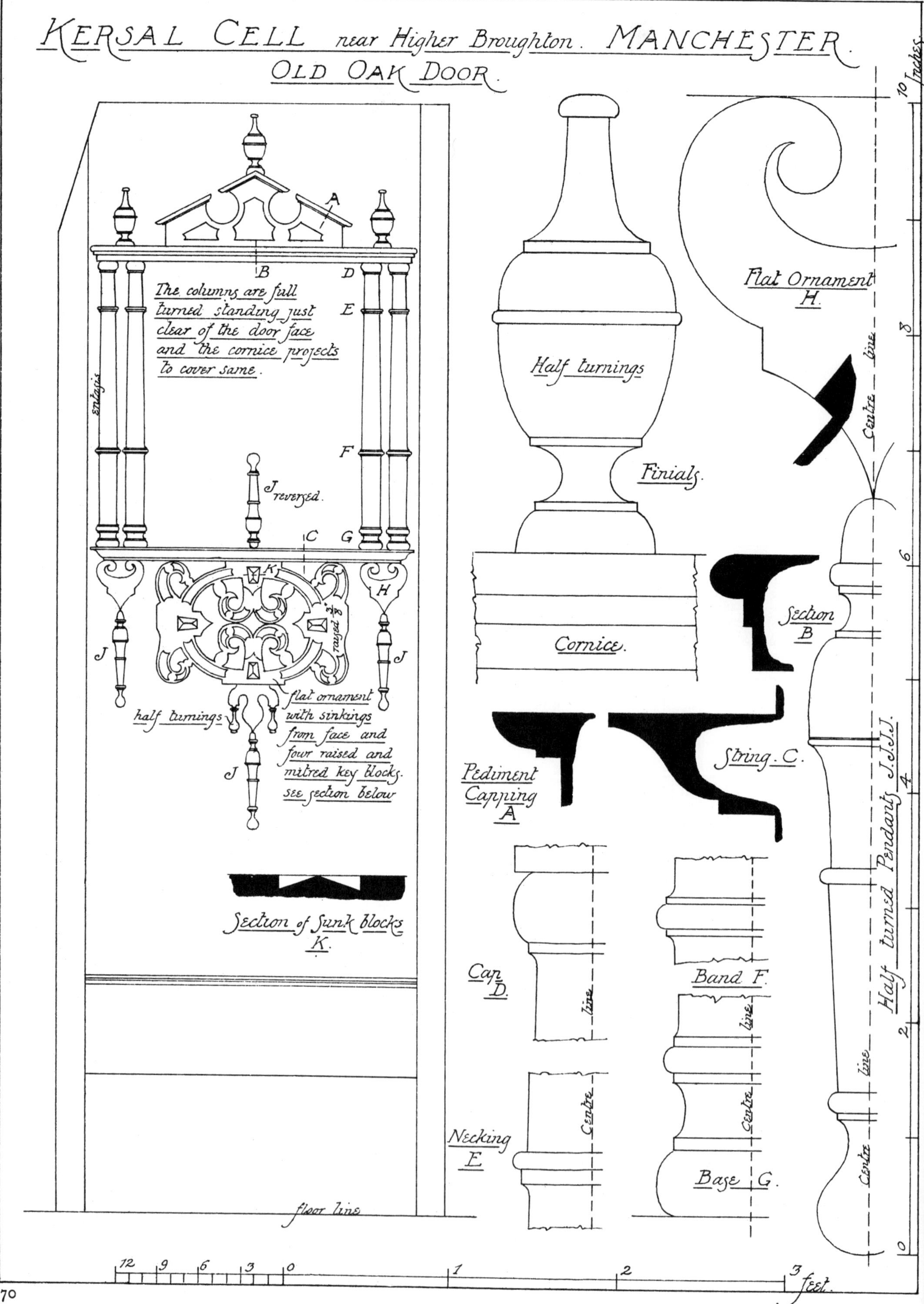

BRAMHALL HALL. CHESHIRE.

Old Oak Door and Dado in Bedroom.

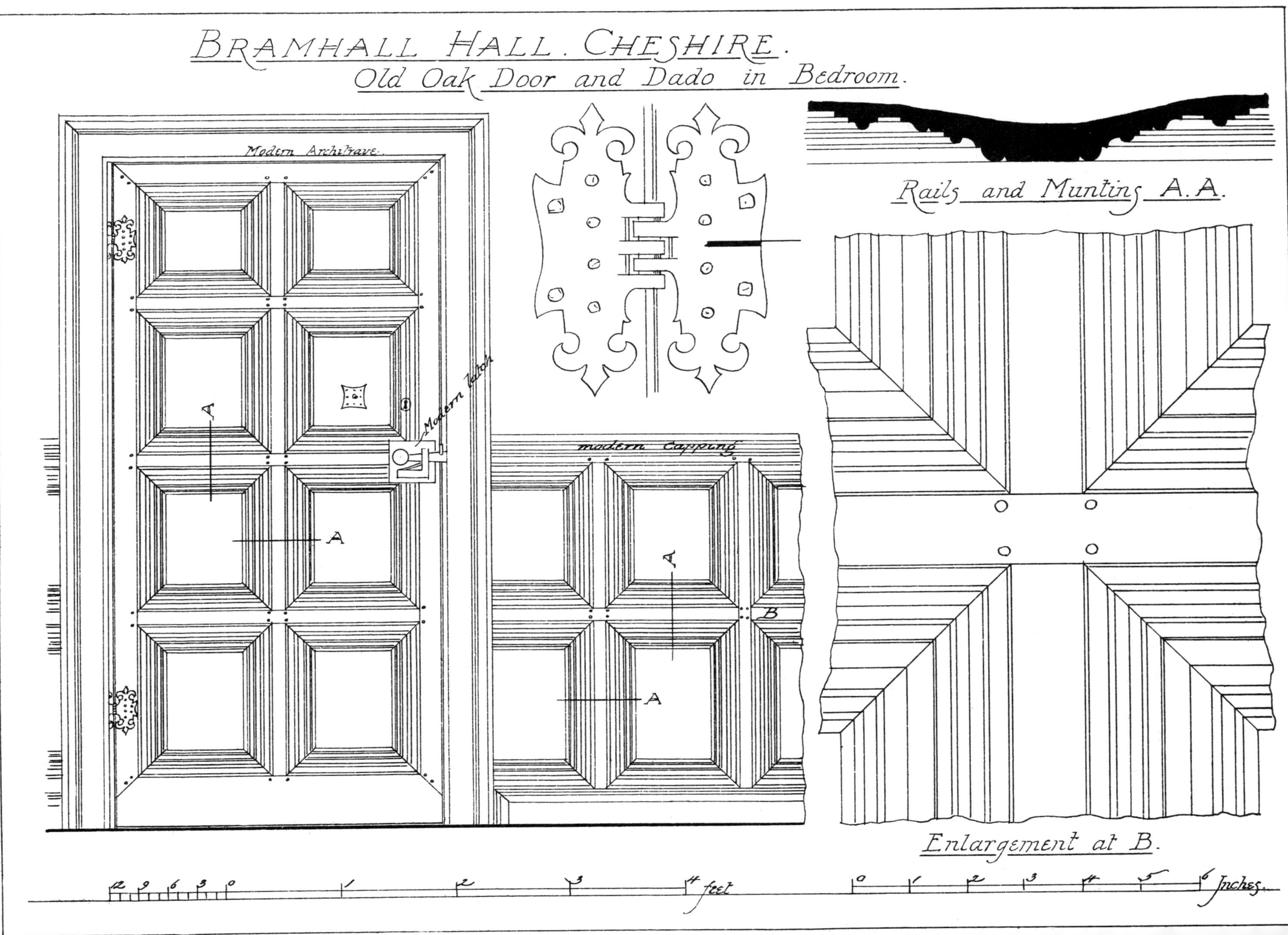

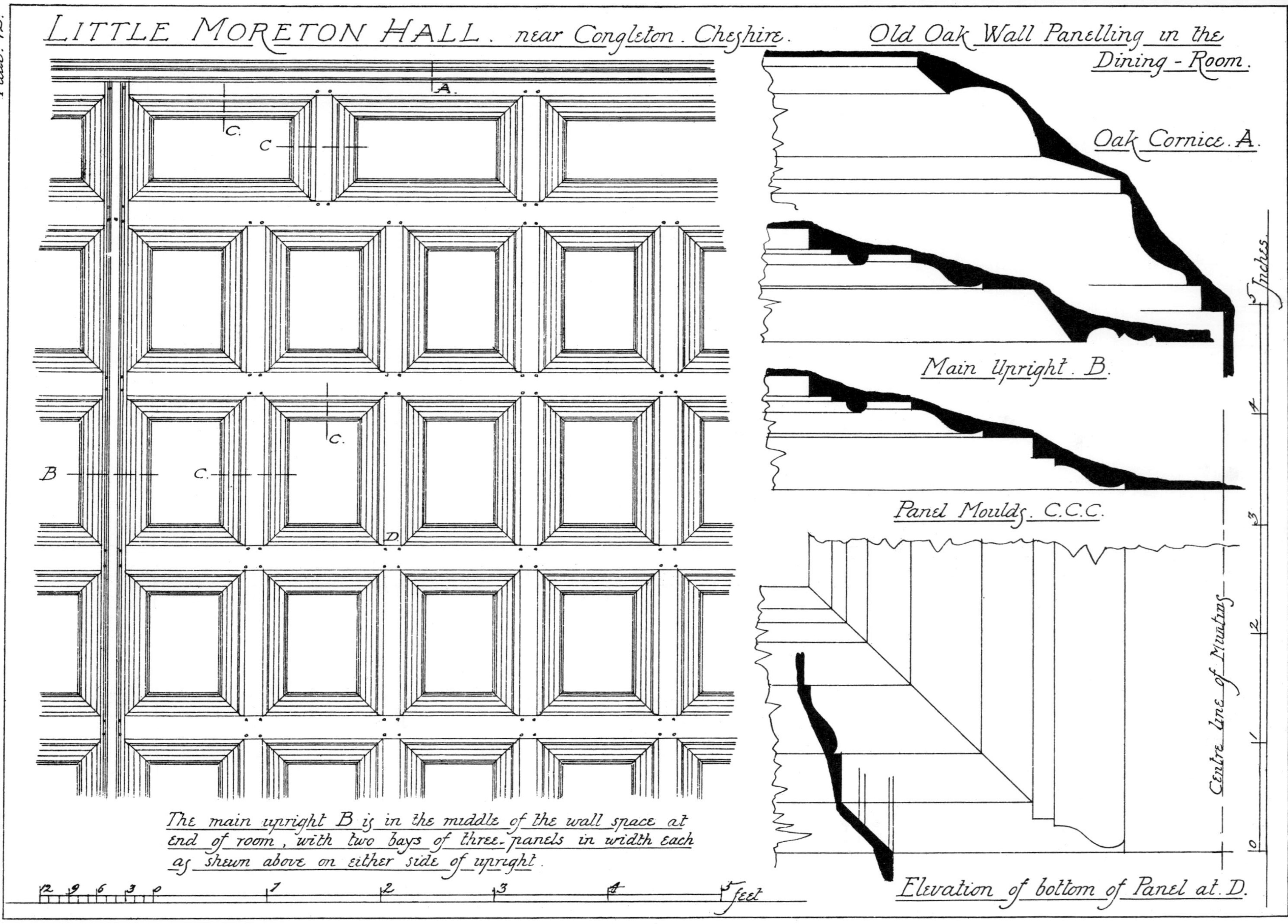
LITTLE MORETON HALL. near Congleton. Cheshire.
Old Oak Wall Panelling in the Dining-Room.
Oak Cornice. A.
Main Upright. B.
Panel Moulds. C.C.C.
Elevation of bottom of Panel at D.
Centre line of Muntins
A.
B
C.
C
D
The main upright B is in the middle of the wall space at end of room, with two bays of three-panels in width each as shewn above on either side of upright.
12 9 6 3 0 1 2 3 4 5 feet
0 1 2 3 4 5 Inches.

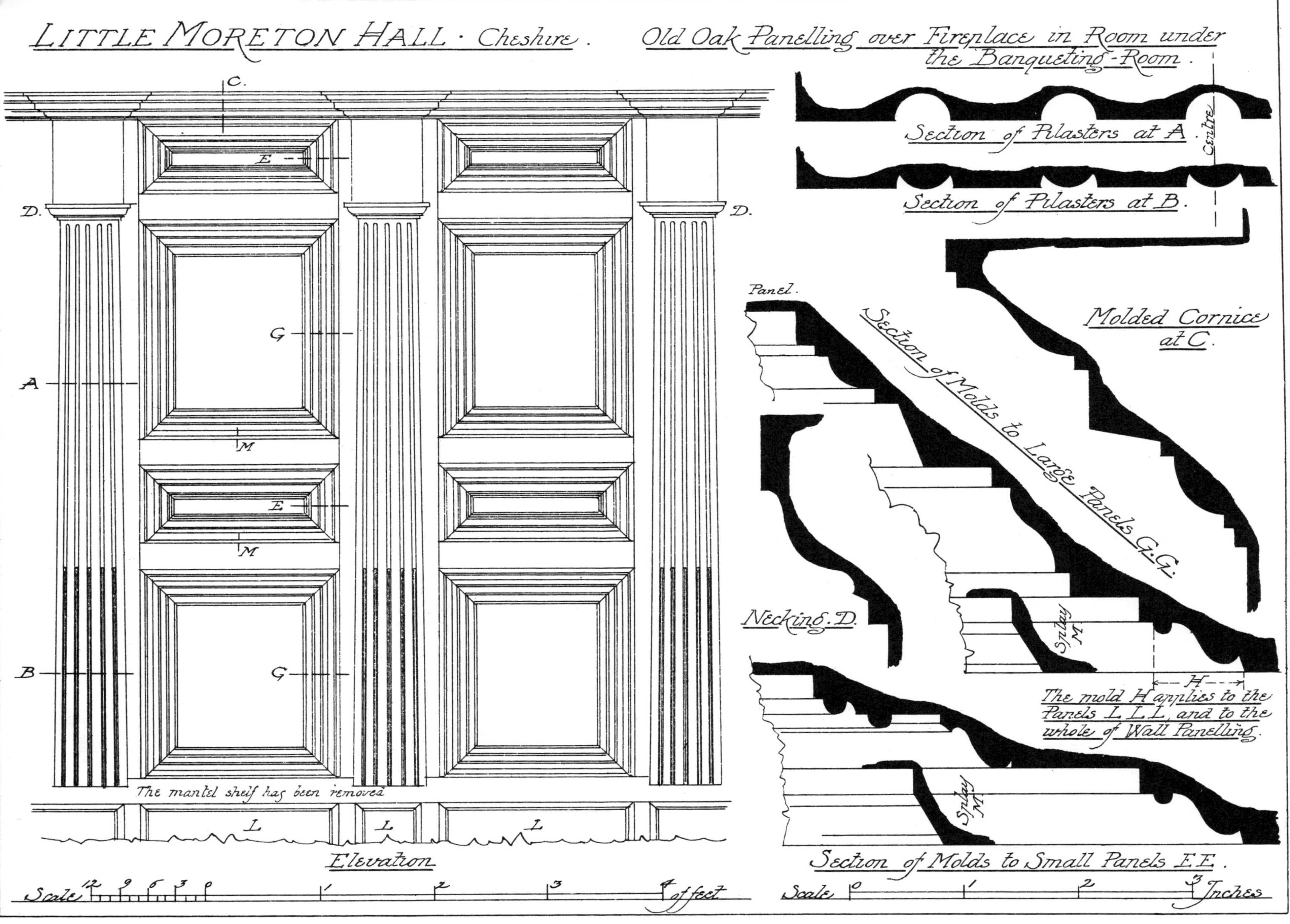
LITTLE MORETON HALL · Cheshire.
Old Oak Panelling over Fireplace in Room under the Banqueting-Room.
C.
E
D.
D.
G
A
M
E
M
B
G
The mantel shelf has been removed
L
L
L
Elevation
Scale 12 9 6 3 0 1 2 3 4 of feet
Section of Pilasters at A.
Centre
Section of Pilasters at B.
Panel.
Section of Molds to Large Panels G.G.
Molded Cornice at C.
Necking. D.
Splay M
H
The mold H applies to the Panels L L L, and to the whole of Wall Panelling.
Splay M
Section of Molds to Small Panels E.E.
Scale 0 1 2 3 Inches

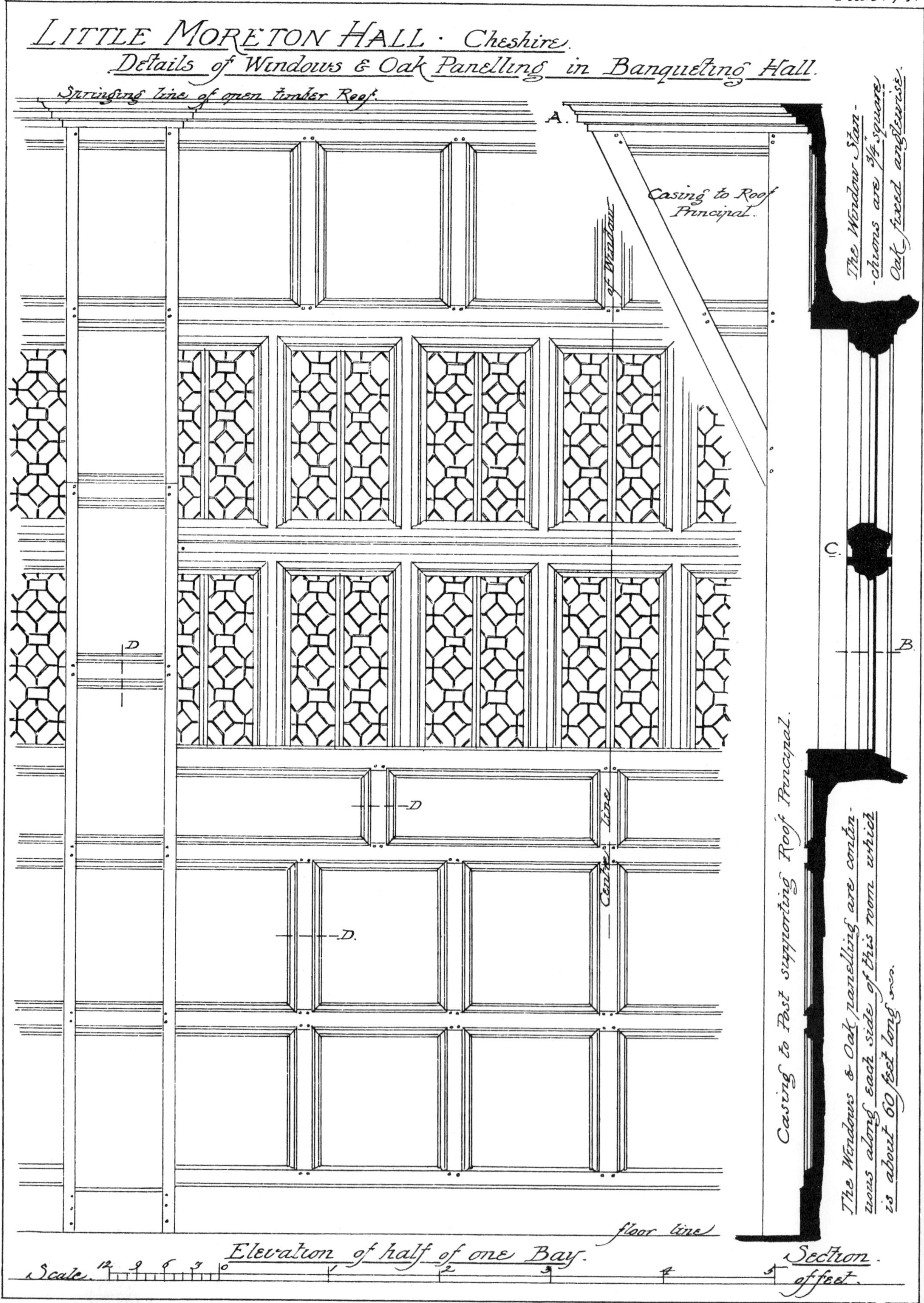
LITTLE MORETON HALL · Cheshire.
Details of Windows & Oak Panelling in Banqueting Hall.
Springing line of open timber Roof.
A.
Casing to Roof Principal.
of Window
Centre line
C.
B.
D
D
D.
The Window Stanchons are 3/4" square Oak fixed anglewise.
Casing to Post supporting Roof Principal.
The Windows & Oak panelling are continuous along each side of this room which is about 60 feet long.
floor line
Elevation of half of one Bay.
Section.
Scale 12 9 6 3 0 1 2 3 4 5 of feet.

LITTLE MORETON HALL · Cheshire
Details of Windows & Oak Panelling in Banquetting Hall.
Section of Cornice. A.
joint.
Elevation of Panel Molds.
Section of Panel Molds at D.
0 1 2 3 4 Inches
Outside
Glazing
Plan of Panelled Casing to Posts.
These Stiles are flush with the outer fillet face of the panel Molds.
12 9 6 3 0 Inches
Glazing
Oak Stanchions.
Outside
Section of Mullions. at B.
Section of Transom. C.
The Head, Sill & Jamb correspond and mitre.
Outside
Stanchion
Inside Elevation of Transom & Mullions.
Scale 12 11 10 9 8 7 6 5 4 3 2 1 0 Inches.

CHETHAM'S COLLEGE MANCHESTER.

Old Oak Wall Panelling in the Library Reading Room.

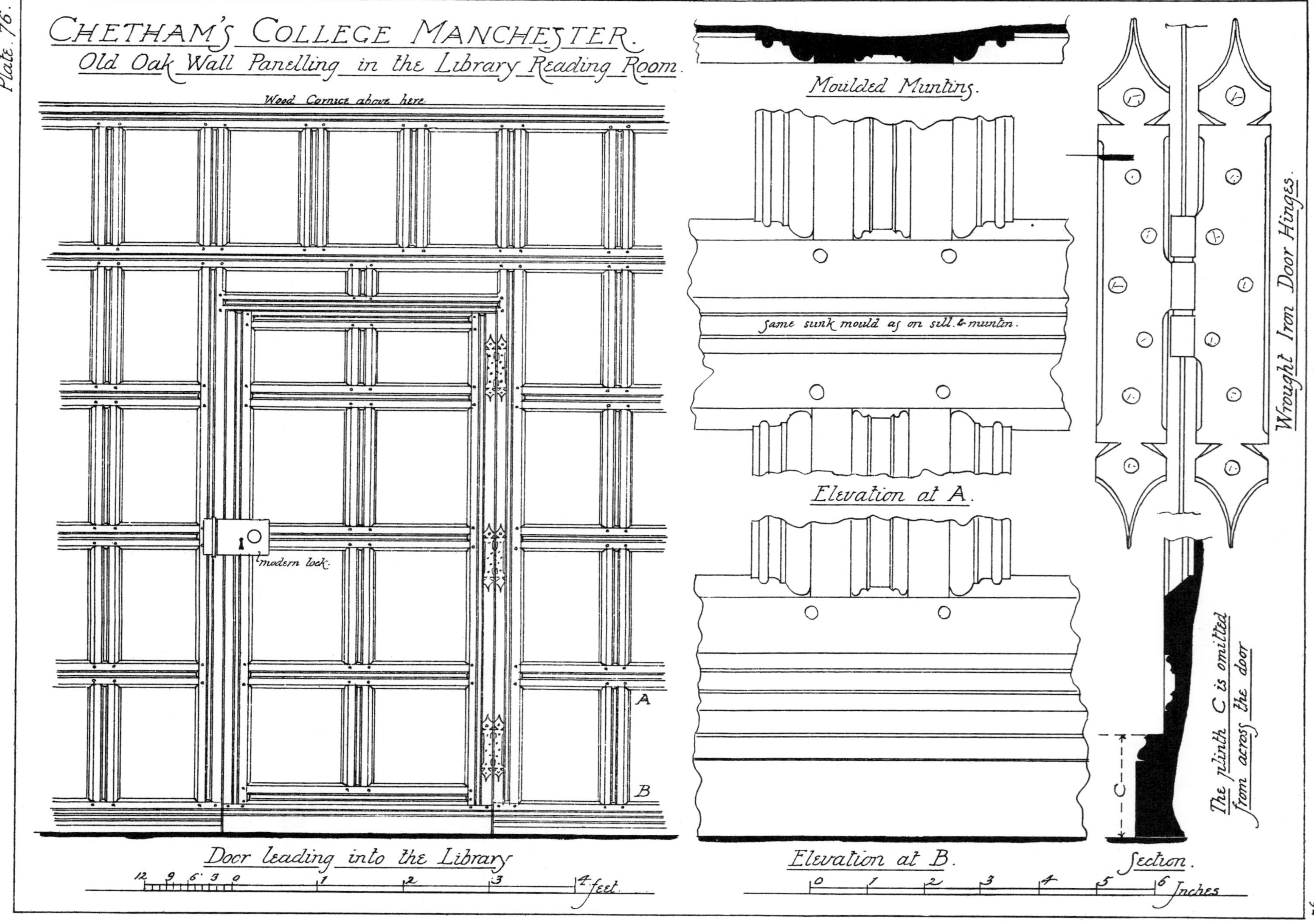

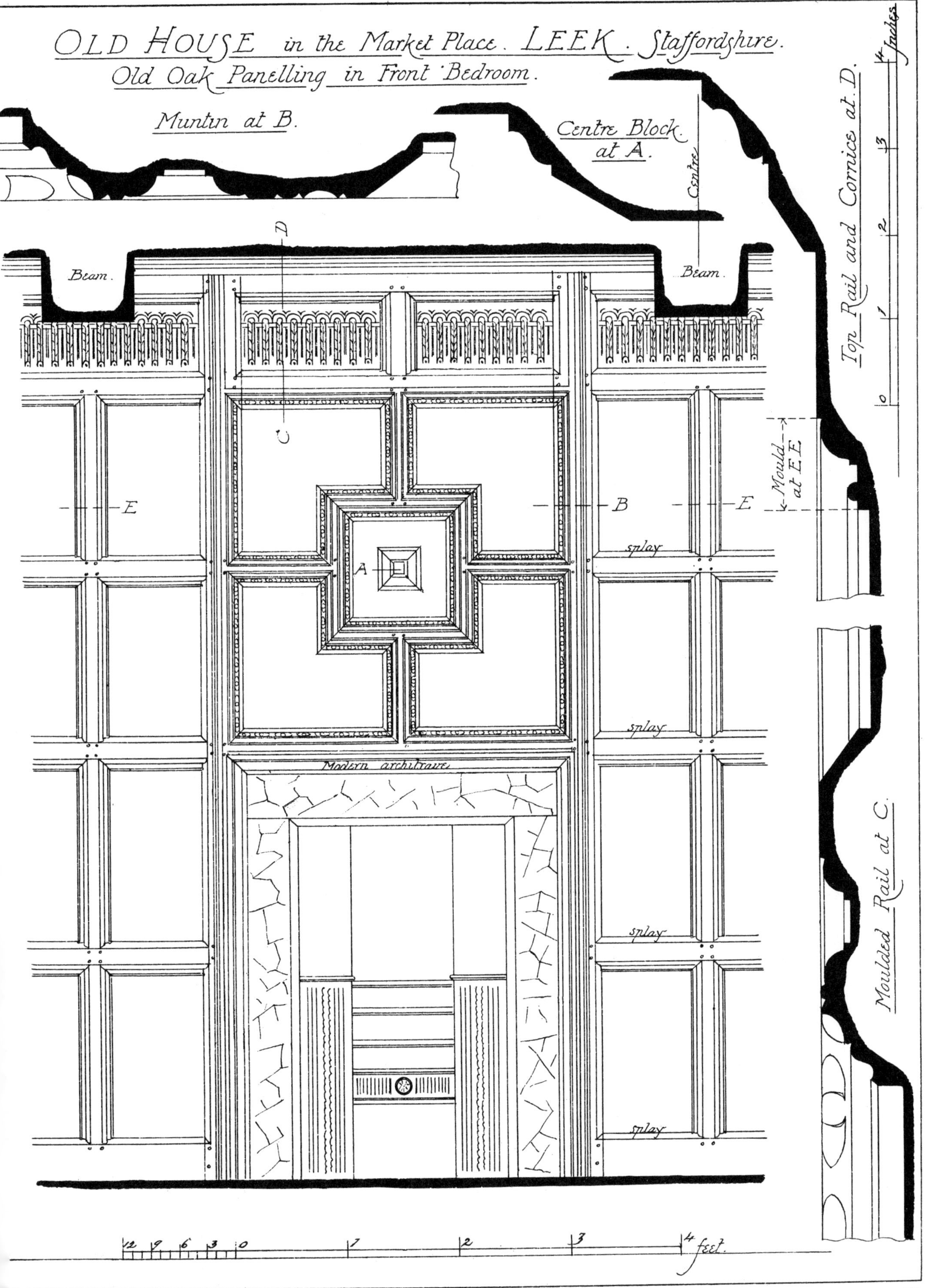
OLD HOUSE in the Market Place. LEEK. Staffordshire.
Old Oak Panelling in Front Bedroom.
Muntin at B.
Centre Block at A.
Centre
Top Rail and Cornice at D.
Inches
0 1 2 3 4
D
Beam.
Beam.
C
E
B
E
A
splay
splay
splay
splay
Mould at EE
Modern architrave
Moulded Rail at C.
12 9 6 3 0 1 2 3 4 feet.

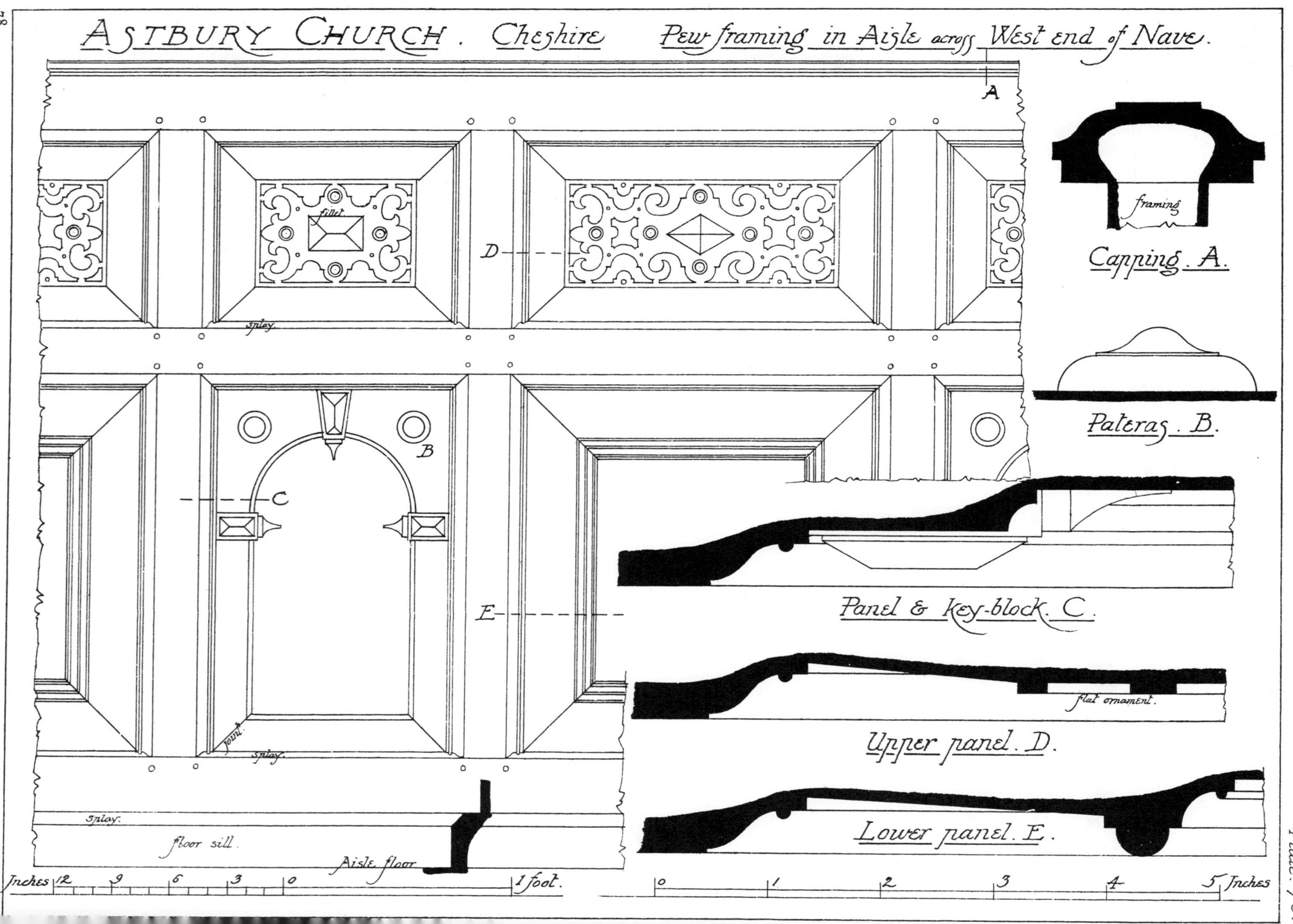

ASTBURY CHURCH. Cheshire. Pew framing in Aisle across West end of Nave.
A
fillet
splay.
D
B
C
E
joint
splay.
splay.
floor sill.
Aisle floor
Inches 12 9 6 3 0
1 foot.
framing
Capping. A.
Pateras. B.
Panel & Key-block. C.
flat ornament.
Upper panel. D.
Lower panel. E.
0 1 2 3 4 5 Inches

Astbury Church near Congleton. Cheshire.

Ornamental Panels of Pew Framing.

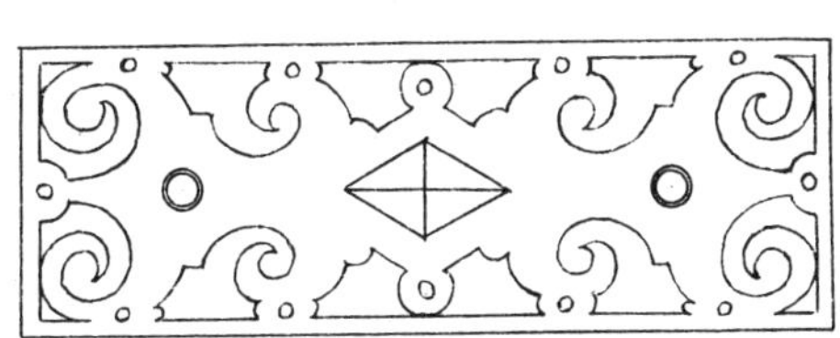

South Aisle.

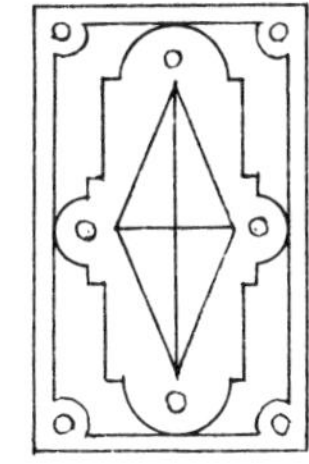

South Aisle.

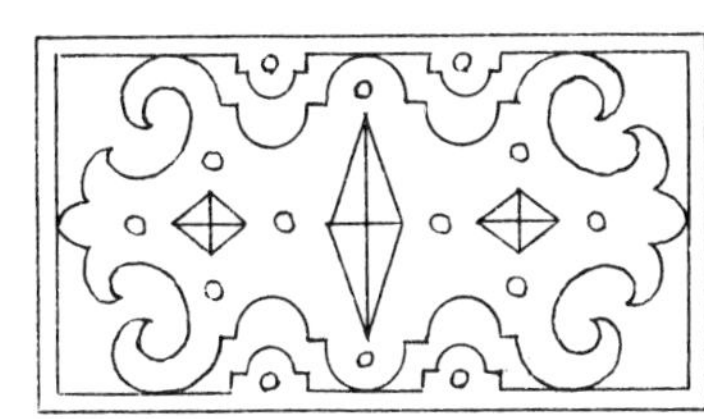

South Aisle.

All the sunk parts are scarcely ⅛" deep.

West Aisle

near South Porch.

West Aisle.

The very small circles are square sunk dots.

Nave Aisle.

West Aisle.

Nave Aisle.

The small circles with two lines are sunk and raised thus.

West Aisle.

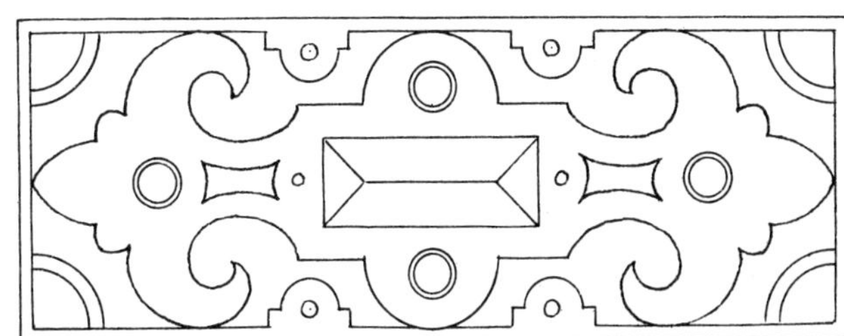

West Aisle.

The whole of the general ornament is flat faced with the centre blocks raised splayed and mitred with small raised fillet around. All the panels have the broad splay and mould mitred around the same as panels shewn on Plate 78.

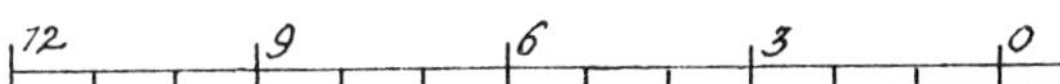

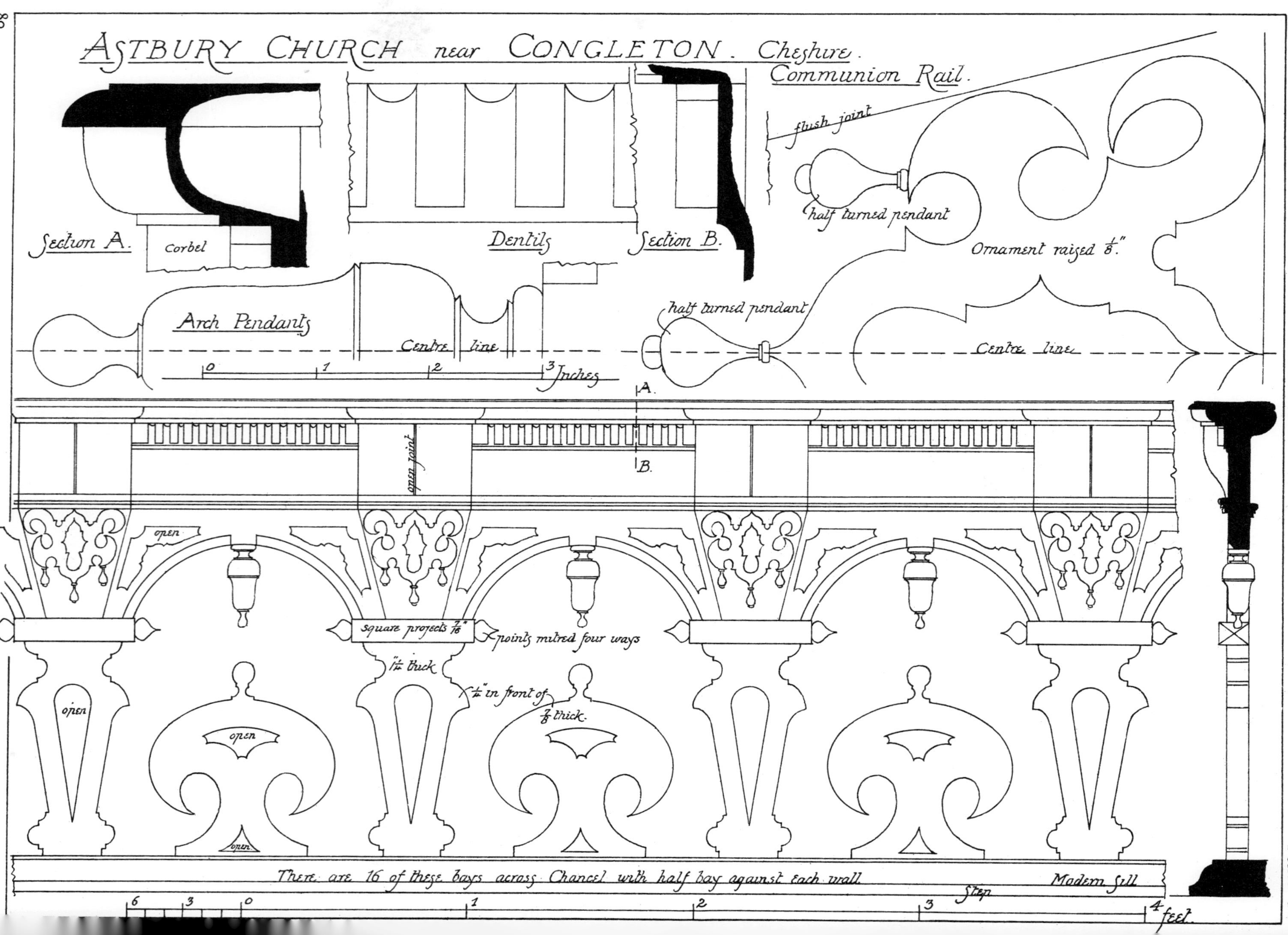
ASTBURY CHURCH near CONGLETON. Cheshire.
Communion Rail.
Section A.
Corbel
Dentils
Section B.
flush joint
half turned pendant
Ornament raised 1/8"
Arch Pendants
Centre line
0 1 2 3 Inches
half turned pendant
Centre line
A.
B.
open joint
open
square projects 7/16"
points mitred four ways
1 1/4" thick
1/4" in front of
7/8 thick.
open
open
open
There are 16 of these bays across Chancel with half bay against each wall
Modern Sill
Step
6 3 0 1 2 3 4 feet

Astbury Church. near Congleton. Altar Table.
Carved Frieze. A.
Fluted Corbels. B.
Plan of End.
Spandrils of Arcading. C.C.
Side Elevation of End Corbels &c. E
Bottom Rails. D.
Small Columns to Arcading.
Four Corner Columns.
Square
turned
Scale for Details
0 2 4 6 8 Inches
flat ornament
The pateras are turned and raised as detail above
half turned pendants
entasis
sinkings
half turned pendant.
C.
D.
12 9 6 3 0 1 2 3 4 5 feet.

LITTLE MORETON HALL · Cheshire : Old Oak Ceiling in Dining-Room.
Section of Main Beams A A.
The whole of the moldings of this Beam are continued around the room as a Cornice. The Intermediate Beams all die square against the upper part of Main Beams. The Panels are in plain wrought close jointed oak boarding in long lengths.
Intermediate Beams B.B.B.
Scale 0 2 4 6 8 10 12 Inches
B.
B.
B.
A.
A.
B.
Plan looking upwards.
Scale 0 1 2 3 4 5 6 7 8 9 10 11 12 13 14 15 16 17 18 of feet.

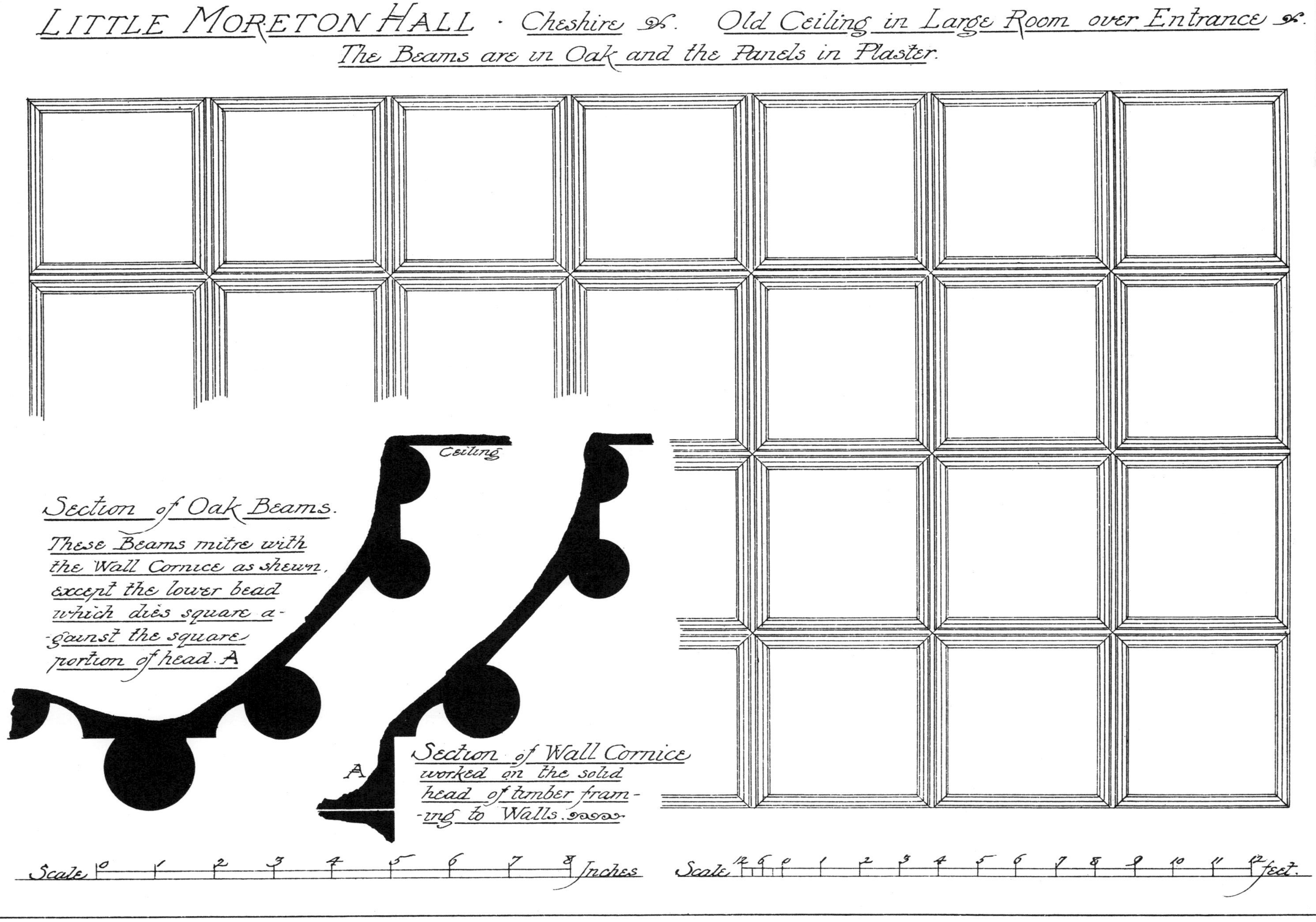
LITTLE MORETON HALL · Cheshire &c. Old Ceiling in Large Room over Entrance &c.
The Beams are in Oak and the Panels in Plaster.
Ceiling
Section of Oak Beams.
These Beams mitre with the Wall Cornice as shewn, except the lower bead which dies square against the square portion of head A
A
Section of Wall Cornice worked on the solid head of timber framing to Walls.
Scale 0 1 2 3 4 5 6 7 8 Inches
Scale 12 6 0 1 2 3 4 5 6 7 8 9 10 11 12 feet.

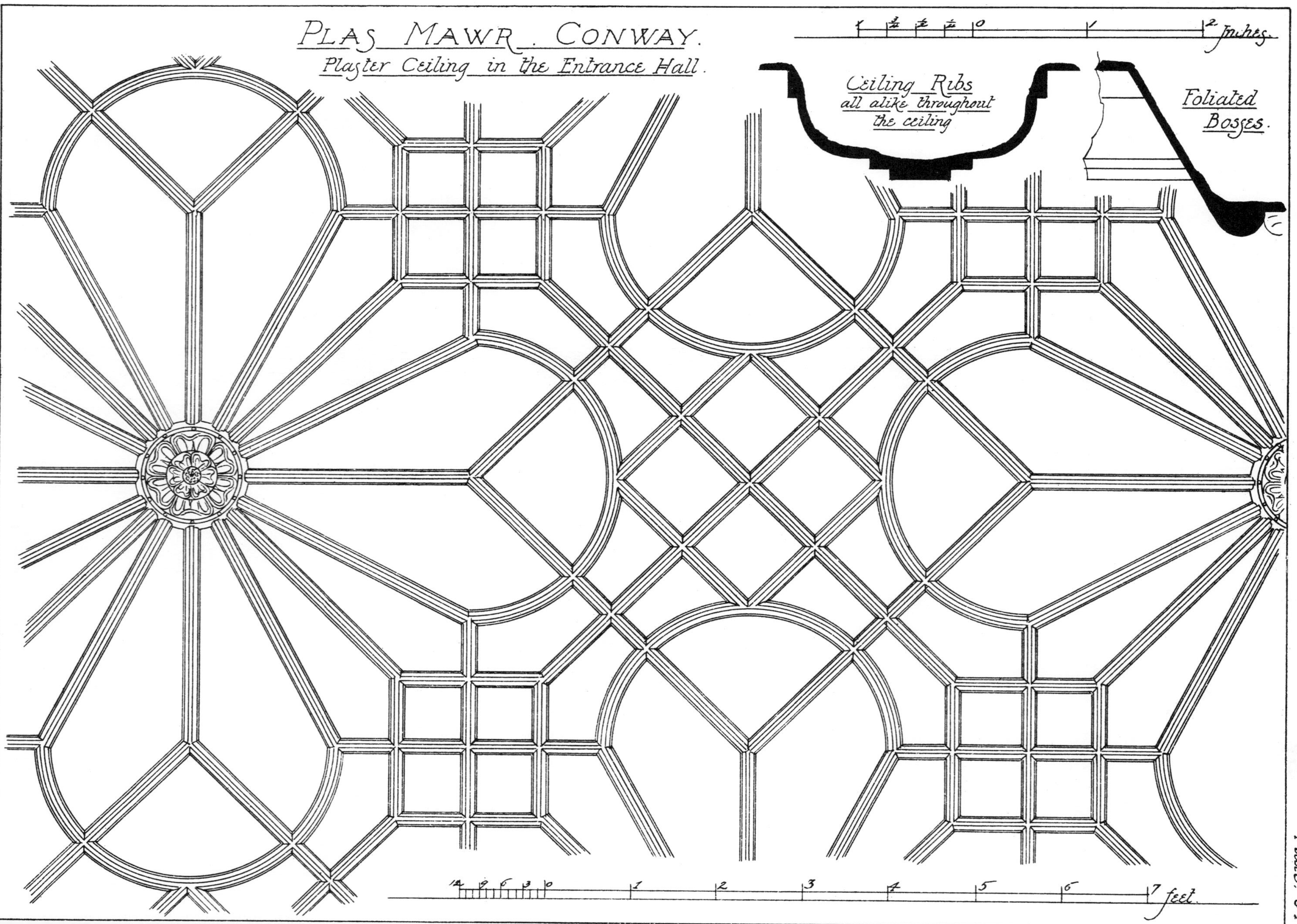
PLAS MAWR . CONWAY.
Plaster Ceiling in the Entrance Hall.
Inches
Ceiling Ribs
all alike throughout
the ceiling
Foliated
Bosses.
feet

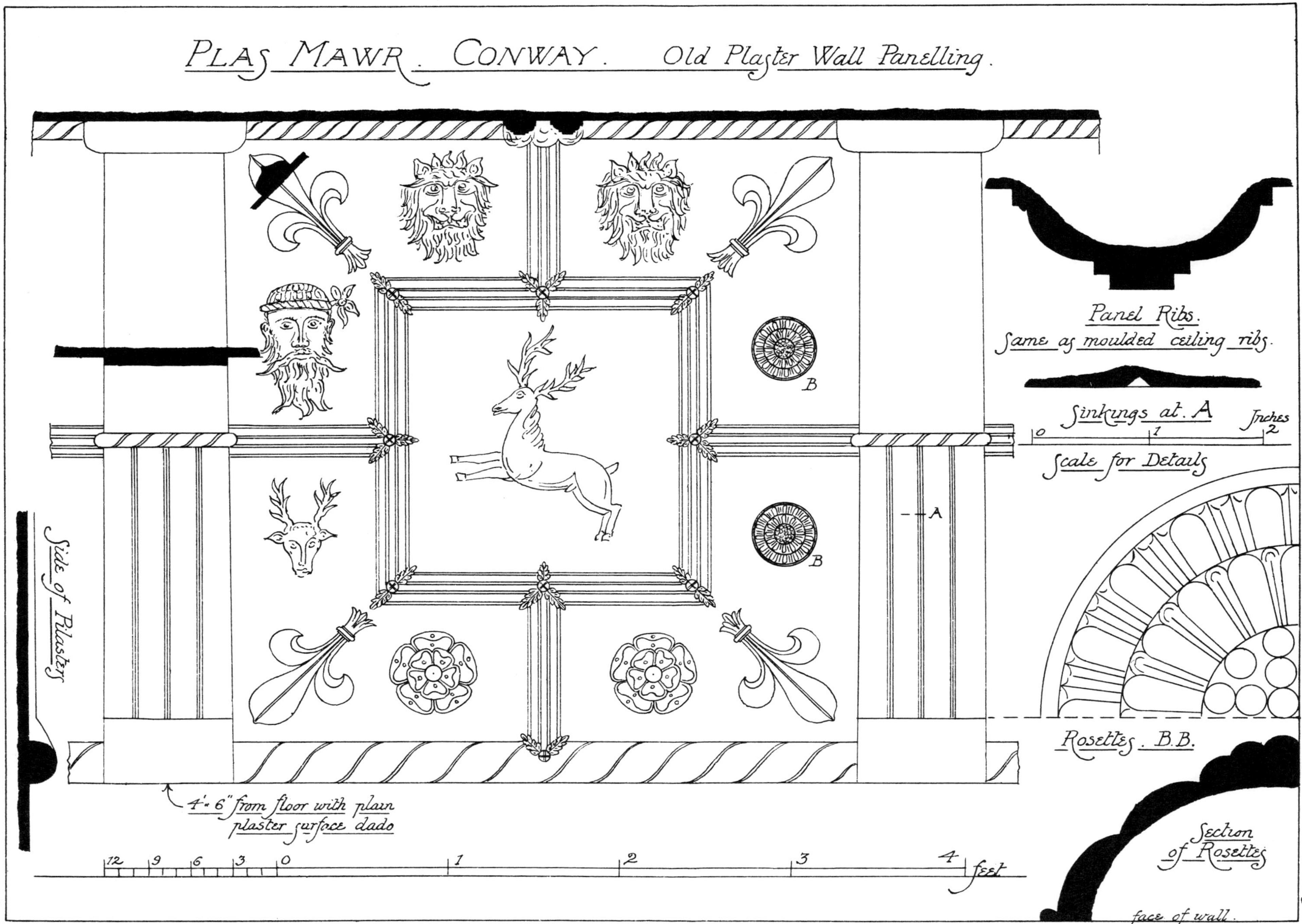

Plas Mawr. Conway. Old Plaster Wall Panelling.

Panel Ribs.
Same as moulded ceiling ribs.

Sinkings at. A

0 1 2 Inches

Scale for Details

A

B

B

Rosettes. B.B.

Section of Rosettes

face of wall.

Side of Pilasters

4'. 6" from floor with plain plaster surface dado

12 9 6 3 0 1 2 3 4 feet

Plas Mawr Conway. Old Plaster Ceiling.

The section of the moulded ceiling ribs and the leaves at the intersections of the ribs are the same as to wall panelling, see plate 85. The rosettes and heads are also similar.

0 2 4 6 8 10 12 feet

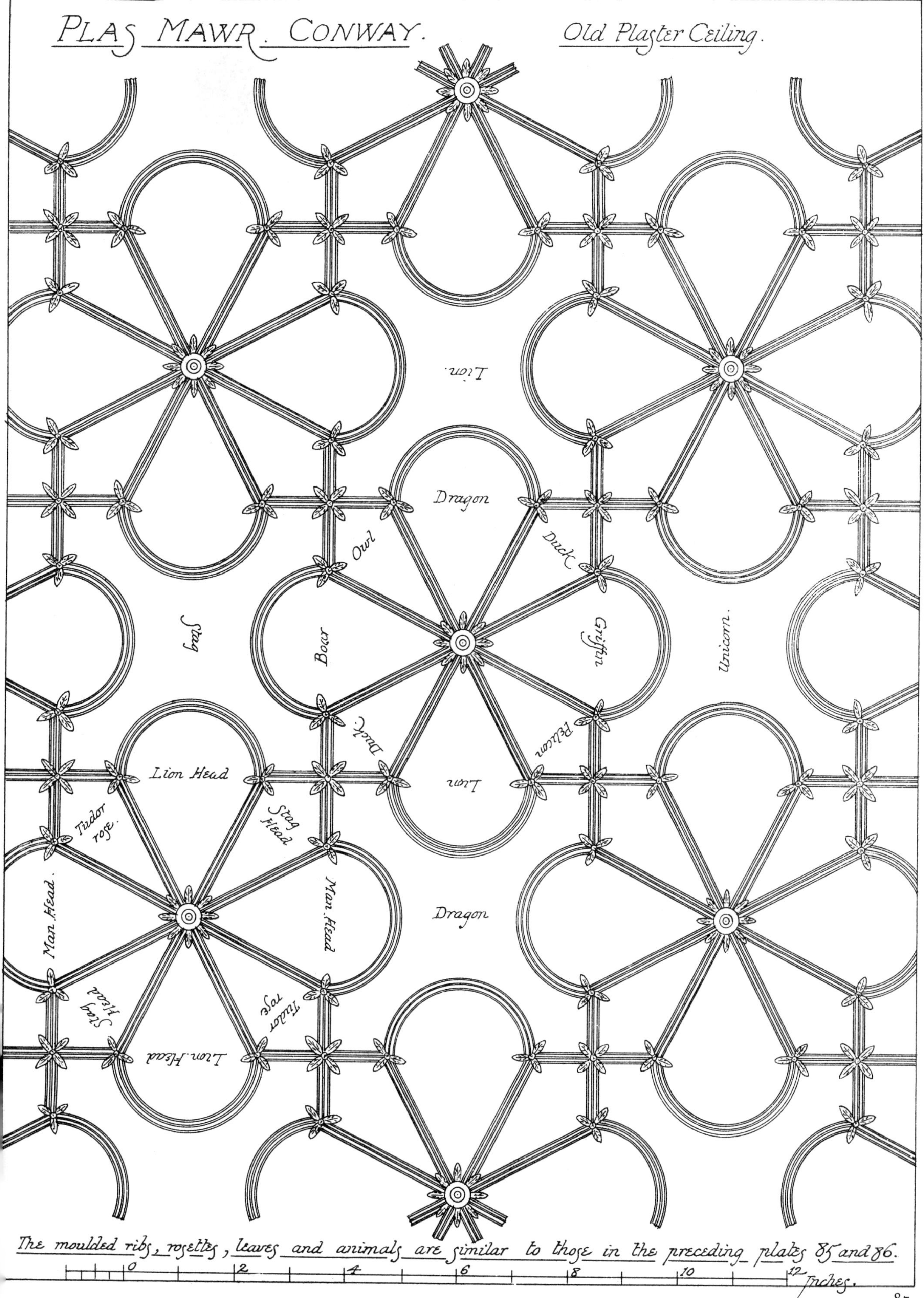
PLAS MAWR. CONWAY.
Old Plaster Ceiling.
Lion.
Dragon
Owl
Duck
Stag
Boar
Griffin
Unicorn
Duck.
Pelican
Lion
Lion Head
Tudor rose.
Stag Head
Man Head.
Man Head
Dragon
Stag Head
Tudor rose
Lion Head
Lion Head
The moulded ribs, rosettes, leaves and animals are similar to those in the preceding plates 85 and 86.
0
2
4
6
8
10
12
Inches.

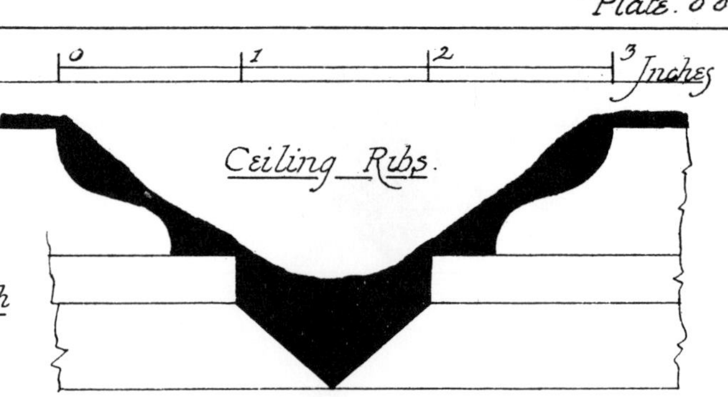

ORDSALL OLD HALL.

SALFORD. Lancashire.

Old Plaster Ceiling.

to room adjoining the Star Chamber in which it is said Guy Fawkes conceived his great plot

0
1
2
3 Inches
Ceiling Ribs.

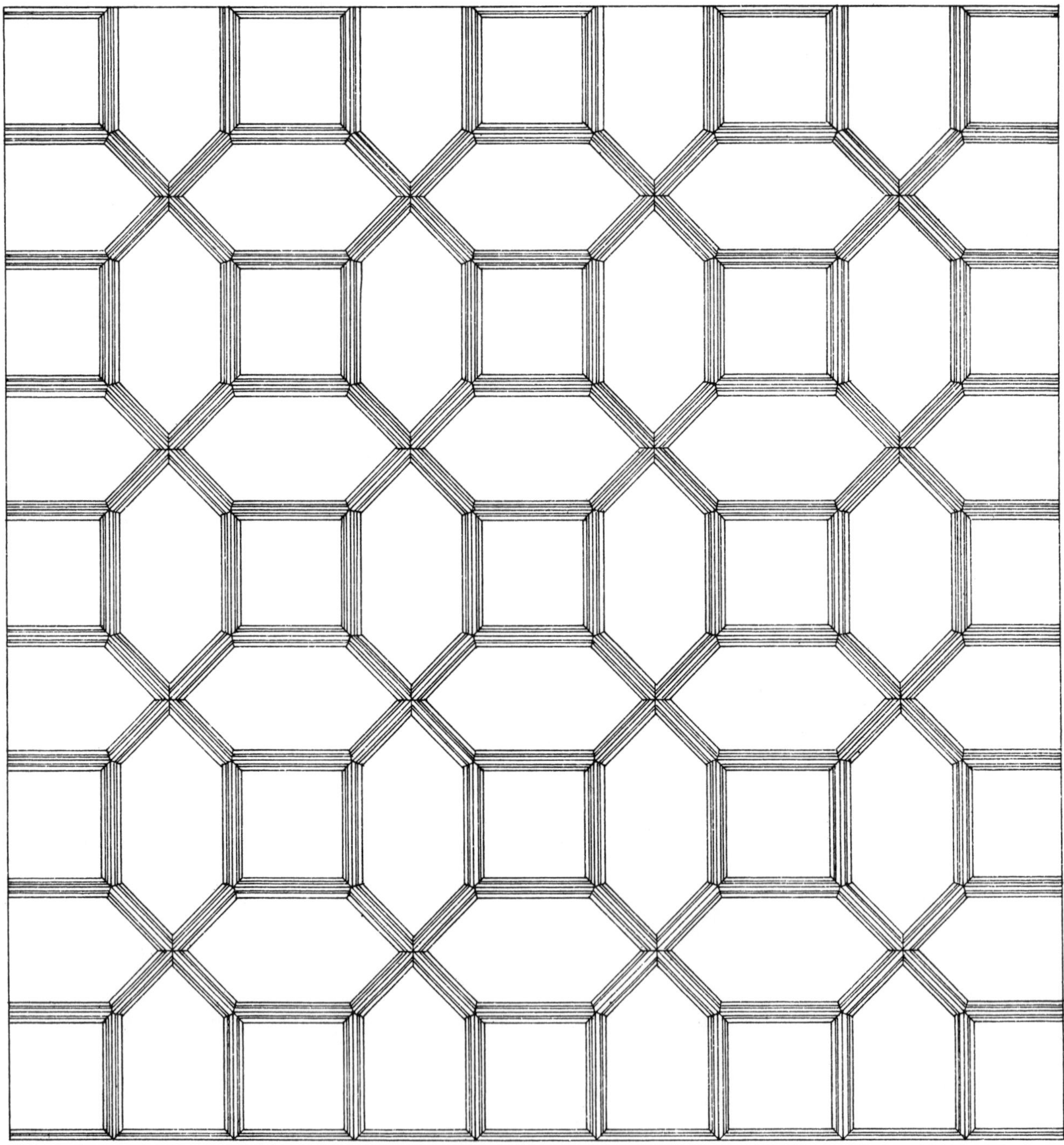

12
6
0
1
2
3
4
5
6
7
8
9
10 feet.

Plaster Ceilings in old House, Market Place. Leek &c pulled down 1897.

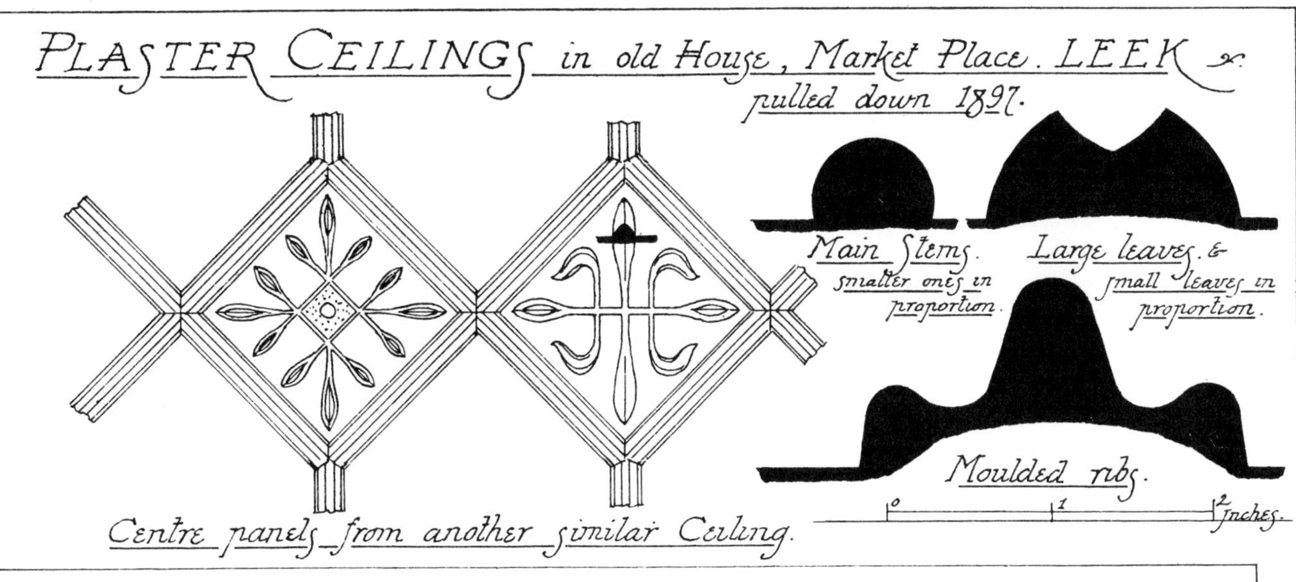

Centre panels from another similar Ceiling.

12 9 6 3 0 1 2 3 4 5 6 7 feet.

OLD LEAD CISTERN at No. 18 Rutland Square DUBLIN
1774
Inches 12 6 0 1 2 3 feet
Two side panels at front.
Centre front panel & two end panels also like this
Centre
Centre
1¼"
Panel Mold
1 1/16"
Base & capping Mold.

LITTLE MORETON HALL. Cheshire. Old Plaster Chimney-piece.
E
F
D
C
B
G
A
Upper Pedestal. F.
Centre line
Lower Pedestal. G.
0 1 2 3 4 Inches
Note. The old grate is missing.
12 9 6 3 0 1 2 3 4 5 6 feet.

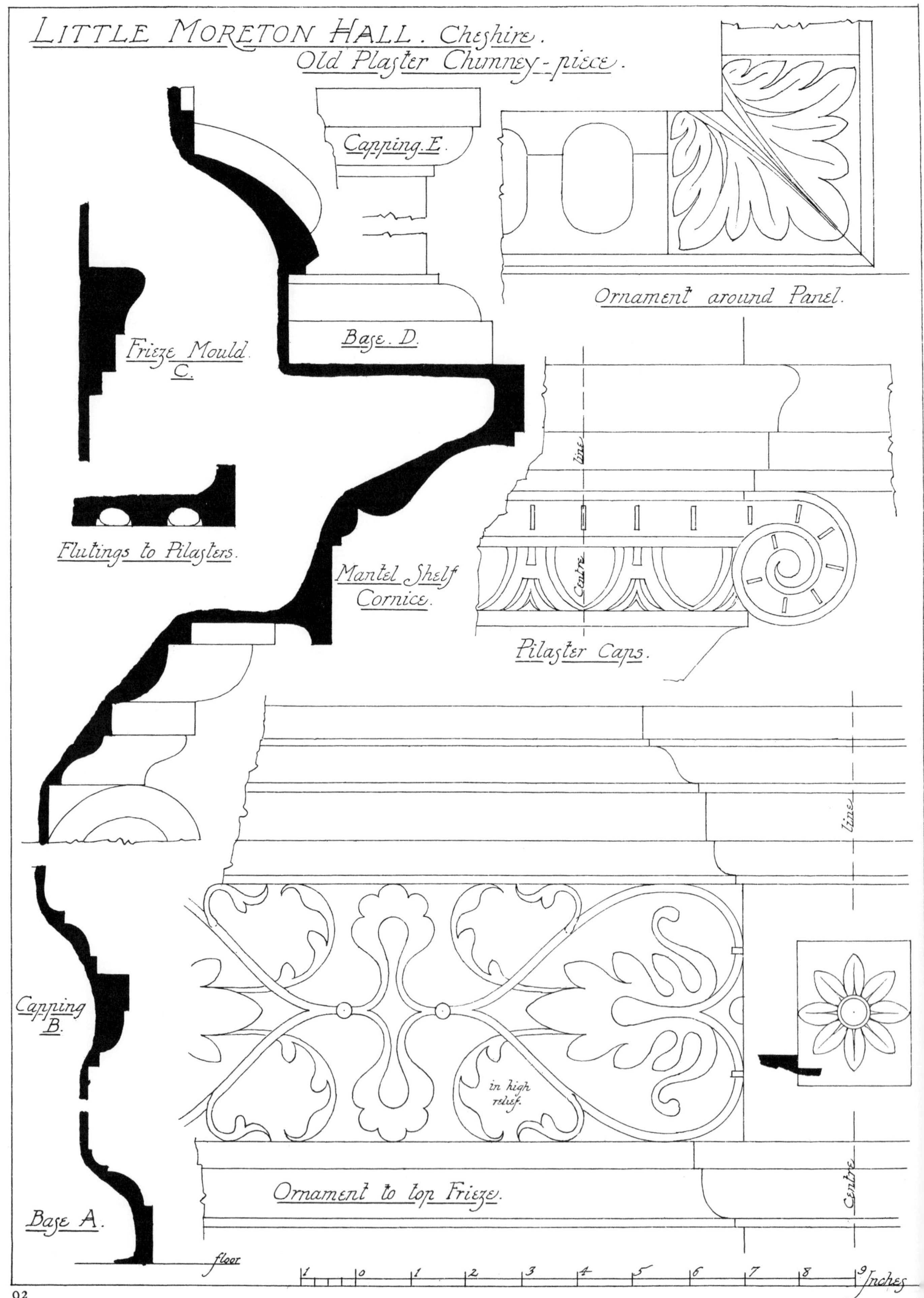
Little Moreton Hall. Cheshire.
Old Plaster Chimney-piece.
Capping. E.
Base. D.
Ornament around Panel.
Frieze Mould. C.
Flutings to Pilasters.
Mantel Shelf Cornice.
Line
Centre
Pilaster Caps.
Line
Capping B.
in high relief.
Ornament to top Frieze.
Centre
Base A.
floor
1 0 1 2 3 4 5 6 7 8 9 Inches

PLAS MAWR CONWAY.
Old Stone and Plaster Chimney-Piece in the Entrance Hall
R
W
15
80
Plaster
Stone
C.
A
Section through Jamb Stop. B
Mantel Cornice
Jamb and Head Moulds A.A
Corbel Shelves C.
A
B
0 1 2 3 4 5 6 7 8 9 Inches
fender
12 9 6 3 0 1 2 3 4 5 6 7 feet

PLAS MAWR CONWAY.

Old Stone and Plaster Chimney-Piece in the Drawing-Room.

A plaster neck mould on same level as the Mantel Shelf, together with the enriched plaster Cornice, are continued around the room with figures between at intervals similar to those in the Chimney-piece below.

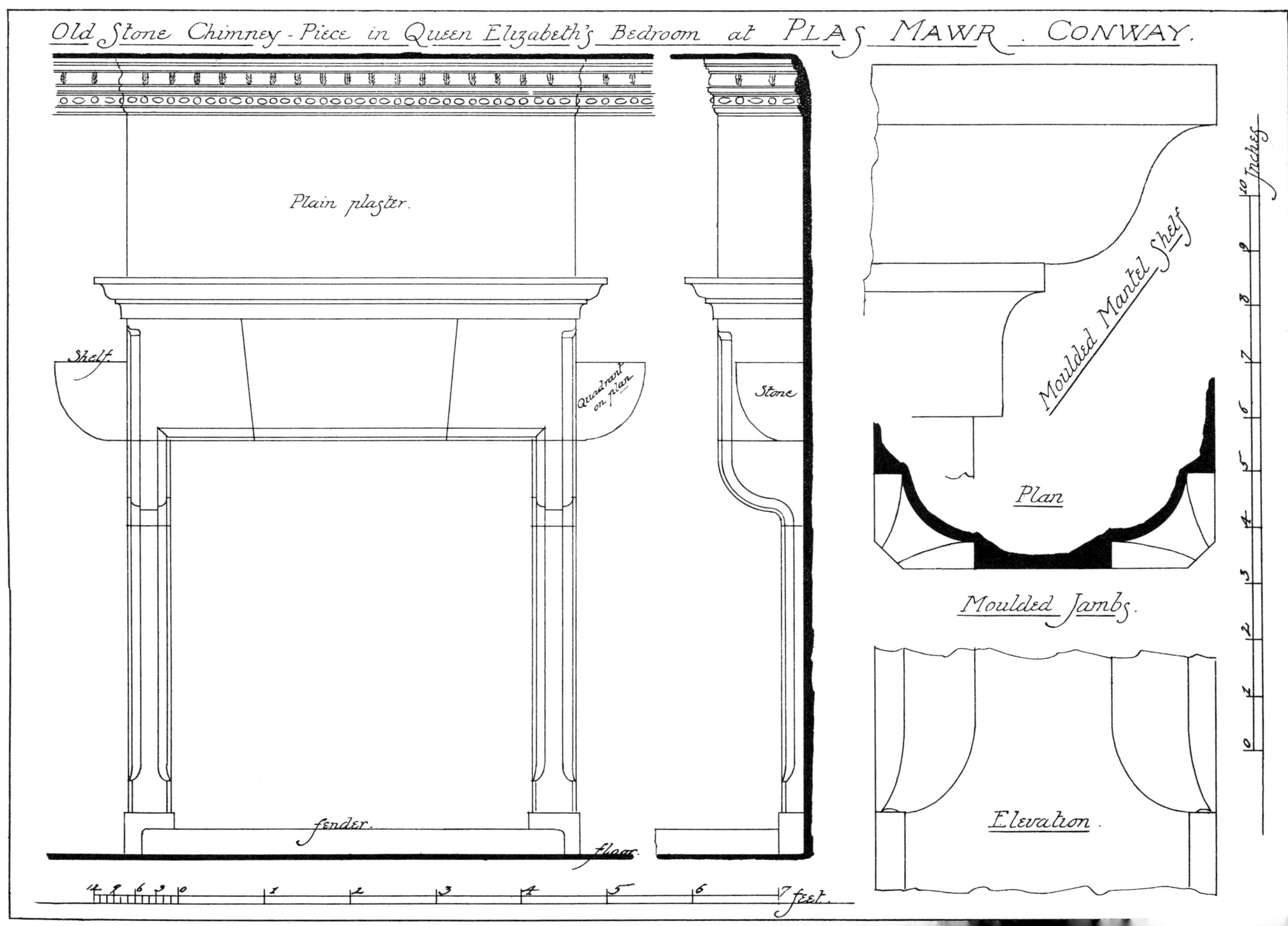
Old Stone Chimney-Piece in Queen Elizabeth's Bedroom at PLAS MAWR. CONWAY.
Plain plaster.
Shelf.
Quadrant on plan
Stone
fender.
floor.
12 9 6 3 0 1 2 3 4 5 6 7 feet.
Moulded Mantel Shelf
Plan
Moulded Jambs.
Elevation.
0 1 2 3 4 5 6 7 8 9 10 Inches

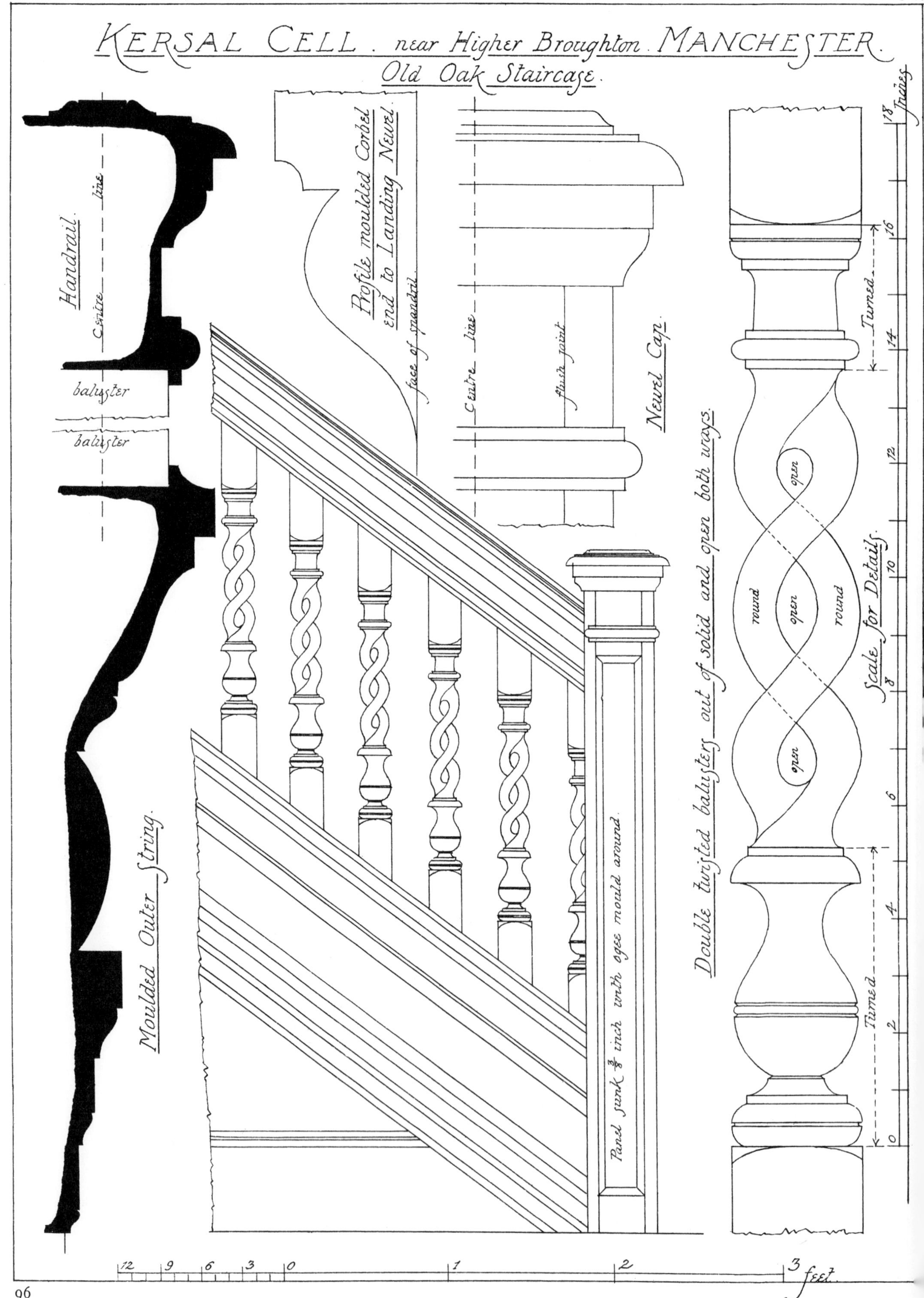
KERSAL CELL. near Higher Broughton. MANCHESTER.
Old Oak Staircase.
Handrail.
Centre line
baluster
baluster
Moulded Outer String.
Profile moulded Corbel end to Landing Newel.
face of spandril
Centre line
flush joint
Newel Cap.
Panel sunk 3/8 inch with ogee mould around.
Double twisted balusters out of solid and open both ways.
open
round
open
round
open
Turned
Turned
Scale for Details.
Inches
18
16
14
12
10
8
6
4
2
0
12
9
6
3
0
1
2
3 feet

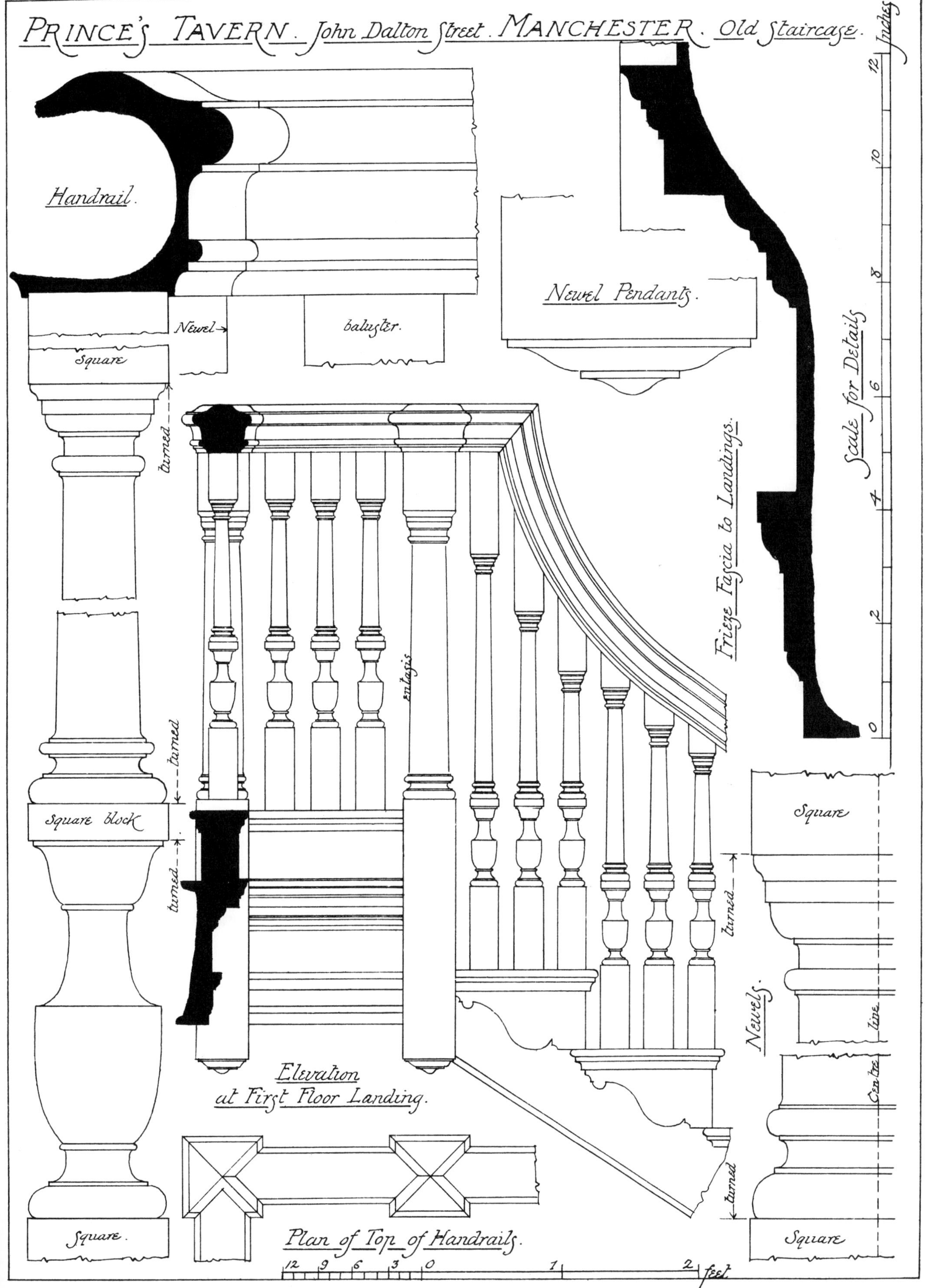
PRINCE'S TAVERN. John Dalton Street. MANCHESTER. Old Staircase.
Handrail.
Newel
baluster.
Newel Pendants.
Square
turned
turned
Square block
turned
Square.
entasis
Elevation at First Floor Landing.
Frieze Fascia to Landings.
Scale for Details
Inches.
12
10
8
6
4
2
0
Square
turned
Newels.
Centre line
turned
Square
Plan of Top of Handrails.
12 9 6 3 0 1 2 feet.

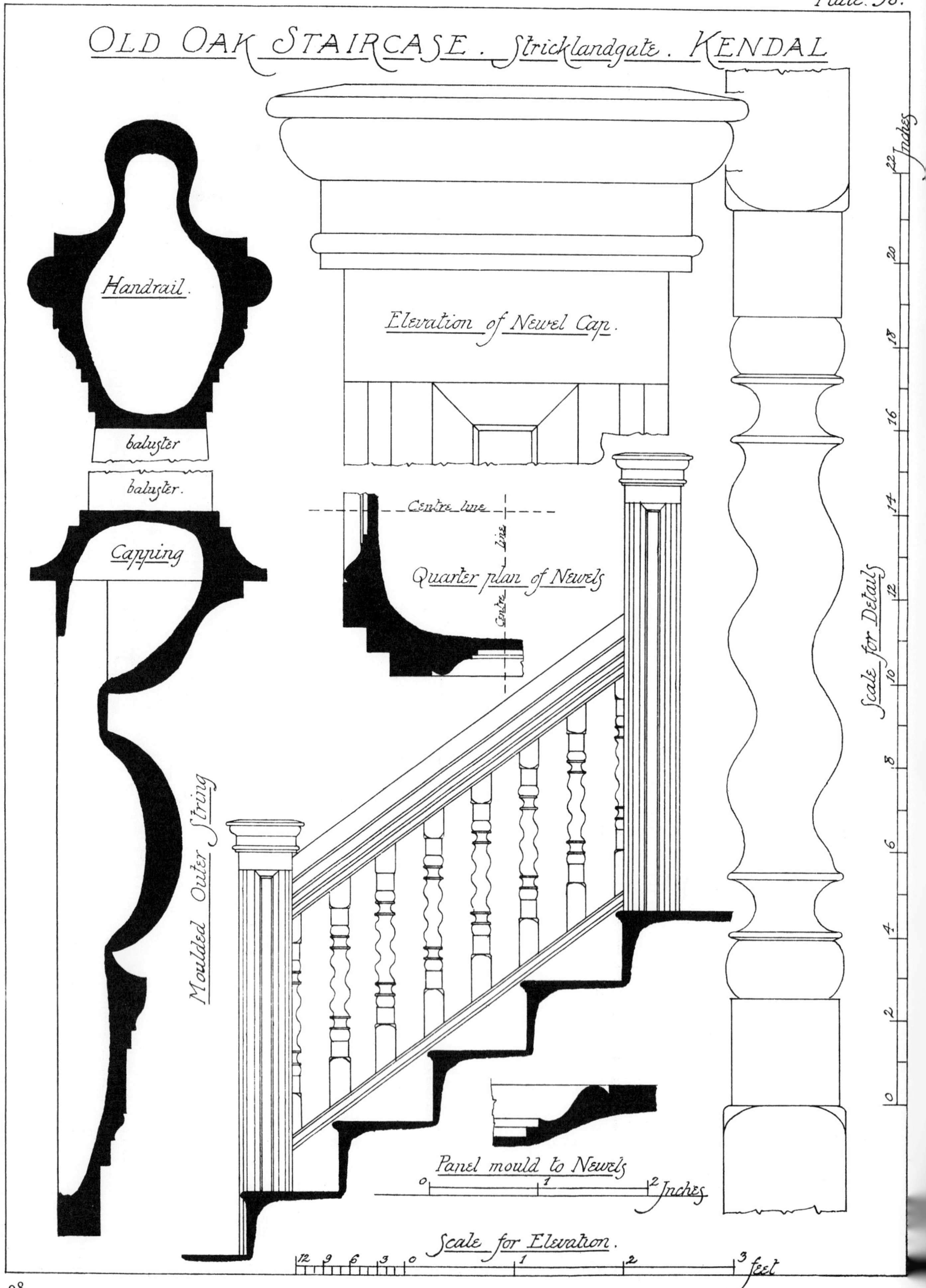
OLD OAK STAIRCASE. Stricklandgate. KENDAL
Handrail.
baluster
baluster.
Capping
Moulded Outer String
Elevation of Newel Cap.
Centre line
Centre line
Quarter plan of Newels
Panel mould to Newels
0
1
2 Inches
Scale for Elevation.
12
9
6
3
0
1
2
3 feet
Scale for Details
0
2
4
6
8
10
12
14
16
18
20
22 Inches

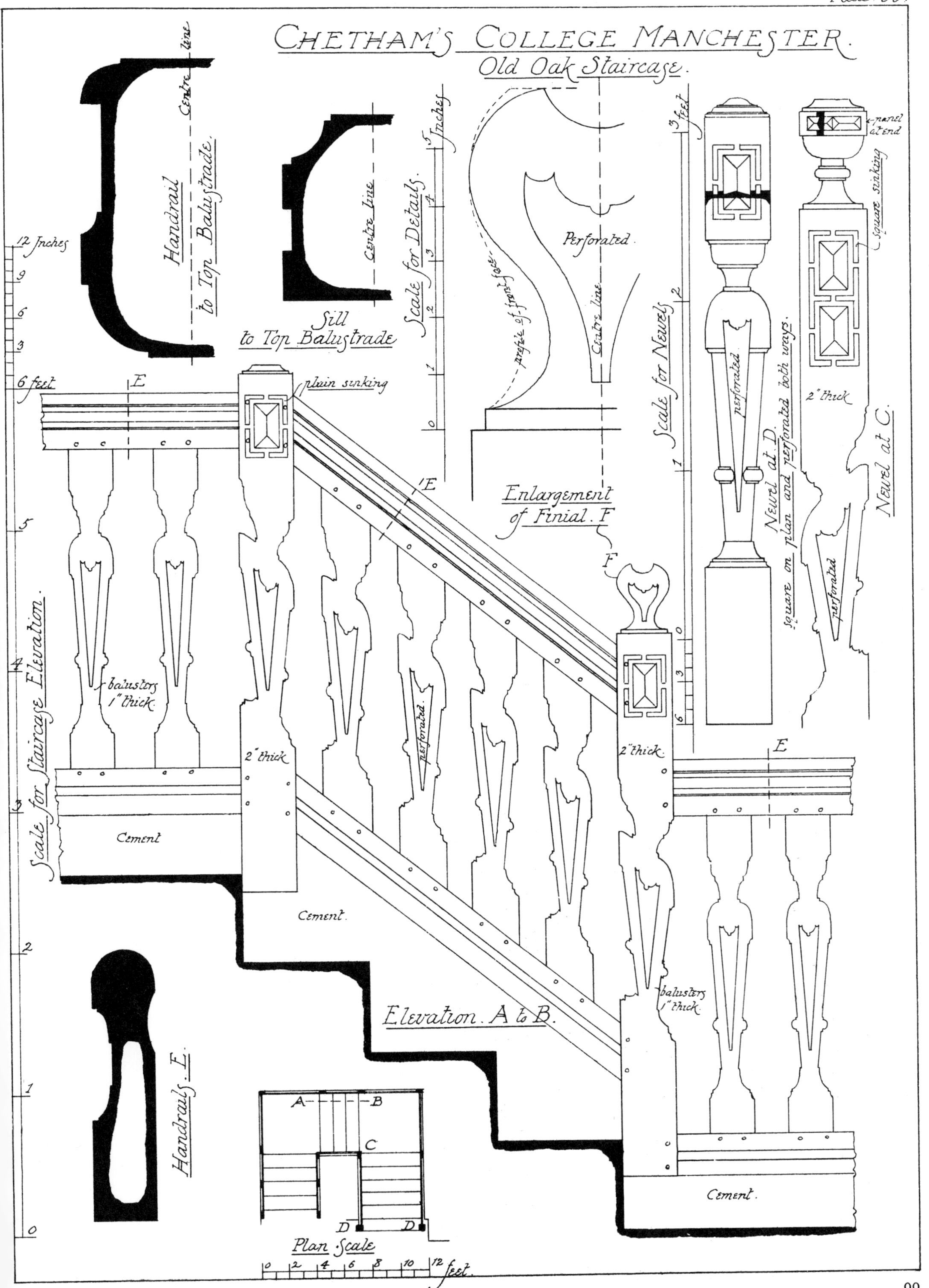

CHETHAM'S COLLEGE MANCHESTER.
Old Oak Staircase.
Handrail to Top Balustrade.
Centre line
Sill to Top Balustrade
Scale for Details.
Inches
Perforated.
profile of front face
Centre line
Enlargement of Finial. F
Scale for Newels
feet
perforated
Newel at D. square on plan and perforated both ways.
panel at end
square sinking
2" thick
Newel at C.
12 Inches
9
6
3
6 feet
5
4
3
2
1
0
E
plain sinking
balusters 1" thick.
2" thick
Cement
Scale for Staircase Elevation.
Cement.
Elevation. A to B.
Handrails. E.
A
B
C
D
Plan Scale
0 2 4 6 8 10 12 feet.

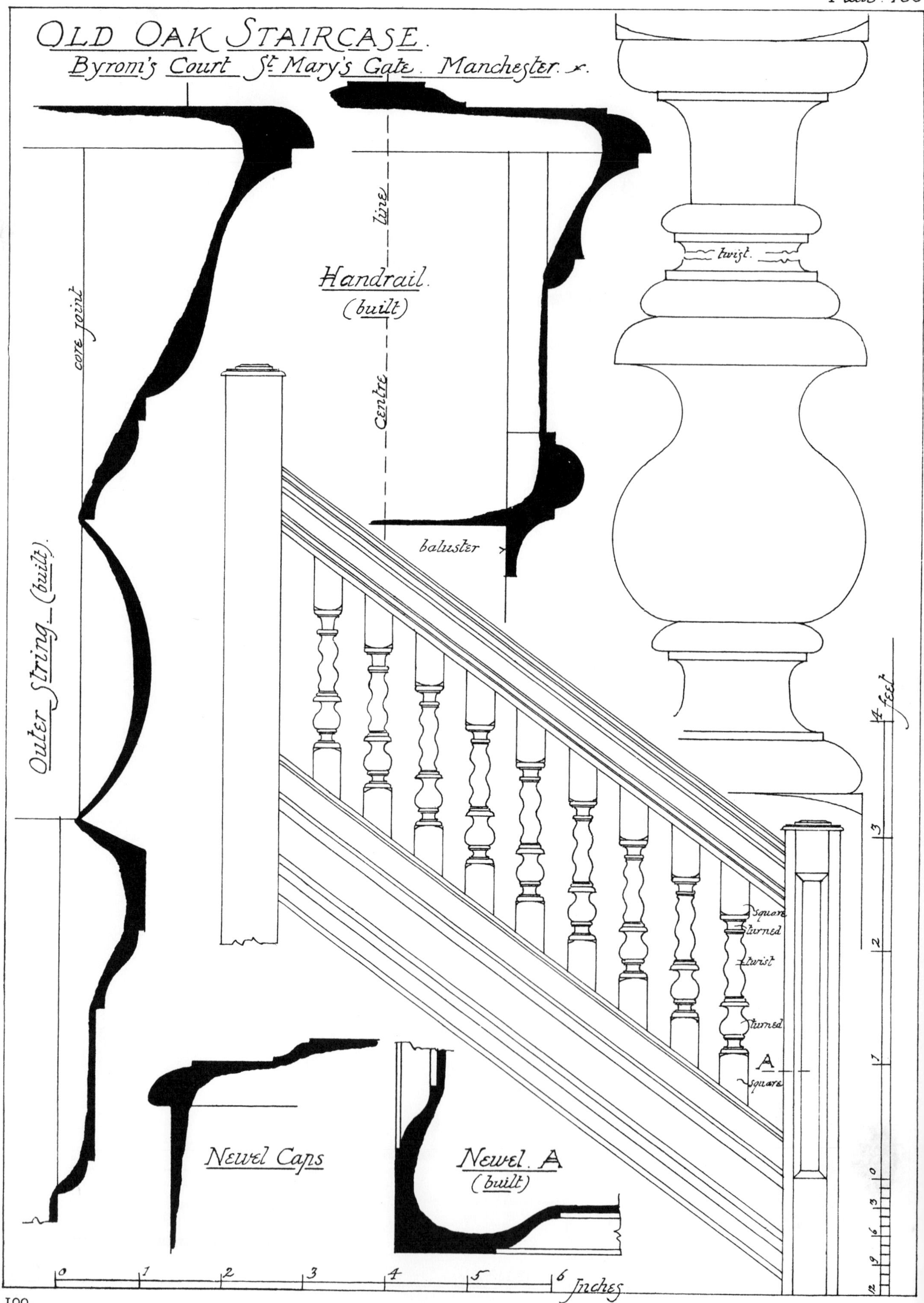
OLD OAK STAIRCASE.
Byrom's Court St. Mary's Gate. Manchester.
core joint
Outer String. (built).
line
Handrail.
(built)
Centre
baluster
twist.
square
turned
twist
turned
A
square
Newel Caps
Newel. A
(built)
0
1
2
3
4
5
6
Inches
4 feet
3
2
1
0
3
6
9
12

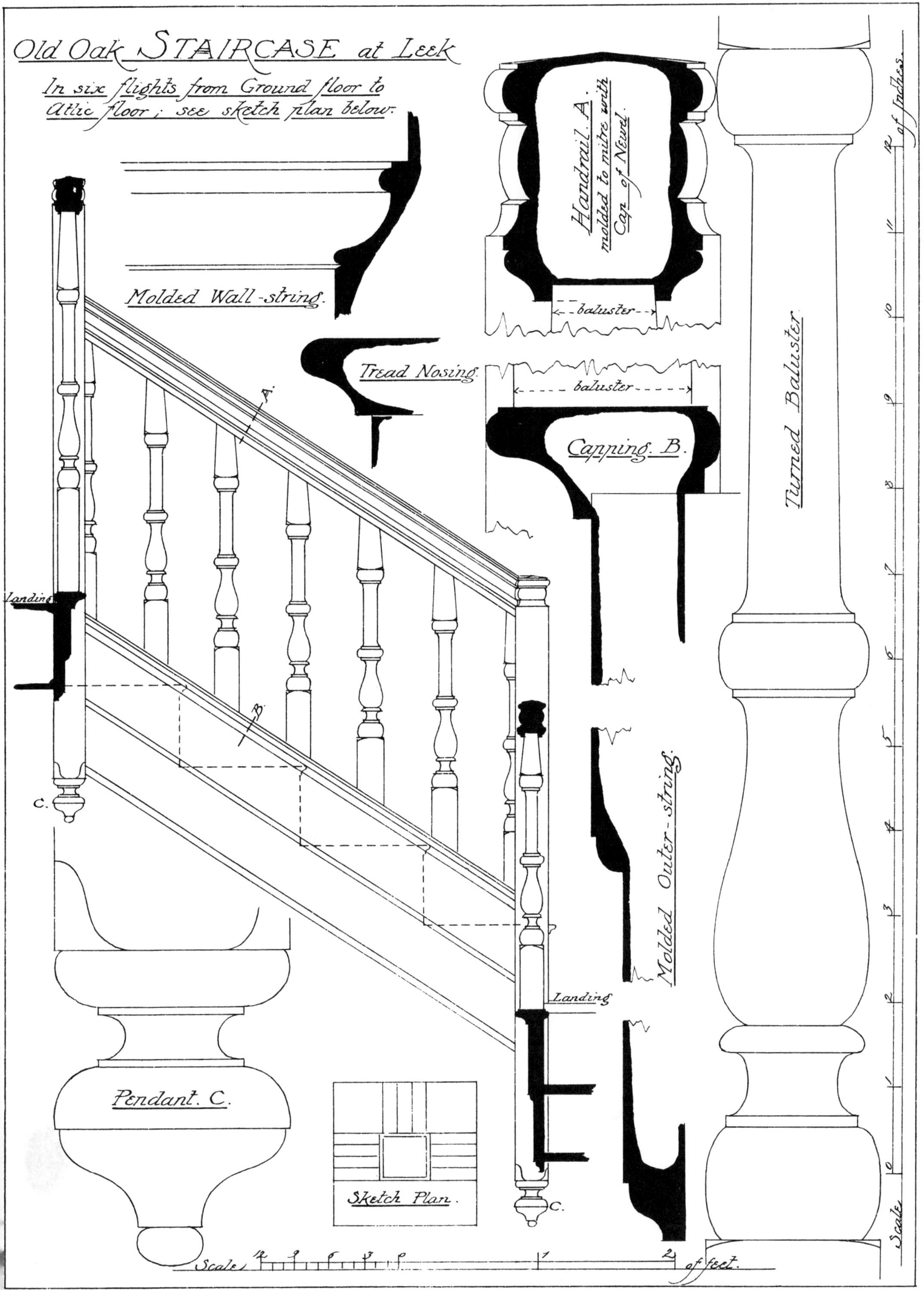
Old Oak STAIRCASE at Leek
In six flights from Ground floor to Attic floor; see sketch plan below.
Molded Wall-string.
Handrail. A. molded to mitre with Cap of Newel.
baluster
Tread Nosing.
baluster
Capping. B.
Turned Baluster.
12 of Inches.
Scale
A.
B.
Landing
C.
Landing
C.
Molded Outer-string.
Pendant. C.
Sketch Plan.
Scale 12 9 6 3 0 1 2 of feet.

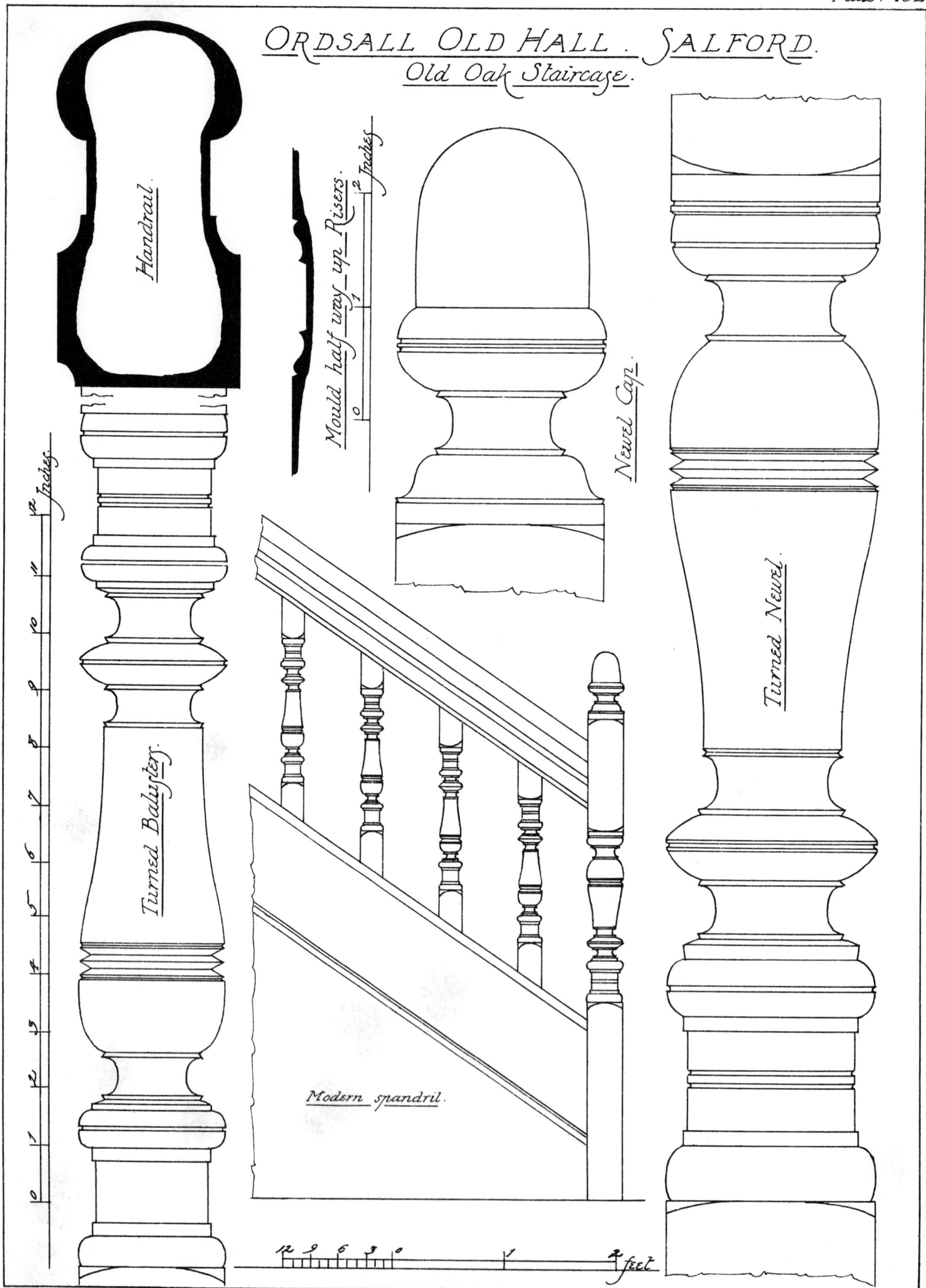
ORDSALL OLD HALL. SALFORD.
Old Oak Staircase.
Handrail.
Mould half way up Risers.
Inches
0
1
2
Newel Cap.
Turned Newel.
Turned Baluster.
Inches
0
1
2
3
4
5
6
7
8
9
10
11
12
Modern spandril.
12
9
6
3
0
1
2
feet

Old Dog Grate.

Belonging to The Honourable Marshall Brooks. Rawtenstall.

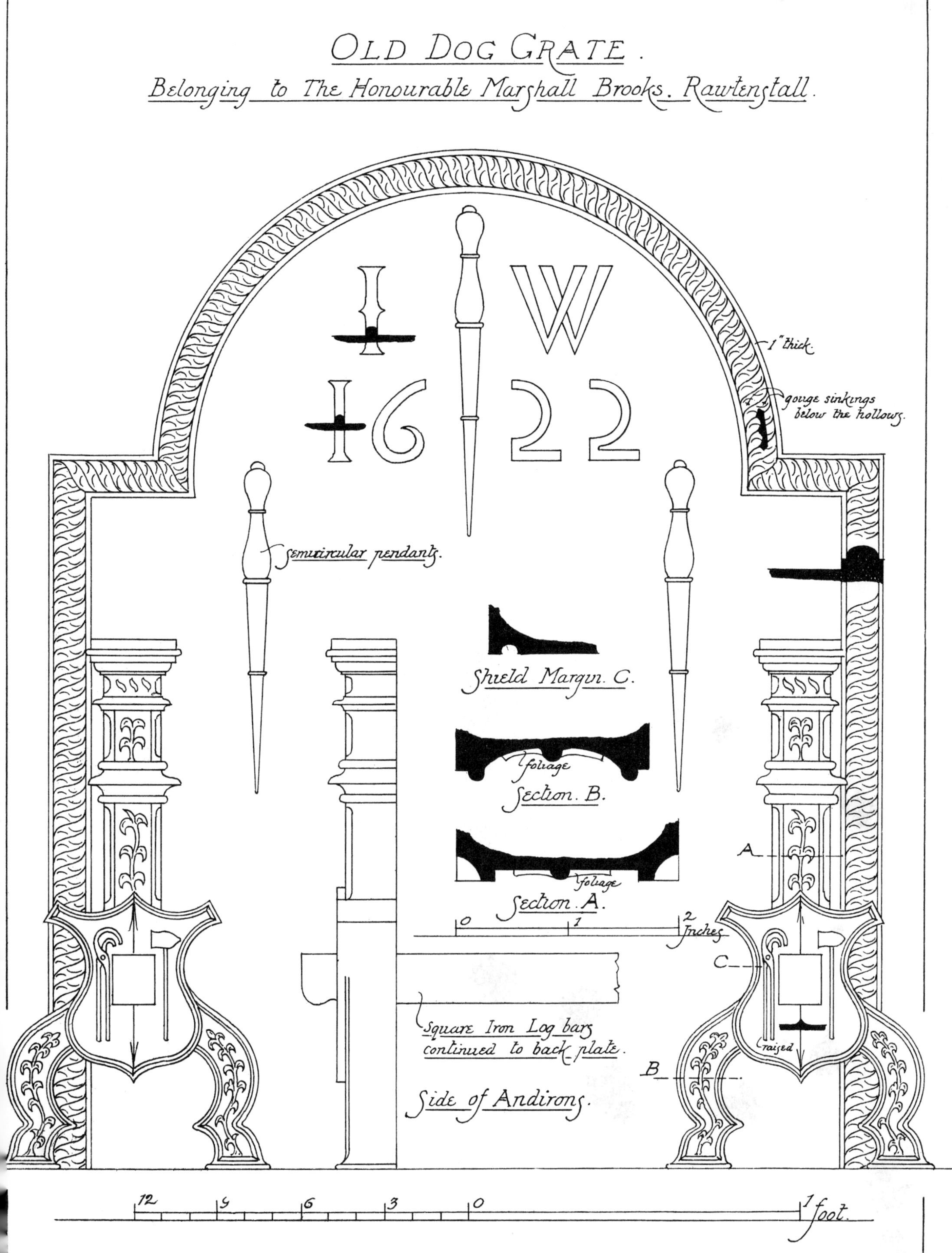

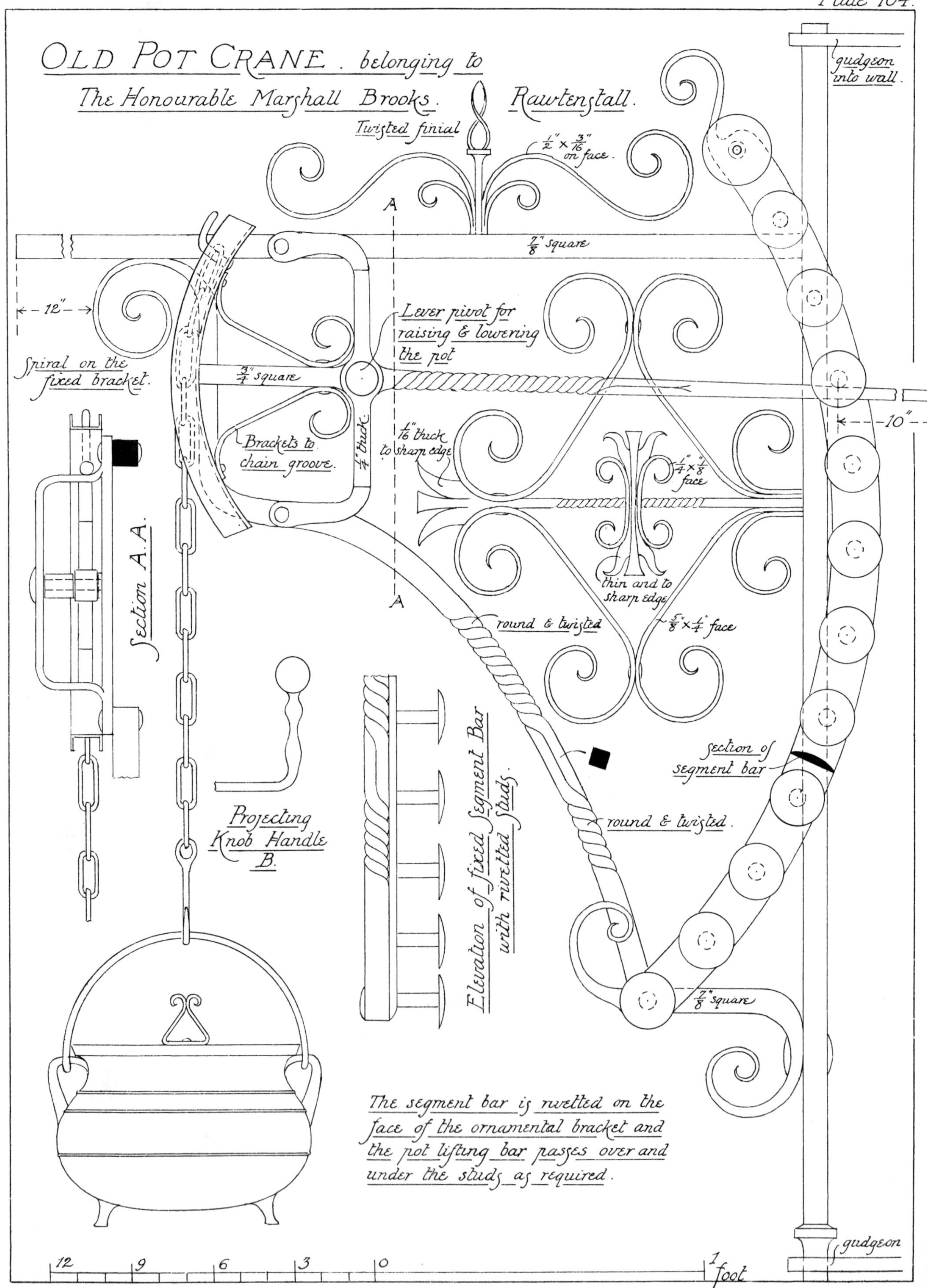
OLD POT CRANE . belonging to
The Honourable Marshall Brooks. Rawtenstall.
Twisted finial
1/2" × 3/16" on face.
gudgeon into wall.
A
7/8" square
12"
Lever pivot for raising & lowering the pot
Spiral on the fixed bracket.
3/4" square
10"
Brackets to chain groove.
1/4" thick
1/16" thick to sharp edge
1/4" × 1/8" face
Section A.A.
A
thin and to sharp edge
round & twisted
5/8" × 1/4" face
Elevation of fixed Segment Bar with rivetted Studs.
Section of segment bar
Projecting Knob Handle B.
round & twisted.
7/8" square
The segment bar is rivetted on the face of the ornamental bracket and the pot lifting bar passes over and under the studs as required.
gudgeon
12 9 6 3 0 1 foot

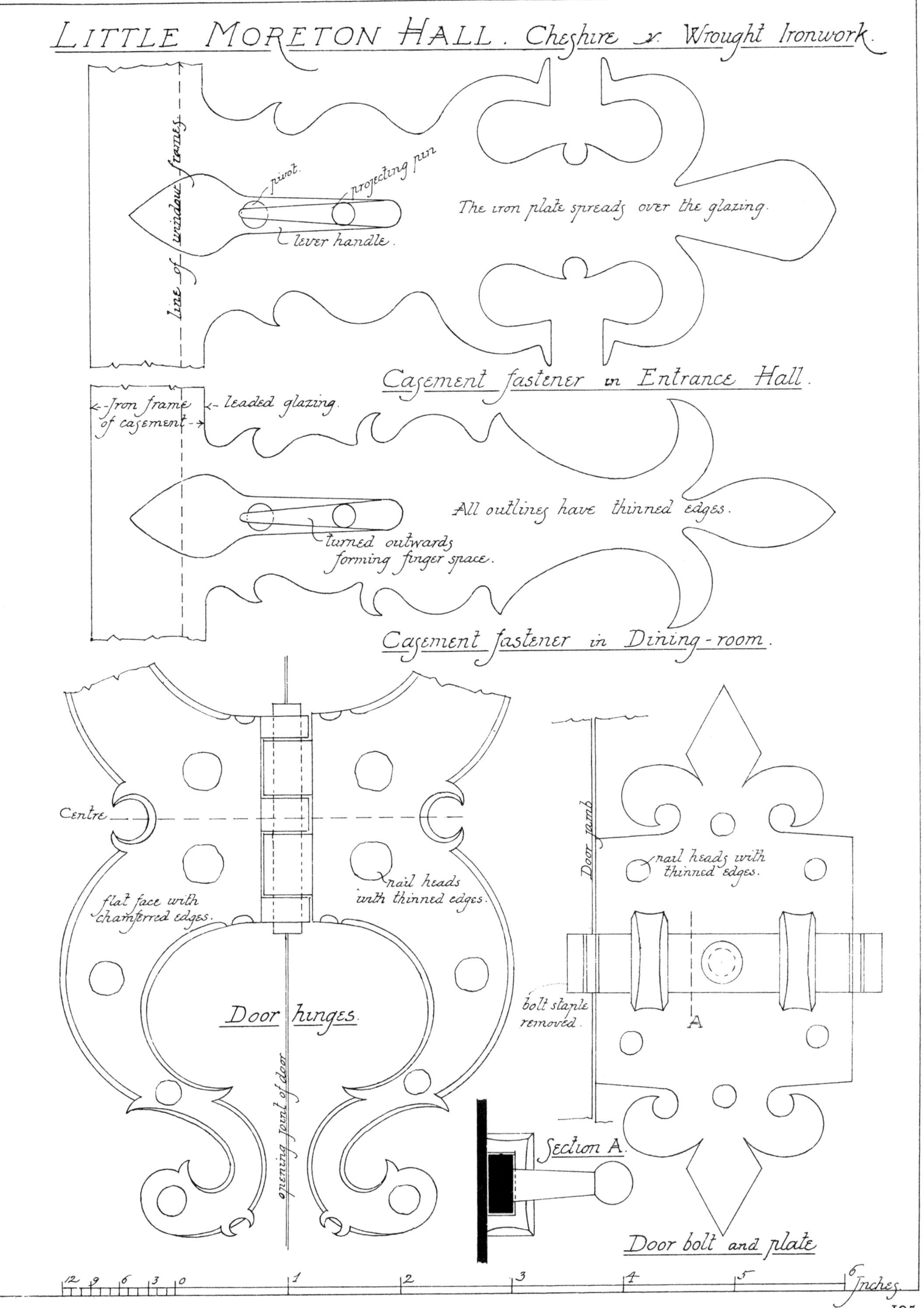
LITTLE MORETON HALL. Cheshire ✕ Wrought Ironwork.
line of window frames
pivot.
projecting pin
lever handle.
The iron plate spreads over the glazing.
Casement fastener in Entrance Hall.
Iron frame of casement
leaded glazing.
All outlines have thinned edges.
turned outwards forming finger space.
Casement fastener in Dining-room.
Centre
flat face with chamferred edges.
nail heads with thinned edges.
Door hinges.
opening joint of door
Door jamb
nail heads with thinned edges.
bolt staple removed.
A
Section A.
Door bolt and plate
12 9 6 3 0 1 2 3 4 5 6 Inches.

EXAMPLES of OLD ORNAMENTAL BRASS-WORK.
Scale 0 1 2 3 4 5 6 Inches
Brass flush inlay along top back rail of Chair at Knutsford.
Clock hour finger.
Minute finger.
Escutcheons & Handles from Old Oak Dressers.

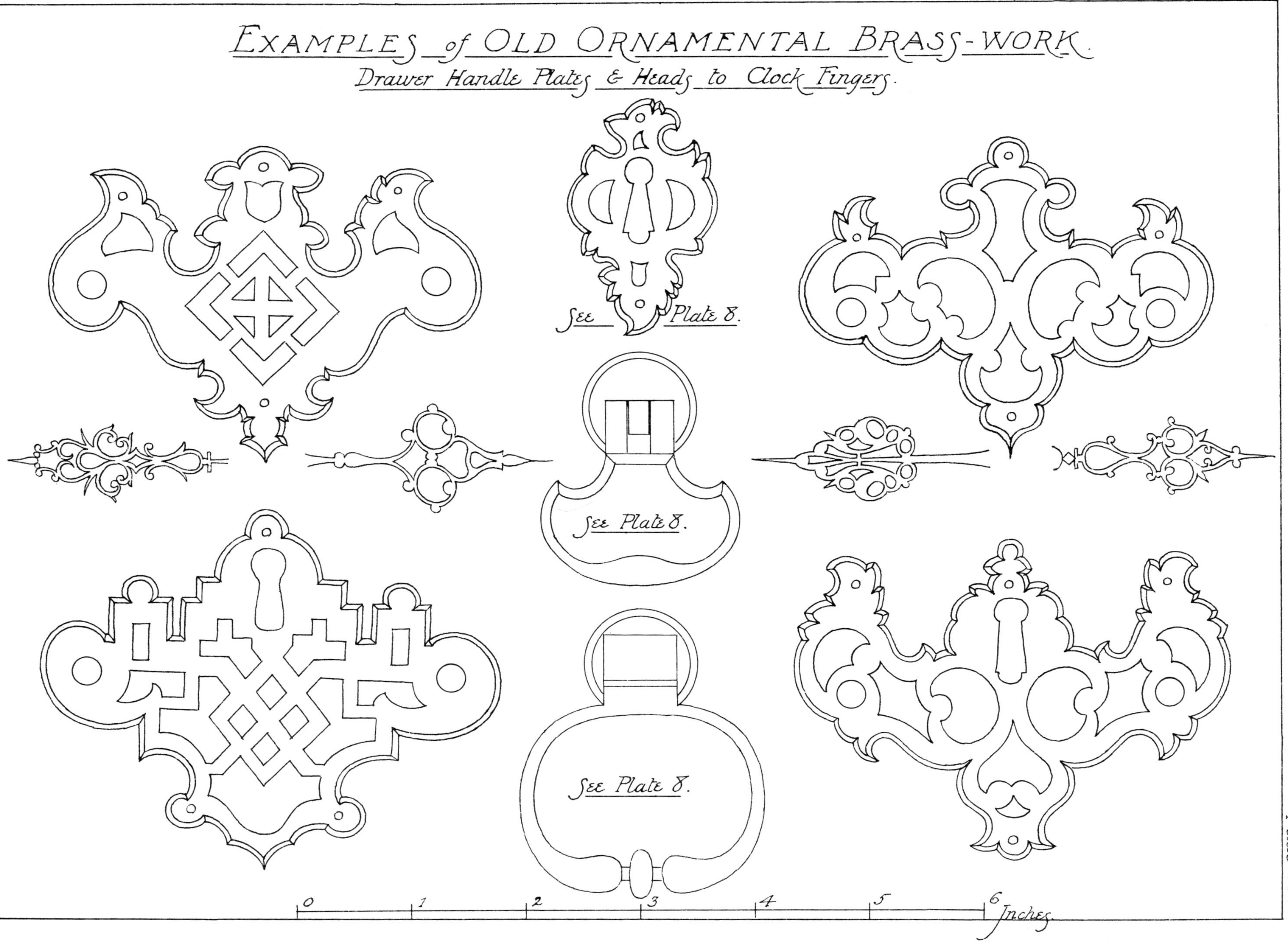
EXAMPLES of OLD ORNAMENTAL BRASS-WORK.
Drawer Handle Plates & Heads to Clock Fingers.
See Plate 8.
See Plate 8.
See Plate 8.
0
1
2
3
4
5
6 Inches.

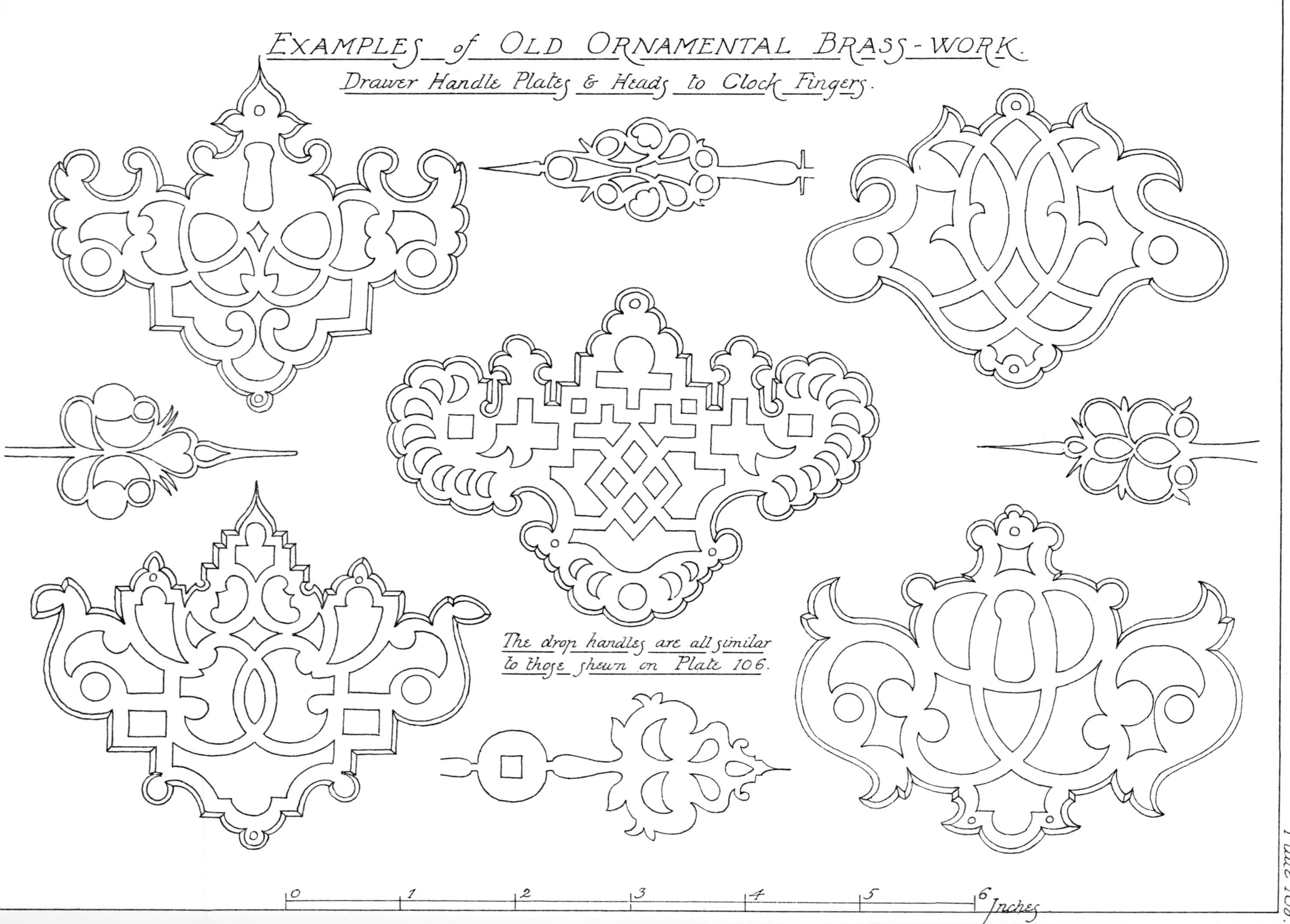
EXAMPLES of OLD ORNAMENTAL BRASS-WORK.
Drawer Handle Plates & Heads to Clock Fingers.
The drop handles are all similar to those shewn on Plate 106.
0 1 2 3 4 5 6 Inches

LITTLE MORETON HALL. Cheshire.

Ornamental Leaded Lights.

Banquetting Hall

Bedroom over Entrance Hall.

Large Room over Entrance Hall.

Entrance Hall.

Entrance Hall.

12 9 6 3 0 1 feet

Bramhall Hall. Cheshire. Ornamental Leaded Lights.

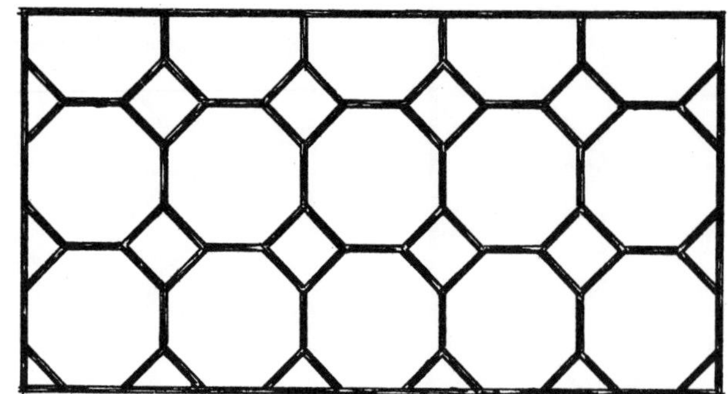

Entrance Hall.

Billiard Room.

Plaster Room

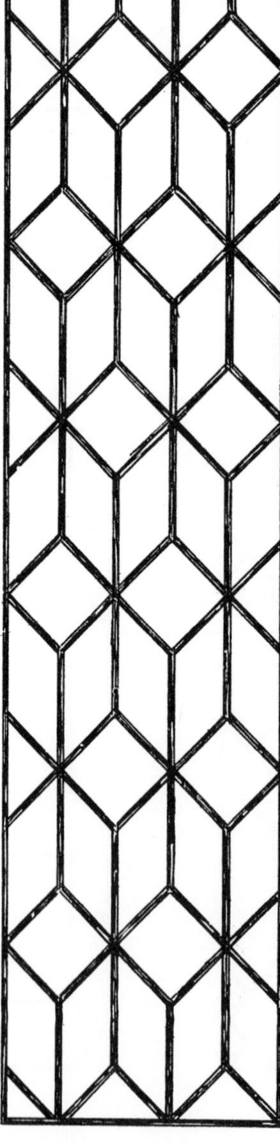

Plaster Room

Billiard Room

12 9 6 3 0 1 2 feet.

A CATALOGUE OF SELECTED DOVER BOOKS

MASTERPIECES OF FURNITURE, Verna Cook Salomonsky. Photographs and measured drawings of some of the finest examples of Colonial American, 17th century English, Windsor, Sheraton, Hepplewhite, Chippendale, Louis XIV, Queen Anne, and various other furniture styles. The textual matter includes information on traditions, characteristics, background, etc. of various pieces. 101 plates. Bibliography. 224pp. 7⅞ x 10¾.
21381-1 Paperbound $6.00

PRIMITIVE ART, Franz Boas. In this exhaustive volume, a great American anthropologist analyzes all the fundamental traits of primitive art, covering the formal element in art, representative art, symbolism, style, literature, music, and the dance. Illustrations of Indian embroidery, paleolithic paintings, woven blankets, wing and tail designs, totem poles, cutlery, earthenware, baskets and many other primitive objects and motifs. Over 900 illustrations. 376pp. 5⅜ x 8. 20025-6 Paperbound $5.00

AN INTRODUCTION TO A HISTORY OF WOODCUT, A. M. Hind. Nearly all of this authoritative 2-volume set is devoted to the 15th century—the period during which the woodcut came of age as an important art form. It is the most complete compendium of information on this period, the artists who contributed to it, and their technical and artistic accomplishments. Profusely illustrated with cuts by 15th century masters, and later works for comparative purposes. 484 illustrations. 5 indexes. Total of xi+838pp. 5⅜ x 8½. Two-vols. 20952-0,20953-0 Paperbound $13.00

A HISTORY OF ENGRAVING AND ETCHING, A. M. Hind. Beginning with the anonymous masters of 15th century engraving, this highly regarded and thorough survey carries you through Italy, Holland, and Germany to the great engravers and beginnings of etching in the 16th century, through the portrait engravers, master etchers, practicioners of mezzotint, crayon manner and stipple, aquatint, color prints, to modern etching in the period just prior to World War I. Beautifully illustrated —sharp clear prints on heavy opaque paper. Author's preface. 3 appendixes. 111 illustrations. xviii + 487 pp. 5⅜ x 8½.
20954-7 Paperbound $7.50

ART STUDENTS' ANATOMY, E. J. Farris. Teaching anatomy by using chiefly living objects for illustration, this study has enjoyed long popularity and success in art courses and home-study programs. All the basic elements of the human anatomy are illustrated in minute detail, diagrammed and pictured as they pass through common movements and actions. 158 drawings, photographs, and roentgenograms. Glossary of anatomical terms. x + 159pp. 5⅝ x 8⅜. 20744-7 Paperbound $3.50

COLONIAL LIGHTING, A. H. Hayward. The only book to cover the fascinating story of lamps and other lighting devices in America. Beginning with rush light holders used by the early settlers, it ranges through the elaborate chandeliers of the Federal period, illustrating 647 lamps. Of great value to antique collectors, designers, and historians of arts and crafts. Revised and enlarged by James R. Marsh. xxxi + 198pp. 5⅝ x 8¼.
20975-X Paperbound $4.50

PINE FURNITURE OF EARLY NEW ENGLAND, R. H. Kettell. Over 400 illustrations, over 50 working drawings of early New England chairs, benches, beds, cupboards, mirrors, shelves, tables, other furniture esteemed for simple beauty and character. "Rich store of illustrations . . . emphasizes the individuality and varied design," ANTIQUES. 413 illustrations, 55 working drawings. 475pp. 8 x 10¾. 20145-7 Clothbound $15.00

BASIC BOOKBINDING, A. W. Lewis. Enables both beginners and experts to rebind old books or bind paperbacks in hard covers. Treats materials, tools; gives step-by-step instruction in how to collate a book, sew it, back it, make boards, etc. 261 illus. Appendices. 155pp. 5⅜ x 8. 20169-4 Paperbound $2.50

DESIGN MOTIFS OF ANCIENT MEXICO, J. Enciso. Nearly 90% of these 766 superb designs from Aztec, Olmec, Totonac, Maya, and Toltec origins are unobtainable elsewhere. Contains plumed serpents, wind gods, animals, demons, dancers, monsters, etc. Excellent applied design source. Originally $17.50. 766 illustrations, thousands of motifs. 192pp. 6⅛ x 9¼. 20084-1 Paperbound $3.50

A DIDEROT PICTORIAL ENCYCLOPEDIA OF TRADES AND INDUSTRY. Manufacturing and the Technical Arts in Plates Selected from "L'Encyclopédie ou Dictionnaire Raisonné des Sciences, des Arts, et des Métiers," of Denis Diderot, edited with text by C. Gillispie. Over 2000 illustrations on 485 full-page plates. Magnificent 18th-century engravings of men, women, and children working at such trades as milling flour, cheesemaking, charcoal burning, mining, silverplating, shoeing horses, making fine glass, printing, hundreds more, showing details of machinery, different steps in sequence, etc. A remarkable art work, but also the largest collection of working figures in print, copyright-free, for art directors, designers, etc. Two vols. 920pp. 9 x 12. Heavy library cloth. 22284-5, 22285-3 Two volume set $40.00

SILK SCREEN TECHNIQUES, J. Biegeleisen, M. Cohn. A practical step-by-step home course in one of the most versatile, least expensive graphic arts processes. How to build an inexpensive silk screen, prepare stencils, print, achieve special textures, use color, etc. Every step explained, diagrammed. 149 illustrations, 201pp. 6⅛ x 9¼. 20433-2 Paperbound $3.50

STICKS AND STONES, Lewis Mumford. An examination of forces influencing American architecture: the medieval tradition in early New England, the classical influence in Jefferson's time, the Brown Decades, the imperial facade, the machine age, etc. "A truly remarkable book," SAT. REV. OF LITERATURE. 2nd revised edition. 21 illus. xvii + 240pp. 5⅜ x 8. 20202-X Paperbound $3.50

THE AUTOBIOGRAPHY OF AN IDEA, Louis Sullivan. The architect whom Frank Lloyd Wright called "the master," records the development of the theories that revolutionized America's skyline. 34 full-page plates of Sullivan's finest work. New introduction by R. M. Line. xiv + 335pp. 5⅜ x 8. 20281-X Paperbound $6.00

VITRUVIUS: TEN BOOKS ON ARCHITECTURE. The most influential book in the history of architecture. 1st century A.D. Roman classic has influenced such men as Bramante, Palladio, Michelangelo, up to present. Classic principles of design, harmony, etc. Fascinating reading. Definitive English translation by Professor H. Morgan, Harvard. 344pp. 5⅜ x 8.
20645-9 Paperbound **$5.00**

HAWTHORNE ON PAINTING. Vivid re-creation, from students' notes, of instructions by Charles Hawthorne at Cape Cod School of Art. Essays, epigrammatic comments on color, form, seeing, techniques, etc. "Excellent," Time. 100pp. 5⅜ x 8.
20653-X Paperbound **$2.25**

THE HANDBOOK OF PLANT AND FLORAL ORNAMENT, R. G. Hatton. 1200 line illustrations, from medieval, Renaissance herbals, of flowering or fruiting plants: garden flowers, wild flowers, medicinal plants, poisons, industrial plants, etc. A unique compilation that probably could not be matched in any library in the world. Formerly "The Craftsman's Plant-Book." Also full text on uses, history as ornament, etc. 548pp. 6⅛ x 9¼.
20649-1 Paperbound **$7.95**

DECORATIVE ALPHABETS AND INITIALS, Alexander Nesbitt. 91 complete alphabets, over 3900 ornamental initials, from Middle Ages, Renaissance printing, baroque, rococo, and modern sources. Individual items copyright free, for use in commercial art, crafts, design, packaging, etc. 123 full-page plates. 3924 initials. 129pp. 7¾ x 10¾. 20544-4 Paperbound **$5.00**

METHODS AND MATERIALS OF THE GREAT SCHOOLS AND MASTERS, Sir Charles Eastlake. (Formerly titled "Materials for a History of Oil Painting.") Vast, authentic reconstruction of secret techniques of the masters, recreated from ancient manuscripts, contemporary accounts, analysis of paintings, etc. Oils, fresco, tempera, varnishes, encaustics. Both Flemish and Italian schools, also British and French. One of great works for art historians, critics; inexhaustible mine of suggestions, information for practicing artists. Total of 1025pp. 5⅜ x 8.
20718-8, 20719-6 Two volume set, Paperbound **$15.00**

AMERICAN VICTORIAN ARCHITECTURE, edited by Arnold Lewis and Keith Morgan. Collection of brilliant photographs of 1870's, 1880's, showing finest domestic, public architecture; many buildings now gone. Landmark work, French in origin; first European appreciation of American work. Modern notes, introduction. 120 plates. "Architects and students of architecture will find this book invaluable for its first-hand depiction of the state of the art during a very formative period," ANTIQUE MONTHLY. 152pp. 9 x 12. 23177-1 Paperbound **$7.95**

THE HUMAN FIGURE, J. H. Vanderpoel. Not just a picture book, but a complete course by a famous figure artist. Extensive text, illustrated by 430 pencil and charcoal drawings of both male and female anatomy. 2nd enlarged edition. Foreword. 430 illus. 143pp. 6⅛ x 9¼. 20432-4 Paperbound **$3.00**

Dover Books on Art

DESIGN AND FIGURE CARVING, E. J. Tangerman. "Anyone who can peel a potato can carve," states the author, and in this unusual book he shows you how, covering every stage in detail from very simple exercises working up to museum-quality pieces. Terrific aid for hobbyists, arts and crafts counselors, teachers, those who wish to make reproductions for the commercial market. Appendix: How to Enlarge a Design. Brief bibliography. Index. 1298 figures. x + 289pp. $5\frac{3}{8}$ x $8\frac{1}{2}$.
21209-2 Paperbound $4.50

THE STANDARD BOOK OF QUILT MAKING AND COLLECTING, M. Ickis. Even if you are a beginner, you will soon find yourself quilting like an expert, by following these clearly drawn patterns, photographs, and step-by-step instructions. Learn how to plan the quilt, to select the pattern to harmonize with the design and color of the room, to choose materials. Over 40 full-size patterns. Index. 483 illustrations. One color plate. xi + 276pp. $6\frac{3}{4}$ x $9\frac{1}{2}$. 20582-7 Paperbound $4.95

A HISTORY OF COSTUME, Carl Köhler. The most reliable and authentic account of the development of dress from ancient times through the 19th century. Based on actual pieces of clothing that have survived, using paintings, statues and other reproductions only where originals no longer exist. Hundreds of illustrations, including detailed patterns for many articles. Highly useful for theatre and movie directors, fashion designers, illustrators, teachers. Edited and augmented by Emma von Sichart. Translated by Alexander K. Dallas. 594 illustrations. 464pp. $5\frac{1}{8}$ x $7\frac{1}{8}$.
21030-8 Paperbound $6.50